AROUND THE BLOC

BLOC AR   OC AROUND THE BLOC A

STEPHANIE ELIZONDO GRIEST

(V)

VILLARD

NEW YORK

AROUND THE BLOC

HE BLOC AROUND THE

MY LIFE

IN

MOSCOW,

BEIJING,

AND

HAVANA

Parts of chapter 13, "The Culinary Revolution," were published as
"A Culinary Revolution" in *Travelers' Tales: Her Fork in the Road:
Women Celebrate Food and Travel,* edited by Lisa Bach (San
Francisco: Travelers' Tales, Inc., 2001). Parts of chapter 26, "The
Rumba Queen," were published as "Sweet Thing" in *Travelers' Tales
Cuba: True Stories,* edited by Tom Miller (San Francisco: Travelers'
Tales, Inc., 2001). Chapter 14, "The Tao of Bicycling," will be
published in *The Best Travelers' Tales 2004: True Stories from Around
the World,* edited by James O'Reilly, Larry Habegger, and Sean
O'Reilly (San Francisco: Travelers' Tales, Inc., 2004).

Library of Congress Cataloging-in-Publication Data
Griest, Stephanie Elizondo.
Around the bloc : my life in Moscow, Beijing, and Havana /
Stephanie Elizondo Griest.
p.   cm.
Includes bibliographical references and index.
ISBN 0-8129-6760-7
1. Griest, Stephanie Elizondo.   2. Journalists—United States—
Diaries.   3. Mexican American women—Texas—Diaries.
4. Mexican Americans and mass media.   5. Communism and
society—History—20th century.   6. China—Description and
travel.   7. Cuba—Description and travel.   8. Russia
(Federation)—Description and travel.   I. Title.
PN4874.G747A3 2004
070.92—dc22
[B]   2003059531

Villard Books website address: www.villard.com

24689753

Book design by Barbara M. Bachman

FOR MY MOM AND DAD,

IRENE AND DICK GRIEST,

WITH ALL MY LOVE

AUTHOR'S NOTE

BETWEEN 1996 AND 2000, I visited the following nations: Russia, the Czech Republic, Latvia, Lithuania, Estonia, China, Vietnam, Mongolia, Uzbekistan, Kyrgyzstan, the former German Democratic Republic, and Cuba. All experimented with communism in the twentieth century, either by choice or by force. None achieved it, but a few are still trying. (I refer to them collectively as "the Bloc," although historically, the term referred primarily to the East European nations that formed the Warsaw Treaty Organization.) This book focuses on the capitals of the three that most intrigued me: Moscow, Beijing, and Havana. As cities, they are about as representative of their nations as Washington, D.C., or New York City is of the United States. To truly appreciate the complexities of Russia, China, and Cuba, one must spend time in its heartlands, its rural towns and mountain villages—the fascinating subject of other books, but not of this.

Translation is a tricky business. I have used a rough English transliteration for the Russian, Pinyin for the Mandarin, and Tex-Mex for the Spanish. My sincere apologies for butchering these beautiful languages as badly in print as I normally do in spoken word.

As for the amazing cast of characters you're about to meet, I have changed the names and identities of most—in some instances to protect their privacy; in others, to ward off possible reprisals. A couple of important characters have been omitted altogether, as per their request. Not all events have been relayed in precise chronological order, and many of the conversations and descriptions are approximations from journal entries and memory rather than formal reportage.

I thank the heroines and heroes of this book immensely for allowing me into their lives and entrusting me with their stories. I can only hope to have portrayed them justly.

CONTENTS

SECTION TWO ★ BEIJING

SECTION THREE ★ HAVANA

RED STAR OVER SOUTH TEXAS

THE BAD DREAMS STARTED right before my high school graduation in 1992. Myself at a washed-up twenty-five, roaming Mary Carroll High's halls in my letterman jacket and getting plastered in the Taco Bell parking lot for fun. I had to get the hell out of Corpus Christi. Wanderlust pumped through my veins: My great-great-uncle Jake was a hobo who saw the countryside with his legs dangling over the edge of a freight train; my dad drummed his way around the world with a U.S. Navy band. I too wanted to be a rambler, a wanderer, a nomad—the kind whose stories began with "Once, in Abu Dhabi . . ." or "I'll never forget that time in Ouagadougou when _____." Who bought her funky jewelry from its country of origin instead of a booth at the mall.

I only needed to figure out the details: how, where, and with whose money?

Around spring break, an invitation to a national journalism conference for high school students found its way into my mailbox. Having toyed since childhood with the idea of being a reporter, I raised a little money, talked my mom out of her frequent flier miles, boarded a plane for the first time in my life, and headed out to Washington, D.C. The keynote address on opening night was given by a seasoned CNN correspondent who had covered the fall of the Berlin Wall and the collapse of the Soviet Union. He vividly described how Lithuanians had flung their bodies in front of Russian tanks to shield their television tower, how Estonians had impaled their Soviet passports upon stakes and set them ablaze in protest, how millions spilled into the street and demanded social change. These images and ideas completely transfixed me. The only thing people took to the streets and shook their fists about in South Texas was football.

This man's job would get me out of Corpus!

When his oratory ended, I darted into the aisle, grabbed a microphone, and asked for advice on how to be a foreign correspondent just like him.

He cocked his head and looked straight at me. "Learn Russian," he replied. "Next question?"

Russian? Half my roots were buried beneath the pueblos of Mexico and I could barely say, *"¿Dónde está el baño?"* How could I possibly learn a language like that? And why would I want to? I'd never met a Russian, and my primary associations with their nation were the cold war and communism. I didn't know much about either, except that my country had recently won the former and the latter made its practitioners psychotic. (Why else were Soviets always building bombs, Chinese drowning their baby girls, and Cubans crossing shark-infested waters on rafts made of tires and plywood?)

Still, he couldn't have been more specific than "Learn Russian." And I had to study *some* language when I started college that fall—and I preferred it not be Spanish. My mom had faced such ridicule for her Spanish accent growing up, she never spoke it around my sister and me, to spare us the humiliation of mispronouncing our *ch*'s and *sh*'s. There hadn't been much incentive to learn it at school, either. Sounding *pachuco* and "acting Mexican" were considered insults in my schoolyard back then, conjuring images of an uneducated someone whose jeans hung around their ankles and who had slicked-back, greasy hair. Spanish for me was a language of hushed whispers followed by laughter, of jokes I was never in on, of rosaries and funerals and *quinceañeras* and weddings, of uncles in cowboy boots calling me *m'hija* and my *abuelita* in an apron feeding me beans. Moreover, it was the language of the place I wanted to leave. If Russian could get me out, I was willing to give it a try. That September, I enrolled in the Department of Journalism at the University of Texas at Austin (UT) and signed up for Russian 601A. That was my first step toward a four-year, twelve-nation tour around the Bloc, but I didn't know it then. When I jetted off to Moscow in January 1996, I was just looking for some excitement. I didn't really care what happened, as long as it was interesting.

born in 1972
graduated 1992
hs
college 1996
1996–2000
travel

Москва

REVOLUTION IS A DIRTY BUSINESS.

YOU DO NOT MAKE IT WITH WHITE GLOVES.

—Vladimir Ilyich Ulyanov Lenin

—

1. MOSCOW MANIFESTO

**FROM EACH ACCORDING TO HIS ABILITIES,
TO EACH ACCORDING TO HIS NEEDS.**
—*Karl Marx*

THEY SAY THE first rule of traveling is packing only what you can carry for half a mile at a dead run. I had every intention of doing this back home in Texas, but my barest essentials filled two huge suitcases and a potbellied backpack. While I could not actually carry all seventy pounds of my luggage, I could push and shove it for small distances. So that's what I did at Sheremetyevo Airport, from passport control to baggage claim to customs. Beyond the exit gate was a mob of onlookers who exuded my first whiffs of Moscow: a scent of equal parts vodka and sausage, leather and tobacco, sweat and strife. For one brief moment, the crowd's collective attention focused on me, taking in my lumberjack hiking boots, Michelin man down coat, and wire-rimmed glasses. *"Inostranka,"* they murmured my nickname for the next half year. Foreign girl. Then the beefy guys in tracksuits and gold chains turned back to their cell phones, the fashionable girls—impeccably dressed in floor-length furs, knee-high riding boots, and fluffy hats—lit up another round of slender cigarettes, and everyone else resumed their stoic stances. I navigated in, around, and through them and emerged smelling vaguely of sausages.

Seeing no other place to sit in the concourse, I plopped down on the floor beside my fortress of luggage to wait for the other exchange students in my group. Within an instant, an ancient woman was hovering over me. She wore thick woolen tights beneath her layers of housedresses and hand-knit sweaters; her silver hair was covered with a brightly colored kerchief. Russians call these walking, talking historical artifacts *babushki*, or grandmothers. When I grinned at her, she latched on to my forearm with an iron grip and plucked me up. "The ground is too cold to sit on. You'll freeze your ovaries," she scolded, then shuffled away so I could ponder the damage done to my unborn children.

Five bleary-eyed Texans soon joined me. Gerad, who was returning for his second semester, ventured outside to look for the van scheduled to meet us at noon. The rest of us—who hadn't slept in thirty-two hours—collapsed in a heap. After an hour had passed, I joined Gerad in the parking lot. "Where do you think our driver is?"

"Passed out on the couch at the dorm," he replied, then pulled out a wad of rubles and handed me a 10,000 note. "Why don't you call Nadezhda?"

Nadezhda was the Muscovite I'd befriended two years before, during her exchange program at my university in Texas. When we'd talked earlier that week, she'd promised to meet me at either the airport or the dormitory, depending on her work schedule. She'd know what to do—if I could find her. I wandered back inside the airport and found a smoky room with a row of plastic red phones stacked atop a counter. Transactions appeared to go through a sour-faced woman seated behind a desk, so I got in line behind three burly men with olive skin and five o'clock shadows. When one cordially asked how to call T'bilisi, the operator glowered. "The instructions are written on the wall! Can't you read?"

The Georgians mumbled their apologies and ambled over to the phones. Then the woman set her ice-pick eyes on me. I dropped the 10,000-ruble note on her desk and darted off to the nearest phone before she could yell. True to her word, the instructions were pasted on the plexiglass partition, but I couldn't decipher more than two consecutive words. Hoping for the best, I simply picked up the receiver and dialed Nadezhda's work number. A woman answered after a few rings.

"Allo? . . . Allo?"

"Hello?" I asked in Russian.

"Allo? . . . Allo!"

"Hello, is Nadezhda there?"

"Allo? . . . Allo! . . . Gospodi!" Then she hung up. It seemed she never heard me.

I got back in line, this time behind a handsome young couple who paid for their phone call, split the change, and walked out the door without ever unlocking their lips.

"It didn't work," I told the operator.

Pursing her lips so tightly they disappeared, she asked why I hadn't followed the instructions *written in plain Russian on the wall.* After I explained that I was somewhat illiterate in her language, she grunted and told me to press something—only I didn't catch what—when I heard a voice. Then she shooed me away.

I returned to the phone and tried again. This time when the woman answered, I pressed nine, as that's what usually gets punched in America. She still couldn't hear me, though, so I pressed one, then zero. Nothing. I started pushing all the buttons frantically. She hung up.

I took a deep breath and retreated to the line.

"Why didn't you press three?" the operator bellowed.

"Why three?" I asked plaintively, then returned to the phones.

This time no one answered at Nadezhda's office, and I let it ring a long, long time, my index finger hovering over the three key. Feeling strangely defeated, I retrieved Gerad's rubles and headed back to my posse. How was I going to survive in a country where I couldn't even make a phone call?

Another two and a half hours passed.

"Well, guys, it looks like the welcome wagon ain't coming," Gerad broke the news. The options that followed were gloomy. The airport was located in the northernmost tip of the city; our dormitory was south of center. The *Mafiya*-controlled taxi cartel would charge about $70 a head—a price none of us could afford. Public transportation was cheap, but how could we get twenty-one pieces of luggage on and off buses that didn't come to complete stops? The only other option was for Gerad to return to the dormitory alone and try to find our driver—meaning the rest of us would have another two- or three-hour wait.

We were about to vote when I heard my Russian name, Stesha, shouted across the concourse. I turned to see Nadezhda running toward me. I whooped for joy, but something stopped me from jumping into her outstretched arms. Last time I saw my friend, she looked like me: hair bedraggled, Levi's ripped, feet sandaled, nose pierced. Now she was draped in fur and riding boots and sported a sleek new haircut.

"You've changed," I breathed.

"You haven't," she quipped before throwing her arms around me.

Nadezhda had spent the past hour and a half waiting on a

couch back at the dorm. When she realized the man crashed out beside her was our driver, she woke him up.

"He's got a hangover, but he's waiting right outside!" she announced cheerfully.

We piled our quarter ton of luggage into the van and clambered aboard. The van lurched out of the congested parking lot and joined the throngs of trams, trolleys, buses, Ladas, and bulletproof Mercedes-Benzes belching exhaust onto the snow-banked highway. Mile after mile of concrete apartment blocs whizzed past, each so randomly placed, it seemed Big Brother had dropped them from the sky. Women chatted on park benches; old men shared dried fish and beer over tree stumps. Kids wore so many layers of winter clothing, their limbs stuck out like a starfish's. Fat gray crows flitted about in pencil-thin trees; the dogs being walked beneath them were, without exception, big, mean, and ugly. (That whole year, I never saw a dog smaller or gentler than a Rottweiler.)

As we approached downtown, the past century of Russian history came into view. After seventy years of exile, pre-revolutionary Moscow was slowly rearing its regal head again, its cathedrals and monasteries receiving full-scale face lifts while its onion-shaped gold domes shimmered in the sun. On the socialist side, ruby red stars crested buildings so massive, they seemed to have been built by titans instead of men. Capitalism had recently seized the skyline in the form of high-rise banks and chic new department stores.

Suddenly, the driver cut across three lanes of traffic to parallel-park beside a whitewashed cathedral with kelly green and electric orange trim. Our new home was the six-story dormitory across the street. We lugged our suitcases up to the lobby, where two guys in jeans and sneakers dozed on the couch in front of the television set. They turned out to be the security guards. During a commercial break, one strolled over to survey the mountain of luggage forming in the foyer.

"The elevator is broken," he said, yawning, and returned to his spot on the couch.

"What floor is our room on?" I asked Gerad.

"The fifth."

Nadezhda took that as her cue to leave. "I'll come see you soon," she promised with a hug and a kiss, then turned on her leather riding boots and left.

I HAD PRACTICED being Russian a long time before moving there. I put cabbage in my tacos instead of shredded lettuce and ate lots of beets. I weaned myself off spices and drowned everything in sour cream. I devoured Russian literature, memorized Pushkin, and sang along to Vladimir Visotsky, the Soviet Union's Bob Dylan. I made the arduous switch from tequila to vodka when I went out at night. I even opted for a non-air-conditioned suite at my group house in college. That's suicide in central Texas heat, but I thought it would build the character I needed for Moscow.

It didn't. Nothing could have prepared me for that student dormitory.

I could handle the fact that our room was on the fifth floor and the elevators never worked. I could live with the chronic lightbulb shortage that left the stairwells and hallways pitch black after sunset. I didn't mind that our wallpaper peeled off in strips, or that our curtain covered only a fourth of the window and our room faced dead east, or that our room was infested with flies. One might assume insects die in Russia's harsh winters, but they actually just migrate into student dormitories.

They hovered over our heads as we brushed our teeth. They circled our skillets when we made spaghetti. They crawled up our noses as we slept. I was once the kind of person who carefully scooped up insects that strayed indoors and carried them outside to the bushes. But within a week of those flies, I joined my roommates' declaration of war. Our first line of defense was a gooey roll of flypaper, which we attempted to suspend from a light fixture with an upside-down hanger. We ran into it more than the flies, however, so we soon made a nightly ritual of shutting the door, closing the window, rolling up some *Pravda,* and going on a killing spree. We became so adept, we sometimes murdered two with one blow.

I could also deal with our bathtub situation. We converted it into a shower by suspending its spray nozzle from another hanger and some masking tape, but our lack of a curtain—or shower rod—meant we either flooded the room when we stood or froze our asses against the porcelain when we sat. (We would all return home to Texas with quads of steel after so many months of squatting.) Our toilet had a room of its own that was so small, we banged our knees against the door when we straddled the pot. Someone hung a portrait of Gogol at eye level, and to this day I associate the literary master with bowel movements.

I didn't even mind our kitchen. Each floor in the dormitory had an oven and two stoves, but only seven of the burners in the whole dorm worked properly. One was on our floor, but our Romanian neighbors were always boiling their beets on it. The kitchens were also home to little cockroaches that—like the flies—periodically peeked over our skillets to see what we were cooking. We were constantly scooping them out and chucking them onto the floor, which grew crunchy as the semester progressed.

Truth is, I rather enjoyed this lack of amenities, as it forced us to be resourceful and inventive—qualities you just can't acquire while living in privilege. We made shelves by yanking off the doors of the cabinets and hanging them on the wall with nails and string. A rope, a bucket, and an empty corner sufficed as our laundry room; we hung our perishables out the window into the icebox of winter. The gaping hole in the ceiling where microphones once recorded late night conversations was our ready reminder of how Soviet life used to be. Gerad said that, back in the day, exchange students used to stand on chairs and bid the bugs *spokounii nochi*—good night—before they went to sleep.

What I couldn't hack in my new home was the cot. The pillow was the width of a pantyliner; the mattress was only marginally thicker than the old army blanket that covered it. Both were smelly and stained. But I probably could have handled even this if it hadn't been for the bedsprings, which bored little holes all over my body. I lost so much sleep, my left eye started twitching. After two sleepless weeks, I sat down for a serious talk with my roommate, Kandy. A native Texan with the Big Hair to prove it—long, strawberry blond, and corkscrew curly—Kandy had financed her entire college education bartending at Tejano and kicker bars and roared around Austin in a fire-engine red sports car. She spoke Russian with a twang but could talk Turgenev like a scholar. She couldn't take our sleeping situation, either, and had already dreamed up a plan.

The second floor of the dormitory doubled as a hotel, and its rooms were rumored to be far nicer than ours on the fifth, with full-length curtains and chairs with cushions. They also had maid service. That last element was key, as it meant a way in when the guests were out. For the next few days, Kandy and I lingered in the stairwell, noting the housekeeper's every move. First she changed the bedsheets and tossed the soiled linens out the door. Next she emptied the trash. Then she dumped a pail of disinfectant onto the floor, splashed it around with a mop, and headed on to the next room, leaving the doors open so they could air out. Most important, tucked in a hallway out of view from the main corridor were three spare rooms that took her about fifteen minutes to clean.

We would have to act with speed and accuracy.

I had never stolen a thing in my life but decided this didn't count. As Proudhon liked to say, "Property is theft." Liberating a mattress was a step toward greater class equality; I could justify my actions in Marxist terms if pressed. Kandy and I took off our hiking boots, put on our *tapochki*—slippers—and crouched in the stairwell as the housekeeper shuffled in and out of the rooms. We waited until she turned the far corner to work on the three hidden rooms, and the instant the disinfectant splashed on the floor we darted into the room nearest the stairwell. Not only was it wallpapered, it had a television set and sofa. Now I really felt no guilt. Kandy went to one bed, I the other. I flung back the bedspread and discovered the same paltry mattress that covered my own cot—except there were four.

"From each according to his abilities, to each according to his needs," I muttered as I pulled out the middle two and covered the remaining two with the bedspread. Kandy took three. We rolled them into bundles along with the fresh linens and crept toward the door.

I heard it first—the clip-clop of the *komandanka*'s orthopedic shoes, coming down the stairwell. The superintendent of the dormitory, the *komandanka* was the in-house tyrant. She crashed all our parties and sent our guests home. She made the hired help cry. Rent raised at her whim. Dubbed "the Poison Dwarf" by exchange students long ago, she was now coming to inspect the housekeeping. My heart leaped into my throat as we made a break for the bathroom and hid behind the door. The footsteps came closer and paused by our doorway. My heart pounded so furiously, I felt light-headed; Kandy's freckles disappeared in a flush.

Were thieves still sent to Siberia in post-Soviet Russia? Would we be summarily denounced? Would she force us to do a self-criticism in front of the other residents?

After the longest thirty seconds of my life, the Poison Dwarf turned on her heels and clip-clopped down the hall. Kandy slipped out of the bathroom to keep watch, then motioned me to follow. We ran for the stairwell with our billowy bundles, flew up five flights of stairs, burst into our room, and slammed the door triumphantly. I stripped off my army blanket and added the two new mattresses and linens. Kandy kicked off her *tapochki* and looked at me. I nodded.

We turned off the lights and slept for the next day and a half.

LIKE MANY AMERICANS born during the cold war, I grew up thinking of the Soviet Union as the Evil Empire. Maps showed it as a menacing red blob gobbling up Asia and Eastern Europe; teachers told how the Soviets had an entire fleet of nuclear missiles pointed straight at us that would knock out not only our country, but theirs as well. When Sting sang, "What might save us, me and you / Is if the Russians love their children too," I actually wondered. So it was something of a surprise to learn in college that communism as an ideology actually had the best of intentions. (I had always assumed oppression was part of its master plan.) The problem seemed to be that the men who led the world's Communist revolutions kept turning out to be murderous dictators. I wondered why: Were they psychopaths to begin with? Was there something inherently corrupting about the ideology itself? Or would the kind of absolute power they each obtained warp anyone's sense of basic humanity?

The only thing I could remotely compare to the mysterious worlds I studied in my post-Soviet classes at UT was the old King Ranch of South Texas. Like the Soviet Union, it was once a vast empire that promised housing, health care, education, and subsistence to its workers in exchange for loyalty and labor. And it too had recently abandoned its principles for reasons that ultimately boiled down to greed.

The King Ranch was "discovered" in 1852 when a captain named Richard King docked his riverboat on the Rio Grande and headed on horseback with a friend to the Lone Star Fair in Corpus Christi. A shortcut landed him in a stretch of mesquite and *zacahuistle* that Mexicans called *El Desierto de los Muertos*— the Desert of the Dead—but King was smitten by its many white-tailed deer and javelina. Sources vary on how he actually acquired the land that eventually became the largest ranch in the world, but many say he rounded up help by venturing into the hills of Tamaulipas, Mexico, and convincing an entire village to join him. According to legend, one hundred men, women, and children gathered up their cattle and burros and followed him across the border. My great-great-grandfather on my mother's side was among them and soon became one of the proud Kineños who braved fires, floods, droughts, cactus, rattlesnakes, and the burning sun as they branded, castrated, inoculated, fed, and bred horses and cattle for their (gringo) *patrón*. In return, the *patrón* paid for their families' housing and medical care, provided their children's schooling, and distributed rations of beans, rice, and *masa*. Kids learned their trades from their parents as soon as they were physically able; the elderly were allowed to remain on the ranch until their final breath. And that is how the medieval fiefdom existed for generations.

My aunts, uncles, and *abuelita* used to reside in the Los Laureles division of the King Ranch in a long block of yellow brick houses. They drove big trucks, ate red meat, drank Miller beer, and wore cowboy hats with cowboy boots and gleaming belt buckles. They felt great security knowing that when they retired, they'd be cared for. But in the late 1980s, King's descendants brought in some outside business executives to run the ranch, and within a few years it became another slice in America's corporate pie, with people rating second to profits. After discovering that a helicopter could do the work of dozens of cowboys at roundup, for instance, the ranch invested in one—causing the Kineños to scramble for ways to justify their employment. Those who couldn't were fired. Rent was also imposed for the first time, including on retirees, at prices few could afford. Within a decade, my entire family had moved off the ranch and taken jobs at places like Wal-Mart to get by.

So I had already witnessed what could happen to a society when the system they had worked toward their entire life collapsed and their cradle-to-grave protection faded away. What I wanted to learn in Moscow was the toll that the dissolution of the Soviet Union had taken on its youth. Would they look on their past with bittersweet memories, like my aunts and uncles? Feel disillusioned, like my cousins? Or would they be determined to seize the momentous shift in their nation's history and forge something altogether new?

If I had paid closer attention, these questions could have been answered before I even left Texas. My last three years in college, I lived with sixteen people in a vegetarian housing cooperative called Royal that was a crunchy granola version of a socialist workers' commune (in my eyes, anyway). We grew our own herbs, brewed our own beer, composted our own waste. The five hours of chores we each contributed once a week—cooking, cleaning, changing the water in the tofu bucket—were monitored by a democratically elected "Labor Czar." We called this little utopia "cooperativism."

But the Russian exchange students who moved into New Guild, a nearby co-op, in the fall of 1995 had a different name for it: "communism."

By mid-September, the cold war had been rewaged. The Russians had been under the impression they were going to live with some nice, affluent family during their year in the United States—not a house full of hippies who asked them to scrub the toilets. But owing to some administrative oversight, our university sent them to us. It was an ill-fated match. To the Russians, our co-ops bore too close a resemblance to the Soviet *kommunalnaya kvartira*, in which half a dozen families got stuffed into two-bedroom apartments. Our "labor holidays"—the one weekend a semester we devoted to group projects like building bike racks—reminded them of the Soviet *subbotnik*, when citizens were riled out of bed to tidy the People's Stadium or spruce up the People's Park.

So the Russian students simply refused to do their share of the labor. Their American housemates tried to explain the virtues of toiling together for the common good, but the Russians didn't buy it. This was, they reminded us, a free country. If they didn't want to scrub toilets, they didn't have to. The Americans accused the Russians of being "un-cooperative." The Russians retaliated by calling us "commies." We deemed them "capitalist bourgeoisie."

Oh, it got ugly.

That experience should have prepared me for the students I would meet in Moscow, but I have a hard time letting go of my illusions. This, I reasoned, was the country that had birthed Sakharov and Solzhenitsyn. Survived seventy years of authoritarianism. Known freedom just five short years. Its college campuses, therefore, would be hotbeds of discourse and political action, teeming with *intelligentsie*, free from the apathy that plagued American universities like mine. I would learn from my peers the very meaning of truth, democracy, and justice— concepts that had surrounded me since birth but which I'd never fully understood or appreciated.

At least, that's what I hoped when I signed up for classes at the Moscow Linguistics Institute (MLI).

THE MOSCOW LINGUISTICS INSTITUTE resided in a nine-teenth-century egg-yolk-yellow building with tall white columns and a spacious courtyard, just a few blocks from Red Square. Its prime real estate had recently made it the target of envy. A businessman purportedly wanted to turn the college into a new bank and had called in so many bomb threats the semester be-fore, the seniors had to postpone their graduation. Resolution was supposedly under way in 1996, but a couple of times we showed up to school only to discover a *NYET UROKOV*—NO CLASSES—sign hanging on the doorway.

Brawny boys in camouflage uniforms demanded to see the *dokumenti* of all who passed through the university's front doors. As the Russian saying goes: *Bez bumazhki ti bukashka; a s bumazhkoy chelovek*—Without papers, you are an insect; with them, you are a person. As foreigners, we had to carry four pieces of *dokumenti* (dormitory ID, university ID, visa, pass-port) at all times to avoid getting shooed away. As we waited in line that first day of school, I caught my initial glimpse of the Russian student body. They were a primped and preened bunch: Their hair was combed, their shoes were polished, their clothes were neatly pressed. The girls wore makeup; the boys wore aftershave. We Texans, meanwhile, had honed the art of rolling out of bed and out the door in ten minutes flat back in Austin. Moscow added a few minutes to our repertoire because we had to wear significantly more clothing, but our jeans were still ripped, our hair was still tousled, our boots were still muddy. Kandy wore lipstick and Durk wore deodorant and that was it.

Inside the building, dozens of students crowded around a poster plastered on a wall. I got excited. Was it a petition against the war in Chechnya? A flyer for a poetry reading? An invitation to an open debate? I squirmed through the body layers and discovered a chart that matched courses, professors, and room numbers with student groups like "Linguistics 6-A." Karen copied the information for "Texas-1"—which we presumed to be us—and we set out for our first class, Russian Grammar. We promptly got lost in the labyrinth of unlit corridors, hallways, and stairwells whose numbering system eluded us. As would happen every day thereafter, one of us flagged down a passing Russian who led us through the mazes and deposited us outside a dark and unmarked room.

Someone flicked on the light switch. Nothing happened. The fixture had no bulb. The chalkboard had no chalk. An empty Coke can and used tissues lay in a corner with no trash can. The room was barren save for three wooden desks defaced by graffiti—"Fak you!" and "Kurt lives!"—and a couple of benches and chairs. We sat down and stared at the jumble of wires dangling from the holes in the ceiling. Outside, all sorts of interesting people passed by—Romanians, Moldavians, Spaniards, Swedes, Russians—but the only ones who entered our room borrowed our extra chairs. (Some of the classes at MLI were so overcrowded, students stood.) A bell soon rang and the sound of doors slamming shut echoed down the hall. Durk stuck his head out and scanned the desolate breezeway. "Maybe they forgot about us," he mused.

Ten minutes later, a petite brunette shot into our room. It

was Alla Bodiereva, the overworked, underpaid, hypercharged professor, dean, and caretaker of foreign students. After welcoming us to MLI, she inquired about our collective level of Russian. It ranged from one to three and a half years, but she didn't find that discrepancy significant. *"Chudesno!"* she chirped. "You'll stay together then!"

Teams—not individuals—make up Russian education. Students typically get placed in groups of ten to thirty at the beginning of their college career and venture through the curriculum as a unit until graduation, with university administrators mapping out their entire course load, assigning their professors, and even selecting their research topics. Decisions are generally made for students, not by them—and that, it seemed, was what just happened to us.

Alla had other business to tend to that morning, so after a quick introduction to her class, she whisked us from one end of the building to the other, dropped us off at the queue to the library, and bolted off to her next engagement. Time all but ceased as we lined up for the books we would need that semester. The library had closed stacks, so students filled out separate slips of paper for each volume they needed and handed them through the window to the librarian, who appeared to be in her upper sixties and—judging by the thickness of her glasses— legally blind. She would squint at each paper for a minute or two before hobbling over to the bookshelves and hunting for the requested volume. The student, in turn, leaned through the window to guide her. "Fourth row, second shelf. . . . No, the second shelf. . . . That's it. See it, right there next to Lermontov?"

If she found it, she removed a card from the book's jacket, fastidiously recorded the student's information, had the student initial it, and filed it into a box. Next, she pulled out a notebook to rerecord the information and made the student initial it. Finally, she handed the book through the window—though she didn't release her grip until she'd harangued the student on how properly to care for it. Then she asked if they wanted another volume—which, naturally, was the case. Russians don't usually buy their textbooks; they borrow them. Every student in that queue needed at least six. So the process repeated itself again and again at an unfathomably slow pace, numbing our minds and trying our souls. It took an hour for the eight students in front of us to collect their books, and an additional twenty stood behind us. One could have distinguished the Americans from the Russians on body language alone: We fidgeted, sighed, grumbled, and bitched; they gazed ahead stoically.

By the time our turn materialized, I had to hold my hands behind my back to keep them from wrapping around the librarian's neck. When at last she returned with our first round of books, she announced there weren't enough—we'd have to share. As she started filling out the paperwork, her pen began to leak. A thin stream of blue ink bled across the note card, forming indigo blobs over the names of generations of students who doubtlessly waited hours to check it out, too. But the librarian continued to record the information in her arthritic script until her pen ran out of ink. Then she proceeded to dip its nub into the little blue blobs—as though they were paint—in between strokes.

All we had to do to end this torture was give the woman another pen, but that didn't occur to any of us just then. The absurdity of the inefficiency caught us in a trance. We couldn't move, couldn't speak. Couldn't do a thing but watch that woman smear blue ink over her cards, her files, her notebooks, and herself.

At some point, I turned around to find Kandy quivering. At first I thought she was laughing, then crying. But when we made eye contact, I saw it was neither. Placing my hand on her shoulder, I steered her out the door to the courtyard, where she shuffled through the mounds of snow until she could finally feel the cold. Then she sat on a bench, lit a cigarette, and inhaled deeply as the bolt of culture shock fizzled away.

After classes ended that day, I visited the university's *stolovaya*, or canteen. One of the few places to congregate on campus, it was always packed with students eating, drinking, and chatting while Russian pop music blared from a small transistor radio. I decided to eat first and meet people second.

At one side of the room was a snack bar featuring Fanta, Coke, Snickers, and Doritos. A dozen students stood in its line. The Russian-style buffet on the opposite side of the room, meanwhile, had two customers—both over the age of fifty. Reminding myself that I had come to Moscow for a cultural experience, I walked over to the buffet and picked up a tray. The special was *bifshteks*, missile-shaped meat chops served with your choice of cold beets smothered in sour cream or egg salad sculpted into phallic mounds by the cook's bare hands and topped with a dollop of mayonnaise and a parsley sprig. Side orders included days-old baguettes and fuzzy cheese, burned rice or scorched potatoes, speckled sausages or greasy soups. Big tin spoons were the only silverware, heavily sugared tea was the sole beverage, and salt was the single spice. Keeping to my vegetarian diet, I asked the woman behind the counter to ladle me a bowl of soup (clear broth seasoned with cucumber slices) and some macaroni; the tea came scalding hot in a plastic cup with no handle. The cashier totaled the cost of my meal on an abacus: 75 cents.

As I maneuvered through the crowd toward a chair, I briefly

crossed paths with a good-looking Russian in a Calvin Klein sweater. His hair was curly, his eyes were blue, his chin was cleft. I smiled. He did, too. Then he pointed at my soup.

"That stuff is for dogs," he said. With a wave of his package of peanut M&M's, he disappeared into the crowd.

ONE OF OUR biggest surprises at MLI was that we got paid to go. Full-time Russian students have traditionally received monthly stipends from the government to help keep them in school, and we did too through our exchange program. Each month we received 300,000 rubles—roughly $60. If I ate the majority of my meals in the *stolovaya* or cooked them myself, used public transportation, and refrained from buying non-essential items, that stipend lasted about ten days. So it was upsetting to discover that 300,000 rubles was not, as we thought, the same stipend given to our fellow students, but rather the starting monthly salary for MLI's highly educated professors. I would run into this system around the Bloc: By virtue of being a light-skinned foreigner, I received perks and privileges that gave me a far higher standard of living than many locals. I never knew what to do in these situations. How do you fight a system that benefits you?

Russian students picked up their stipends at the end of the month, but we received ours at the beginning, as did the professors. The first time Kandy and I went to retrieve them, the line was long and testy. We shuffled in behind the professors, but a guard noticed us and waved us to the front. We shook our heads vehemently—the last thing we wanted to do was cut in front of professors—but the guard insisted. As it turned out, there were two money lines: one for foreigners and one for Russians. Trying to ignore the penetrating stares of the professors, we took the rubles and hurried off, feeling as though we'd stepped back in time to the days of Jim Crow in the Old South.

The next month, the ruble line was even longer than the previous had been and twice as disgruntled. The professors had received only half their paychecks the month before and anxiously awaited their new ones. At that time, the government owed about 28 billion rubles in delayed wages. In some parts of the nation, workers were paid in food, coal, or—if things were really bad—vodka to drunken (and shut) them up. According to Alla Bodiereva, it cost nearly 1 million rubles a month to feed a family of three in Moscow. That was roughly the combined income she earned as professor, department head, and dean and her husband as a doctor. Since the Soviet Union's collapse, they had both taken side jobs to supplement their salaries. Receiving only half a paycheck meant Alla had to double her tutorials with foreign students and borrow money from her family and friends. (It seemed that everyone I met "borrowed" money from their friends, but I never once encountered any lenders.)

Kandy and I couldn't tell from the back of the line if the foreigners window was open or not, and we debated what to do. The Russian line looked to be an hour long. We started to wait in it, but after fifteen minutes passed without movement, we stole forth to investigate, prompting angry pushes and shoves. Just then, the guard—the same guy as before—noticed us. "The foreigners window isn't open today," he snapped.

"Zhdai kak Russkie!" a professor yelled. Wait like Russians! The others joined in. *"Zhdai! Zhdai! Zhdai kak Russkie!"*

Wishing the floor would swallow us whole, we scuffled back to the end of the line, elbows jostling us every step of the way.

Once again, the professors received only half their paychecks. One by one they filed away, the women with pursed and pointy lips, the men steely and distant.

Kandy and I got our stipends in their entirety, however. We blew them on tickets to a Sting concert in Red Square.

RUSSIAN SCHOOLS were no longer required to devote a quarter of their curriculum to the tenets of Marx and Lenin in 1996, but few had the money or resources to fully utilize their new freedoms. Conditions had plummeted at most universities, which were now starved of government funding. Education had been free to all in the Soviet Union, but increasingly, only the wealthy were able to afford the exorbitant tuition of specialized, private institutes. State-run universities were still relatively cheap (although preparation courses for their placement exams cost millions of rubles), but even they were seeing sharp decreases in enrollment. In the mid-1990s, it simply behooved would-be students to delve straight into the market economy rather than toil at a university for five years. Those who stayed shied away from sciences and liberal arts in favor of more profitable arenas like accounting, finance, computers, and languages.

Our own performance at MLI was rated by our ability to rote-learn massive amounts of material and regurgitate it on command. In Classical Literature, for instance, our professor made us repeat random passages of eighteenth-century literature until we committed them to memory. That would have been palpable if it had been poetry, but she picked sentences from texts with grammatical monstrosities like "He went to the station to change his horses, cleaned his musket, continued over to tea with Dunya and her father, and then left with his friends." Since the Russian word for "to go" has a dozen variants alone, that one sentence took up an entire class period. In Phonetics, our instructor passed out long lists of similar-sounding words and conducted our rounds of repetitions like a linguistic orchestra.

Conversation class entailed reading questions aloud from our workbooks and then answering them. "Did you buy apples at the store?" could be answered in one of two ways: "Yes, we bought apples at the store" or "No, we did not buy apples at the store." I once tried: "We were going to buy apples, but there weren't any, so we settled for pears." It wasn't until the professor looked at me quizzically that I realized how profoundly Russian that statement sounded.

Two of my classes reflected the changes of time. In one, a graduate student who wore platform shoes and black leather skirts assigned us readings from the Russian edition of *Cosmopolitan*. In the other—Mass Media and Information—we answered questions about current events clipped from a variety of Russian newspapers, including *Kommersant*, *Moskovskii Komsomolets*, and *Nezavisimaya Gazeta*.

Sensing my building frustration with her class, a professor pulled me aside one day. "You ought to be more grateful, Stesha," she reprimanded me gently. "Ten years ago, you would have been translating propaganda straight out of *Pravda*. At least now we have different points of view."

AMONG THE FREEDOMS Russians gained in 1991 was the right to assembly. Students at MLI celebrated that freedom's reverse—the right *not* to gather. In Former Times (that is, while the Soviet Union was still intact), every Russian who wanted a decent future joined Octobrists at age seven, Pioneers at nine, Komsomol at fourteen, and the Communist Party thereafter. These youth organizations were like coed scouting troops, only instead of vowing to "Serve God and my country, to help people at all times, and to live by the Girl Scout law," they promised to be *vsegda gotov*—always ready.

"Ready for what?" I once asked Nadezhda.

"Revolution," she said with a sigh.

For the most part, Russians my age had attended a few thousand too many meetings during their childhood, and the majority now despised most forms of organized activity. MLI, consequently, was dead after class. I never heard of any distinguished speakers lecturing on campus. There were no film festivals or theatrical productions or sporting events. When classes were over, students left.

My friends at the co-op in Austin and I often debated why American college students were so disengaged and decided it was because our lives lacked Struggle. Our country's economy was thriving. We weren't at war. We had social problems, of course, but no single Cause that could unite our entire student body (besides football). The Russians, on the other hand, had the war in Chechnya, ethnic conflict, widespread corruption. This was the first time in recent history that students could rally and protest on their own free will. Why weren't they?

Over the course of that year, I took an informal survey of young people and found their responses to be remarkably similar. As Nadezhda put it, they considered themselves to be the "sacrificial generation" that straddled two major epochs of their nation's history. Democracy would be a long and painful process whether or not they participated. Why get involved in something they couldn't change?

There was an element of truth to this argument. It probably would take Russia generations to reach anything resembling a Western-style democracy (if that, in fact, was what they ultimately chose to do). But hadn't history shown them what students were capable of? Lenin, Bukharin, Stalin, and Trotsky had all been student leaders known (and later expelled) for their radicalism—look what they did!

But my friends seemed too busy deciding between a life of honest labor or fast rubles to contemplate social change. Should they toil for years at a government job to earn paychecks that would barely keep their heads above the poverty line? Or should they join the burgeoning *Mafiya* that infiltrated every level of Russian society—from beggars row to the gilded seats of the Kremlin—and kept its men and molls in bulletproof BMWs? Either way, they couldn't seek much counsel from their parents, who were too preoccupied with trying to keep *borscht* on the table while their economy lay in ruins. *Their* parents— the old-age pensioners—usually had definitive convictions, but they generally wanted a return to the past (and could often be seen marching through Red Square, brandishing banners of Lenin). So it really was up to the youth to plot Russia's next course.

"Don't you think if we held a rally against the war, people would come?" I once tried to cajole Nadezhda. "It would be so great! Come on. Whatever happened to *'Vsegda gotov'*?"

"You need to understand something, Stesha. The Revolution is dead," she said flatly.

SIX THOUSAND MILES AWAY

IT WAS JUST after midnight. Kandy and I had taken the last train of the evening, and the Metro *babushka* locked the station's carved wooden doors behind us. We'd been out celebrating the end of our first month in Moscow, and it was the latest we'd ever returned. Two things we failed to take into consideration: the darkness and the cold. Shivering spastically, we wondered how to get home.

We usually walked along the kiosks that stretched two city blocks, but they had closed for the night and turned off their lights. The drunks and ice patches that lurked along that path were hard enough to avoid in daylight: How could we navigate them in total blackness? The other option was to walk along the street, but that would add at least five minutes to the journey— and my teeth were already chattering so violently, I had to roll up my tongue so it wouldn't get bit.

While we could condemn the city's dearth of street lamps for the darkness, we could only blame vanity for our skimpy attire. We had spent our entire lives in tank tops and sandals, so the frumpy layers of longjohns, undershirts, overshirts, sweaters, scarves, mittens, boots, hats, fleece, and Gore-Tex we now had to don before so much as opening a window had become a serious affront to our femininity. Reasoning that our dorm and the Taganka Theatre were so close to linking Metros that we'd be exposed to winter's elements for only "ten minutes max," we had seized that evening's performance of Mikhail Bulgakov's *Master i Margarita* as an opportunity to reassert our womanhood, stripping off the thermals and sliding on the hose. But that miniskirt and Navy peacoat I'd put on so happily a few hours ago now felt as insulated as cheesecloth, while a swarm of hornets seemed to be sucking on my toes straight through my cute leather shoes.

Erring on the side of safety, Kandy and I shuffled through the snow toward the street, where the occasional passing car cast a wan light through the icy sleet. It couldn't have been more than ten degrees, and the temperature seemed to drop every minute. I was so focused on retaining body heat, I didn't even notice the tinny gray Lada trailing behind us until it pulled right up beside me. The window rolled down and a man poked his head out. *"De-vu-shka,"* he called out.

That was another name I'd acquired in Russia. It means "young, presumably unmarried woman" and is actually quite handy. Rather than saying, "Excuse me!" and hoping the right person in a crowd turns around, it is perfectly polite to be specific in Russian, as in *"Dedushka!"* (Hey, you, old man) or *"Devochka!"* (Yo, little girl, I'm talking to you).

In this context, however, *devushka* sounded sinister.

"It's too cold to be out on the street, *devushka*," the man slurred. "Come inside, where it's nice and warm."

"Ne nada," I said brusquely. That was the second mistake of the evening: He could tell by my accent and word choice that I wasn't Russian.

"Amerikanskie devushki!" he exclaimed triumphantly. Ameri-

can girls! Laughter erupted from inside the car as more windows rolled down. There were four men altogether. I could smell the vodka on their breath.

Fuck.

Kandy and I quickened our pace, but the Lada followed so closely behind, its heat singed the backs of our legs. We soon reached a video store that had also closed for the night. A thigh-high snowbank loomed behind it.

"Let's lose them in there," I whispered to Kandy.

"Go for it."

On the count of three, we darted behind the store and promptly sank into the snowbank, which soaked our hose and filled our shoes with slush. The Lada, however, sped on down the street as we tromped through the snow toward the kiosks. The dorm was still a block away, with only the glimmering steeples of the distant Church of St. Nicholas of the Weavers to guide us. Back on the icy kiosk trail, we hurried in silence. My worries shifted from the men back to the cold. What happened to my feminist virtues? I resolved never to compromise body heat for fashion again.

Suddenly, two bright lights pierced the darkness. It was the same Lada as before, only now it was in front of us and approaching rapidly. *"A-mer-i-kan-skie devushki!"* they called out.

We were so astonished, we could only stand and gape— until a hunchbacked man staggered into the Lada's light. He was one of those kiosk bums we'd been trying to avoid, but it occurred to us—simultaneously—that we might be safer with him, if only because he was male and we were not. We darted over to either side of him, grabbed an arm, and held on tight.

"Could you walk us back to the dorm?" Kandy asked in as conversational a tone as possible.

"*Kuda?*" he inquired, spraying us with toxic spittle.

Using the drunkard as a shield, we approached the car blocking our way home. When we got within a few feet of it, the doors opened and all four men climbed out. The car's inner light spilled onto the snow as vodka, leather, and cigarette smoke thickened the air. I watched in disbelief as the driver's shoes sauntered toward me. My eyes ran up from his socks to his jeans, his black leather coat, his jutting chin, and finally his glassy eyes, peering hard at me. When invited, the stare of a man feels so warm and wet. It turns your insides out, quickening your breath, swelling your breasts, parting your thighs. But a predatory stare feels cold and dry. Muscles lock, hairs stand, lips dissolve, thighs press tightly together.

"*Amerikanskaya devushka,*" he said, then reached out for me.

"Leave us alone!" I hollered in English, backing up.

Kandy and I exchanged a final glance. We'd seen enough movies to know that women in these situations had only one recourse.

RUN!

Down the dark alley, across the glittering snow, in little black heels designed to make me feel like a woman. (They were doing their job tonight.) Don't slip, don't fall, don't look back, never look back. You're already going to be haunted by their sound, their smell, their pursuit, your fear. Don't add the sight of them chasing you, too. Focus on those steeples of St. Nicholas, gleaming golden in the distance. SCREAM! (How do you call for help in Russian? They didn't teach us that!) Remember that ice patch that has wiped you out so many times before. JUMP! Feel the solid concrete beneath your feet. You're almost there. The security guards! They're probably drinking on the couch in front of the TV. They need to open the locks before you get there. SCREAM!

As I rounded the final corner, two guards miraculously

appeared. I slid right into them. "Men—in the street!" I cried.

Understanding immediately, they took off running.

Kandy. *Where's Kandy?* I screamed out her name, panic riddling my body. And then she too appeared—silky blouse soaked, hair tangled, mascara everywhere. We exchanged wide-eyed looks before she beelined through the foyer and up the stairs. But I couldn't make it through the doorway just yet, electing instead to stand and shiver.

After some time, the *komandanka* appeared, ostensibly to shut the door. She gasped at the sight of me. *"Idi syuda!"* she demanded, grabbing me by the arm and yanking me inside. "You're wearing a skirt? In this weather? Do you want to catch a cold? *Uzhasno!*"

My suitemates sat up with me in shifts that night, holding me as I contemplated the horrible fates we had narrowly escaped. Of course, drunk men chase women down dark alleys the world over. I just hated being reminded of the universal vulnerability of my sex so soon after my arrival to an exciting new place.

When the sun rose the following morning, I placed a collect call to my parents at a phone downstairs. Mom answered on the first ring. She asked what was wrong, as I normally called during their Sunday mornings—not early Thursday evenings. I couldn't tell her the truth, though: My parents already worried so much about me. Instead, I mumbled about homesickness, and she promptly began to soothe me with peaceful, calming words. Then she passed the phone to my father, who continued where she left off before handing it to my sister, her husband, and a succession of *m'hijita*-crooning aunts and uncles. I was so caught up in my own life, I didn't even question the occasion that had brought them all together. I just assumed fate had gathered them to field my call, never fathoming they'd have their own traumas to tend to.

—

IT WAS A Friday night, two weeks later, around 7:00. Not yet knowing the best places to shop, Kandy and I had spent hours tramping through the snow for dinner, only to return with pasta, onions, a kilo of walnuts, and some mealy red apples. Our suitemates, however, had found sour cream, raspberry jam, and a kilo of mutant mushrooms that the vendor swore hadn't been gathered in Chernobyl. Our mood lifted considerably when Katie popped some Irish tunes in our cassette recorder. She hacked away at the onions while Kandy buttered some bread and Karen and I improvised a walnut-butter-cream sauce. We had just set the table when David, the grad student UT shipped over to be our "group leader," came in with the mail he had retrieved from the embassy. Only soldiers huddled in foxholes could have been happier to see that bundle of letters. Kandy pried them away and launched them one by one across the room. "Katie, Karen, Stesha, Stesha, Karen—oy! *Moya!*"

Six letters, all for me. My hands quivered with excitement as I thrust my thumb under the first flap and unsheathed its precious contents. So much news from my housemates back in Austin! Jason's band lined up a new gig, Arthur was rebuilding a keyboard he found in a garage sale, Joy bought an iguana and named it Ayla, Michelle and Ari finally hooked up. For a moment, I was swinging my legs from our communal kitchen's countertop while Tyra filled me in on the past month's gossip.

Then Karen started sobbing.

" 'Sometimes I miss you so much, I just go and sit in your room and cry,' " she read her best friend's letter aloud as tears streamed down her face. The rest of us dutifully put down our mail and went over to console her. Then Katie started sniffling over her boyfriend's card. We walked over to rub her shoulders. Kandy also received upsetting news and retreated to the hallway for a smoke.

Finally I returned to my cot, where I'd saved the biggest and thickest letter from my parents for last. I paused for a moment, savoring the anticipation, before unfastening its metal clasp and spilling its contents onto my blanket. My eyes landed first on an image of the Virgin Mary in mourning. This was death's calling card for Catholics, but it couldn't have been anyone close to me: I'd just shared a pleasant conversation with my mother a few days before. Must have been some long-lost uncle or twice removed aunt (I had lots of those). I flipped it over to read the fine gold print.

"In memory of Nicole Elizondo."

Nicole. Elizondo. Nikki? My cousin? My beautiful, twenty-three-year-old cousin? She can't be dead. I just saw her at Christmas. My whole family went to that barbecue place where she waits tables. She bought us cheesecake and ice cream. Called my parents Aunt Irene and Uncle Dick. She's not dead. She wants to be an airline stewardess.

What else is in this envelope? Newspaper clippings. Black-and-white mug shots of Nikki everywhere. Here's a letter. Folded twice. Written by my mother. So many words that make no sense. The sentences just dance together. But then the first one stands still: "It is with a sad, sad heart that I write you about Nicole. . . ."

It was late. The manager of a nightclub offered her a ride home on his motorcycle. He was drunk. Had only one helmet, and he wore it. Rammed right into his own jeep. Nikki was thrown thirty feet. That shattered her spine, punctured her lungs, and incapacitated her brain, but her heart continued to beat a whole extra week while my family kept vigil by her side and I, back in Russia, conjugated verbs of motion.

That's why everyone had gathered at my house that night—so they could pray for Nikki. But instead, I'd made them comfort me.

Images. Thanksgiving at *Tía*'s house. Playing "Bloody Mary" in the shed while our fathers dealt poker chips and drank beer and our mothers basted turkeys and gossiped. Easter at the King Ranch. Nikki showing me where she'd hidden a whole crate of *cascarones* (painted eggs filled with confetti) for us to use once the tradition of cracking them over everyone's head began. Junior high. Nikki sticking up for me, the nerdy little cousin relegated to the sidelines.

Of my several dozen cousins, I had always related to Nikki best—probably because she, like me, spoke little Spanish and was blue eyed and fair skinned in a dark-eyed, caramel-skinned, *r*-rolling family. But while my racial loyalties used to fluctuate with my company, Nikki always claimed a Mexican heritage.

"You don't look Mexican," people would tell her.

"Well, I am!" she would say.

I admired her for that. I wouldn't take that sort of pride in my culture until college, where it was more acceptable—even cool—to be Chicana.

Suddenly I was screaming and then I was crying as arms wrapped around my body and squeezed me tight. More hushed words, more sweet soothing.

A long time later, the four of us stumbled back to the table. Our pot of cold Stroganoff and loaf of buttered bread were now coated with flies.

"What have we done to ourselves?" Kandy asked gloomily.

"Well," Katie surmised, "the countries with beaches were just too expensive."

We looked at her and then each other before breaking down

once more, this time in laughter. After picking at the mushrooms, I retreated downstairs to call my parents.

"I got the letter," I said when they picked up.

"Oh, hon," my mother said, heavy with grief. "We were afraid you would have wanted to come back home, and there was nothing you could have done. It's better you're there in Russia. We know we should have told you when it happened, honey, but we just couldn't bear to . . ."

When I packed my bags for Moscow, I somehow thought I was simultaneously wrapping twenty-one years of personal relationships into a box, tying it neatly with a ribbon, and setting it off to the side so that nothing would change in my absence. I didn't fathom that Nikki would die, or that one of my best friends would sink into manic depression, or that my mother's hair would further gray. I didn't consider what it might feel like to know my sister was giving birth to her first child and I wasn't there to greet him.

That's because true travel, the kind with no predetermined end, is one of the most selfish endeavors we can possibly undertake—an act in which we focus solely on our own fulfillment, with little regard to those we leave behind. After all, *we're* the ones venturing out into the big crazy world, filling up journals, growing like weeds. And we have the gall to think *they're* just sitting at home, soaking in security and stability.

It is only when we reopen these wrapped and ribboned boxes, upon our triumphant return home, that we discover nothing is the way we had left it before.

4 · THE ABANDONED

DURING A ROUTINE food-finding mission one evening, I happened upon a bakery and slipped inside. Russian bread smells just like where it came from—the moist, sweet earth—and this bakery was stocked full of freshly baked loaves. Breathing in the delicious air, I slowly made my way through the crowd of shoppers toward the Borodinskii loaves cooling on a distant shelf. Suddenly I tripped over something and stumbled onto the slush-streaked floor, nearly knocking over two shoppers in the process. As I picked myself up, I saw that I had almost landed atop a middle-aged Russian man wearing a furry *shapka* with earflaps. I apologized profusely, but he didn't respond. His eyes were closed and he was stretched out on the floor, as limp as he was muddy, moving not a muscle. Timidly I touched him. He felt frightfully cold.

Moscow has a reputation for being a rough-and-tumble place, and most Russians and expats have grisly stories about running across dead bodies.

Had I just discovered mine in the biscuit aisle?

I darted over to the *kassa*, or cashier's. The queued customers protested as I pushed to the front and cried out: "There is a man on the floor!"

The *kassa* lady didn't even blink.

"I think he's hurt!"

She told me to get back in line.

"Maybe he's dead!" I gasped.

That got a reaction. She stood up on her stool, peered into the crowd, and spotted him.

"I don't know him." She shrugged.

If she had, she would have crossed the Volga River to reach him. Since she didn't, even a stretch of parquet was too far. Swallowing hard, I pushed my way back through the crowd, trying to remember the CPR I had learned in my eighth-grade health class. To my relief, the man was no longer alone: a *babushka* in a thick woolen shawl was crouched beside him. I squatted behind her and formulated questions in my mind: What can I do? Is there a police station close by? How do you call for an ambulance in this country?

Then I realized what the old woman was doing.

The man had apparently been shopping prior to his collapse. He held in his hands a muddied baguette; dented canned goods peeked out of his plastic bag. The *babushka* slapped him on the cheek a few times and then, when he did not stir, began to swipe his cans and plop them into her own bag, which bulged with the empty beer bottles she'd probably been collecting to recycle for rubles. Then she removed the soggy baguette from his arms and carefully wiped it off on her shawl. Sensing my presence, she turned around to face me. Her indigo eyes seared straight through me.

What could have brought this old woman to steal from a fallen man? The humiliation of gathering recyclables in her retirement years because her hard-earned pension yielded little more than a few sacks of potatoes? The insult of working a life-time for an ideology, only to see it fall by the wayside? And what about the other shoppers in that bakery? How could they so nonchalantly step over a man lying in the middle of a muddy floor? After seventy years of reporting their comrades' actions, did they now rebel with indifference?

Or maybe I was making too much of this. The situation was really quite simple: He no longer needed food, and she did. So she took it. I was just witnessing survival in its rawest state—and couldn't take a moment more. Though I would forever regret not seeking medical attention for that man, I bolted to my feet, barreled out the door, and ran through the streets until I slipped on an ice patch and sliced open my palms. Only at the sight of my own blood did I finally break down.

UP TO THAT point, my foremost concern had been my own survival, which I roughly defined as scrounging enough food for three vegetarian meals a day and keeping my feet warm. But stumbling upon that comatose body—and then doing nothing for it—caused me to question the validity of my time in Russia. How could I justify the space I took up in the Metro? I decided I needed a Cause or a Project. Something that would separate me from those sombrero-toting tourists I used to make fun of on the Mexican border, whose interactions with locals was limited to bartering and photographs.

Volunteering in a society that has no real word for it isn't easy, though. My dictionary offered only *bezplatno rabota*, work without pay, but no one took me seriously when I asked where I could do it.

"That's Communist!" one student cried when I asked if there was a volunteer center at MLI, as there had been at UT. "We don't have to do that sort of thing anymore."

That got me thinking about where I could realistically volunteer without a useful degree like public health or social work. And then it occurred to me: an orphanage. I saw a documentary about Soviet orphanages back in high school, and the images had haunted me ever since—of malnourished children rocking back and forth on their haunches, ramming their heads against dingy walls, of babies lying in filth. I didn't know enough Russian to work with adults, but I could probably hold my own with little kids. So I got off at a random Metro stop one day and roamed around, asking everyone who passed if they knew where I could find one. Amazingly, one lady actually did and led me through a labyrinth of concrete slab buildings before depositing me on a doorstep. A small blue sign read DYETSKII DOM, or CHILDREN'S HOME. My stomach tingling with nerves, I knocked on the door and a woman in a white lab coat and hairnet flung it open.

"What do you want?" she asked suspiciously.

"Can I work for free here?" I asked, smiling with all my teeth.

"Nevozmozhno," she clipped before slamming the door shut.

I wouldn't have let me in, either, in retrospect, but at the time, I was crushed. I later learned, however, that most dyetskii dom had been off-limits to foreign volunteers since journalists and human rights organizations started exposing their squalid conditions in the late 1980s. While documentaries laudably call attention to social injustices and rake in badly needed donations and resources, they can leave the unfortunate legacy of distrust for anyone else who wants to "understand" or "see" or "help."

Through the grapevine at the dorm, however, I eventually

learned about a *priyut*—a temporary children's shelter—in southern Moscow that welcomed foreign volunteers. I tried to prepare myself for swaddled babies and half-starved children on my first Metro ride over, but to my relief, this particular *priyut* was a cheerful redbrick building surrounded by a big yard with a garden and a jungle gym. The director of the shelter, an energetic Tartar in his early forties, had no qualms about my "Can I work here for free?" approach. He put me to work the moment I knocked on his office door.

"The youngest children are in art class," he said as he briskly led me down a hallway lit by the sun that spilled through the windows. We entered a room full of listless children dressed in thirdhand clothing. Half a dozen lounged on a sagging couch, watching cartoons of the *Brothers Grimm Fairy Tales;* another group painted old magazines with watercolors at a table. It smelled like a pediatrics ward: three parts disinfectant, one part urine.

"Dyeti," the director called their attention. "This is our guest, Stesha."

A child with hair so short that I mistook her for a boy leaped into my arms, grabbed fistfuls of my hair, and squealed.

"This is Annya," he told me.

"Privyet, Annya," I greeted her.

She squeezed my breasts and giggled, making clear she had no intention of unhooking the scrawny legs wrapped around my waist. I carried her on my hip the rest of the day.

Hair length, it turns out, is the quickest way to tell how long a child has been in a *priyut:* It's all shaved off upon their arrival to rid them of any lice or mites. Cuts and bruises reveal other details, like how their father beat them between drinking binges. Neglected bodies read like books—every wound another chapter—and even more life experiences are exhibited through behavior. Five-year-old Kostia, for example, knocked girls to the ground with a gruff "You're my wife" and rubbed against them, making carnal noises. Little Nastia often spoke about an invisible man in the corner who would kill us all at her command.

The thirty residents of this shelter ranged in age from four to twelve. Police found some of them scavenging the trash bins in train stations, while others were squatting in abandoned apartments. Only one ten-year-old boy was a genuine orphan: Many of the children had been dropped off at the shelter by their own down-and-out moms and dads. Most stayed about six months, although a few remained for years. If the courts still deemed their parents unfit for child rearing by the end of their stay, they could either go up for adoption, move in with a foster family, or be sent to a *dyetskii dom*. The director lobbied hard to keep his kids from heading down that last route. According to a 1998 Human Rights Watch report, of the 15,000 children who leave *dyetskii dom* each year, 5,000 can't find work, 6,000 go homeless, 3,000 rack up a criminal record, and 1,500 commit suicide—all within a few years. If kids aren't mentally disturbed before they arrive, the director once remarked, the *dyetskii dom* will see to it soon enough.

I sat upon a three-legged stool at the art table with Annya perched on my lap. She grabbed a brush and smeared blue paint on magazine advertisements of women modeling lingerie. Next to me, a boy with black hair and vacant eyes cut a magazine into slivers.

"What are you making?" I asked brightly.

"Pieces of paper," he mumbled without lifting his head.

"I'll help," I offered, reaching for a pair of scissors and a magazine. "What's your name?" I asked as I cut out a big heart.

"Ivan."

"How old are you, Ivan?"

"Nine."

He was so small, I mistook him for six. Not knowing what else to say, I laid my heart on top of his pile of slivers.

"Thank you," he mumbled as he picked it up and shredded it into bits.

Just then, a counselor in a white lab coat and hairnet poked her head through the doorway. *"Dyeeetttiiii,"* she called. Ivan brushed the confetti into a trash can and sprinted out the door. After sloshing a wet rag around the floor, Annya grabbed my hand and headed out, too. *"Davai!"* she cried. Let's go!

We clambered down the stairs into a locker room. The kids kicked off their *tapochki*, put on their snowshoes, and looked at me disapprovingly for not doing the same. I glanced down at the hiking boots I had worn all morning. It's bad manners to keep your street shoes on in Russian homes; I made a mental note to bring *tapochki* next time.

Just then, two boys disagreed over who should take the volleyball outside and started slugging each other. Having worked at summer camps back in Texas, I had seen my share of kid fights, but never one like this. One lunged for the other's throat; the second aimed straight at the groin. They hit with calculated accuracy. All I could think to say in Russian was, "Let's be friends," which proved ineffective. So I jumped in between them and promptly got kicked in the rear by one and in the shin by the other. I hollered an obscenity (in English) and bent over to shield my more vulnerable body parts.

That's when Masha—a stout five-year-old with a fading black eye—joined in. With stunning force, she knocked over the seven-year-old and rammed the eight-year-old against a locker. Then she calmly walked over to her own locker, pulled out a faux fur coat and a baby doll, and sauntered outside. I trailed behind until she turned around and shouted: "Stop following me."

When the police first brought Masha to the shelter, she was battered with bruises, having lived on the street for unknown months. If anyone got within three feet of her, she lashed out like a wounded animal. Her street sense had earned her the respect of every kid in the *priyut*, but she preferred solitude to company and could often be found in the garden, playing quietly with her doll.

As I watched Masha go, Annya resumed her spot on my hip. "Swing me," she instructed. I obediently carried her to the jungle gym, where a little girl was being swung by a woman wearing a lab coat over blue jeans. The metal swings were connected to the set by bars and yowled like cats when pushed. As I swung Annya, I struck up a conversation with the woman, first in jumbled Russian and then—when we realized neither was a native speaker—in English. A social worker who grew up in the German Democratic Republic, Ines was volunteering at the *priyut* as part of her graduate studies program. I asked what she knew of the children.

"Well, Annya, you see, she and her brother, Maksim, arrived not long ago," she began. As if on cue, a lanky little boy trotted over and threw his skinny arms around Ines's waist. *"Privyet!"* Ines greeted him, smoothing back his blond crew cut.

Annya and Maksim's father was a drug dealer, their mother a prostitute. Both ran their businesses out of their apartment. During a raid, police found the children cowering in a corner, naked and hungry. Neither had ever gone to school and had apparently learned only enough Russian to communicate their most basic needs (although Ines said they sometimes spoke in their own special language, like twins). The day I met them, I took their ages for three and six. They were actually six and nine.

Annya used her underdevelopment to her advantage, carving out the role of the smallest and sweetest in the *priyut*'s hierarchy. The older girls carried her around like a doll, and she reveled in their attention. Maksim's shortcomings were more of a liability. His chest was so sunken, he could hardly stand straight; his speech impediment—a telltale sign of fetal alcohol syndrome—made him sound as though he were speaking through a bottle. He struggled with physical activities that boys half his age performed with ease, like climbing up the slide backward.

A staff nurse interviewed Maksim and Annya about their home life soon after they were brought in. When Maksim refrained from answering her questions, she dismissed him as incapable of remembering and classified him as an *imbetsil*—imbecile—in his papers. If the director hadn't intervened, Maksim could have been dispatched to a mental ward for life then and there. Soviet propaganda long ago instilled the notion that strength, beauty, and cleverness were the essential characteristics of a *Homo sovieticus*. Even today, children who fail to meet these standards are often scorned. According to Human Rights Watch, *internat*—boarding schools for the "ineducable"—are full of children whose sole disability is a cleft palate or club foot. They also found that 30 to 60 percent of the children labeled "mentally deficient" after being interviewed by a panel of psychologists, doctors, and government officials actually have average or better than average mental abilities.

Maksim reminded me of a parakeet I once saw at a pet store that had a beak deformity. The other parakeets tormented him for this imperfection, pecking his head each time they flew past. But he'd grown so accustomed to it, he hardly flinched anymore. When I asked the shopkeeper why he didn't put him in a separate cage, he laughed. "That would be interfering with nature. Those birds know what they are doing." Maksim showed a similar resignation when the other boys ganged up on him— at most dropping to his knees and covering his head with his bony arms. He never attempted to fight back, not even against the littlest ones.

My second day at the shelter, I realized Maksim couldn't tie his shoes. I attempted to teach him on his dirty laces, but his clumsy fingers couldn't form a proper loop. Frustrated, he screamed, *"Ya ne umeyu"*—I am incapable—as tears slid down his pasty cheeks, but that only made me more determined. Insisting he pay attention, I showed him again and again, until a group of children gathered to watch.

"Maksim ne umeyet," they teased. Maksim is incapable.

"Umeyet!" I snapped back.

But Maksim ran away before I could prove it, his shoelaces flapping against the snow. I later asked a counselor why a nine-year-old hadn't been taught to tie his own shoelaces.

She shrugged nonchalantly. *"Maksim ne umeyet."*

THE ALPHAS OF the *priyut* were three prepubescent boys who wore jean jackets, spoke the slang of the streets, and had been in and out of group homes and shelters for much of their lives: Volodya, Vova, and Dima. Volodya, a twelve-year-old with ice blue eyes and a strong Slavic jaw, was the leader and could usually be found pacing along the fence that enclosed the *priyut*, checking his watch as though waiting for important business. Neither Ines nor I could engage him in a game or conversation. He distanced himself even from his two younger siblings— Nastia, the morbid little girl who threatened everyone with phantom killers, and Alyosha, a gorgeous five-year-old boy who could have been the pride and joy of a functional parent.

About a month into my volunteering at the *priyut,* Ines approached me one afternoon with troubled eyes. "Volodya ran away last night. They think he may have gone home."

The prospect of the latter clearly worried her more than the fact of the former. The police originally brought the siblings to the shelter because Volodya's teacher complained he was always drunk or hung over. An investigation revealed that his alcoholic parents not only knew about their son's habits—they supplied the liquor.

I went off looking for Alyosha and found him sitting forlornly on the porch steps, hugging his knees to his chest. Beside him was the nurse's twenty-four-year-old daughter, who played piano for the kids on Friday afternoons, and the counselor who reacted so ambivalently to Maksim's inabilities.

"What's wrong, Alyosha?" one asked as she lit up a cigarette.

"You miss your brother, don't you?" the other chimed in.

"He ran off and left you all by yourself, didn't he?"

Alyosha buried his head in his hands and started sobbing.

"What are you doing now, Alyosha?"

"Don't you know big boys don't cry?"

When I first began working at that shelter, I vowed not to be an Indignant American who thought her method of conducting affairs was morally superior to that of locals. So I bit my tongue when the counselors harangued the children for dropping the soap in the bathroom or speaking without being spoken to during meals. I apologized when they lectured me about playing with the children without a lab coat or walking into the dining room without a hairnet or anything else they deemed "undignified" or "improper." I conjured up dozens of historical, political, and cultural excuses for their unsparing behavior and reminded myself that—at the end of the day—I was just a volunteer with no concept of what it must be like to work full-time with children whom an entire society had neglected.

Watching those women tease Alyosha after his big brother had just ditched him, however, was more than I could take. I scooped the child into my arms, carried him as far away as we could get, and covered his tear-streaked face with kisses—all the while wondering if I was adding to his feelings of abandonment by showing up for a few hours, drowning him in affection, and then leaving him until my next visit.

At about $55 a month, the counselors at that *priyut* were severely overworked and grossly underpaid. Theirs was a thankless job with virtually no opportunity for advancement. But while I empathized with their discontent, I couldn't fathom their severity. Even the young pianist conducted her lessons like a tyrant. She would teach the children lyrics to five different songs one week and expect them to sing flawlessly the next. If they made any mistakes, she screamed. Ines told me about the day she picked on Maksim.

"He really tried, Stesha, and I think he was in fact singing. We just couldn't understand him because of his speech impediment. All the children started laughing at him, but the teacher wouldn't stop. She made him stand up and told him to sing louder and louder. Finally he just started crying—and then *she* began to laugh."

Interestingly enough, the children turned to the two men at the shelter for love and tenderness. The children so adored the director, they called him Papa, and their collective big brother was Slava, the happy-go-lucky graduate student who worked the night shift. Rugged and kindhearted, Slava connected with even the most withdrawn of children. For weeks, he was the only person Masha trusted enough to come near her. Slava could also handle the most troubled children, like Kostia.

A policeman discovered Kostia begging for food in front of a meat market. Since he wore nice clothing, the officer told him to go back home. When he replied, *"Nyetu"*—I haven't got one—he brought him to the *priyut*. Kostia was a good-looking kid with black hair and glittering eyes, and exceptionally bright (I have him to thank for finally mastering such grammatical nightmares as Russian's instrumental case), but at the ripe old age of five, he had issues. He roamed the halls of the *priyut* like a pint-size gangster, back arched, chest inflated, picking fights with anyone who got in his way (but rarely winning). He even bit Ines on her thigh once, cutting straight through her jeans and breaking the skin beneath.

During naptime one afternoon, I poked my head into the bedroom he shared with three other boys to check on them. When he saw me, Kostia put a pillow between his legs and proceeded to hump it while staring straight at me. The other boys, thinking it a game, quickly followed suit, laughing all the while, but this was no joke for Kostia. He was imitating something he had seen before. When he began to slap the pillow around with his little fists, I shut the door and darted upstairs to the office, where Slava and Ines were having tea. Russian failing me, I simply said, "Kostia," and pantomimed a pelvic thrust. Understanding immediately, Slava bolted out the door and down the stairs. I flopped on the chair beside Ines, grabbed a cup of tea, and swallowed it in one gulp.

"Ah, Kostia . . ." Ines sighed as she stirred a spoonful of sugar into her cup. "I hope I never run into him in a dark alley someday."

—

ONCE THE SNOW melted off the birch trees and the dandelions puffed out their bouffants, Slava organized an afternoon excursion to a nearby wood. He got some friends to clear a picnic space and build a fire there while we readied the children at the *priyut*—changing them into jeans and stuffing their backpacks with Frisbees, balls, and thermoses of tea. The kids were beyond excited: This was a rare opportunity for them to be like normal children and rejoin the free world. But as we were about to depart for the Metro, the nurse ambled over with a clipboard and demanded to examine the children first. She scrutinized each child with a tongue depressor and scribbled half a pad of notes, then announced everyone could go except Kostia, Alyosha, and Maksim.

"*Pochemu?*" Slava gasped.

"It is too hot in the forest and too cold in the shelter," she snapped as she tucked her pen behind her ear. "They'll get sick."

Alyosha and Kostia started screaming in protest, but Maksim just stood and quivered. When Ines bent down to comfort him, he shrugged off her hand and ran away.

Once again, I felt torn in two. What right did I have to question a nurse's authority in a workplace and a nation not my own? At the same time, how could I allow such a ludicrous verdict to stand?

Only one person had the power to overturn the nurse's decrees at the *priyut*, and that was the director. I dashed up the stairs to his office and—forgetting to knock—burst in on a meeting. As seven distinguished heads turned to face me, Russian failed me again. "The nurse . . . Maksim," I stuttered. The director sighed knowingly, excused himself from the others, followed me outside where Slava and the nurse were locked in a fiery debate, and joined in the fray. I stepped back into the heap of wide-eyed children to watch the two men use every possible diplomacy to get that steely woman to acquiesce.

"*Klassno!*" the kids shouted when she finally did.

I ran back into the shelter to tell Maksim the good news and found him lying facedown in bed, sobbing as Ines massaged his bony shoulders. I crouched by his pillow and whispered into his ear: "*Davai!*"

Two splotches of red sprang across his chalky cheeks. "To the forest?" he asked.

"To the forest."

Maksim leaped out of bed, darted toward the door, and promptly tripped on one of his shoelaces. He squatted, tied it perfectly, and then ran to catch up with the rest of the group, his lanky limbs flailing like wings.

MY GOOD FRIEND Elena was one of those Russian exchange students who got sent to live in the co-ops in Austin the year before, but unlike most of the others, she rather took to our quirky ways. "Our system really *can* work," she marveled when I gave her a tour of our industrial-size kitchen, where Jason, Jon, and Sonya happily brewed wheatberry beer and Tyra baked vegan pumpkin muffins.

Born in the provincial town of Balakhna, half a day's drive from Moscow, Elena had been plotting a way out for years. She chose languages because her mother taught English at the local elementary school and somehow managed to achieve a high rate of fluency in both British and American English and German despite the fact Balakhna was closed to foreigners until 1990 (as a military complex lurked nearby). She beat out hundreds of students at her university when she won the coveted ten-month scholarship to UT, and made the most of her time abroad, studying business and finance in addition to languages. But now she was back in Balakhna, where the largest employer was the paper mill. She wanted to relocate to the capital, but a paper bureaucracy that dated back to the days of Peter the

Great prevented it. Russians need a special residence permit called a *propiska* to move to large cities like Moscow or St. Petersburg, and unless their parents or spouse have one, they can legally obtain the document only through an employer with money and clout (that is, one in Moscow or St. Petersburg). Therein lay the catch-22 for small-town Russians: How are they supposed to land a high-end job in a city in which they aren't allowed to live?

During my second month in Moscow, Elena invited me to Balakhna for a four-day weekend. Realizing that buying a train ticket would be a considerable undertaking, she faxed over an extensive set of instructions stating that I needed to go to Window 14 at the Yaroslavskii Station. She also noted that while she lived in Balakhna, I should buy a ticket to Nizhnii Novgorod (the nearest big city), and if my ticket happened to say Gorky, that was okay because they were the same thing. (Mapmakers and city planners had been busily renaming revolutionary-honored cities, towns, streets, schools, libraries, parks, and bridges since communism's collapse.)

I approached the ticket agent at Yaroslavskii's Window 14 the following morning with passport in hand and dialogue memorized but was greeted with a *nyet*. Not only was I at the wrong window, the agent informed me, I was at the wrong depot. I needed to go to Kievskii Station.

"But my friend . . . ," I objected, unfolding Elena's fax.

"Nyet, devushka," she repeated, and swatted me away.

I had actually grown accustomed to this. I must have learned a dozen synonyms for "no" my first week in Moscow alone. *Nel'zya. Nevozmozhno. Nikogda. Nichevo. Nikak. Nyet.* It's not allowed. It's not possible. Never. No way. Nohow. Uh-uh. I got rejected at least five times a day—by sales clerks, security guards, waitresses, fruit sellers, postal employees. *Nyet,* I couldn't squeeze their eggplants to see if they were ripe. *Nyet*, they wouldn't look in the back for a pair of shoes in my size. Or check to see if my fax had arrived. Or take my order, or pour me a refill, or bring me the check. Couldn't I see they were busy smoking cigarettes and staring into space? Why didn't I just go away?

So I stuffed the fax into my pocket and headed back to the Metro *babushka* style. (After weeks of coming home speckled with elbow-shaped bruises, I decided that you can't walk in a normal fashion through a monstrously crowded Metro. I had recently adopted the strut of the *babushki:* chin up, elbows out, full steam ahead. Kinda like a chicken, but with the force of a bull.)

Window 14 at Kievskii Station was staffed by an agent intently filing her nails. I launched into my monologue but got interrupted.

"*Nyet, devushka.* Kazanskii Station," she said flatly.

When I protested that the agent at Yaroslavskii Station had just sent me all the way over here, she pulled down the blinds that separated us. You kind of have to admire a society like that. Not yet having made the transition to full-blown consumer culture, mid-1990s Moscow was still refreshingly bereft of superficiality. If someone treated you civilly, they genuinely liked you.

I turned around, trudged back to the Metro, and headed to the third train station of the day.

Kazanskii Station is the hub for trains from the southern Caucasus. While the first two stations had a largely white clientele, the bulk of the vendors being *babushki* peddling moonshine and guys in Nike tracksuits hawking gold chains, Kazanskii attracted a far more colorful crew, namely nomadic Romani families (aka *Tsiganie*, or Gypsies) whose women wore floral head scarves and patchwork skirts and strapped olive-skinned babies to their backs. Many Russians looked upon these people the way certain Texans did *mojados* (or "wetbacks"), claiming they did nothing but beg, cheat, and steal. But how can you blame a nationless people who have been persecuted, enslaved, deported, forced to assimilate, and—by the Nazis— nearly exterminated for committing a petty crime now and then? Routinely denied employment and housing, traveling Romanies often could find no other way of feeding their children than picking a pocket or two.

Kazanskii Station also teemed with street kids high on glue, ticket scalpers, prostitutes, peddlers, and beggars. I burrowed beneath them all and eventually popped up by yet another window staffed by a sour-faced agent. Dog tired, I simply unfolded Elena's fax and held it up for her to see.

"*Nyet, devushka.*" She glared at me through her turquoise-frosted lashes. "You have to buy your ticket at Yaroslavskii Station."

Frustration having devoured the last of my patience, I started hollering in the most fluid Russian to ever pass through my lips. First I ranted about how I tried to buy a ticket at that very station two hours prior and had been sent all the way over here; next I raved about how rude every attendant had been. Then I folded my arms and said that I would not leave until she sold me a ticket.

At that, she raised one eyebrow.

I have tried for years to get my eyebrows to do that—it would add so much to my interviewing repertoire—but they refuse. So I flared my nostrils instead.

She pursed her lips.

I did something I have never done in my life: I growled. I didn't exactly mean to. It just slipped out from my throat.

Her face went absolutely stony.

I'm sure mine did, too.

Before I realized it, we had engaged in a stare-down that must have lasted at least a minute. Then my left contact dried, puckered, and fell out. If they had been disposables, I would have let it go, I swear. But I only had one spare pair. I scooped it off the ground with as much dignity as possible and stalked off, cursing Bausch & Lomb along the way.

I knew I'd been framed when the agent at Window 14 at Yaroslavskii Station saw me across the crowded room and started snickering. I was so mad, I could hardly breathe. Then my eyes fell upon the hours stenciled on her window's pane. She'd go on break in twenty minutes. So I sat down and schemed until I devised a plan.

Russians have never gotten much merely by asking for it. As Communists, they had to bribe bureaucrats for telephones, plumbers for toilets, butchers for sausages, gravediggers for plots. As capitalists, they "tip" nurses for anesthesia, teachers for good grades, and cops to kindly look the other way. Only when I learned to apply such tactics to my own affairs did my vocabulary expand with affirmatives like *mozhno, konechno, pozhalyusta, davai, da* (you may, of course, please do, go ahead, yes). Slipping the dorm's security guards a can of beer before I went out for the evening, for instance, guaranteed they would let me back inside after curfew. A bottle of vodka gained admission for any guests I may have picked up along the way. Passing out flowers and cigarettes to the ladies in the dormitory's canteen ensured that I received my yogurt each morning for breakfast.

The instant the attendant pulled down her blinds to go on break, I set the time on my watch back ten minutes so that I could argue she'd left too early. Then I ran up to her window, peeked through the slits until I could make out someone walking by, and pounded on the window like mad. My idea was to flat-out bribe whoever answered into selling me a ticket before my nemesis returned, but when the blinds parted and a *babushka* poked her head out, I had a better one.

"*Babulya!*" I cried, the diminutive for *babushka*.

The old woman squinted suspiciously as I lied about how I had just skipped class to come to the train station and buy a ticket. If I had to wait a whole hour for the agent to return, I would miss a very important lecture on Pushkin. Then I showed her my watch, which backed my claim that five minutes remained until the agent's break officially began. But the *babushka* just snapped the blinds shut.

Great. Maybe I could hitchhike to Nizhnii with the Romanies. I was about to look for some when two slits in the blinds parted. In a muffled voice, the woman asked where I wanted to go.

"Nizhnii Novgorod," I whispered.

The blinds flipped open. "*Konechno, devushka,*" she cooed, and sold me a ticket.

According to the ticket, the train to Nizhnii departed out of yet another station—Kurskii. Since my journey would commence at 7:00 the following morning, I decided to give it a trial run. I hopped back on the Metro and headed to the fourth station of the day, exhausted but under the soothing misconception that this battle was over.

RIDING DOWN THE escalators of the Moscow Metro is like descending into hell. They sink so deep into the ground that halfway down, you can't see where you're going or where you've been. It's just a chasm of *shapka*-covered heads. Locals have invented numerous pastimes for these interminable rides.

Friends face one another and gossip all the way. Lovers make out. *Huligani* throw coins down the dividers, which make a terrific noise as they crash toward the ground. (I found that deviant behavior somewhat reassuring: At least I knew there was an end to the escalator ride when I heard those coins hit bottom.)

The greatest fixtures of these escalators are the employees who anchor the ends in plexiglass boxes. Among other things, they monitor the little lever that halts the escalator when pulled. This usually occurs when someone, like a drunkard, falls. Suddenly stopping the escalator for stumbling drunks is problematic, however, as it puts others at risk of falling, too. (One of my recurring dreams that year in Moscow was of getting crushed at the bottom of the escalator after a long line of Metro riders toppled over me like dominoes.) The stations also come equipped with microphones, which the attendants utilize at whim: "Respectable passengers, keep to your right. I said the *right*, not the *left*. You, the old man in the muskrat *shapka*, *move it*!"

So when the escalator at Kurskii Station deposited me into a pit with several tunnels but no clear way out, I rapped on the door of the attendant box.

"*Babulya*," I purred, "can you please help me?"

The old woman looked me up and down. "Where are you from?"

"Texas, but I'm going to Nizhnii Novgorod. Do I take this tunnel or that one?"

"You're from where?"

"Texas. It's in America. Now how do I get to the train station?"

"You're an American?"

"*Da.*"

"An American?" she repeated. By this point, she had risen from her stool and opened the door. A lapel pin of Lenin gleamed from the collar of her navy blue uniform.

"*Da*. I need the train to Nizhnii Novgorod. Which way do I go?"

Rather than reply, she wrapped her short arms around my neck.

"American! Leave my country! Get out of Russia!" she cried as she proceeded to shake me. She had shrunk so much in the latter years of her life, she barely came up to my shoulders, but her grip was strong and firm.

I covered her wrinkled wrists with my hands and met her livid gaze. Never before had I been held accountable for what I represented. (That's one of the few perks of being ambiguously biracial: In times of trouble, you can always try claiming your other heritage.) But this woman was holding me responsible for the actions of my government, from our eastward expansion of NATO to our role in her nation's fall from superpower status. Conflicted emotions boiled inside me: indignation (But I took care of the children her people abandoned in Metros *just like this*!), guilt (What if she's right?), and fear (What if I can't unlock her grip?).

Throughout our altercation, scores of people passed by. I often tried to construct stories out of Muscovites' expressionless faces. A *devushka* might be on her way to a mail-order bride photo shoot; a bedraggled veteran, to a meeting of the Communist Party. While that old woman shook me, however, I scanned the crowd to see who might join in. That pensioner scrounging for recyclables? Or that mother of four calculating the rubles she had left over for groceries?

Yet no one seemed to notice us.

I turned back to the *babushka*. Her storm subsided as

quickly as it fomented. After releasing her hands from my neck with a sigh, she pointed at one of the tunnels and then returned to her plexiglass box. The door slammed behind her.

MY SECOND-CLASS ticket to Nizhnii Novgorod put me on a train car that resembled an army barrack, complete with bunk beds. My travel companions included a stylish *devushka* wearing a silky black skirt and heels, a matronly blonde who gave her entire bag of boiled eggs to a beggar who sneaked aboard the train moments before it departed, and a crotchety lady in stretch pants who drank six bottles of home brew and belched for the duration of the trip.

Riding a Russian train is like being on the set of the Home Shopping Network. Every few minutes, someone new stands at the entrance of the car, gives a thirty-, forty-five-, or sixty-second monologue about their wares, and then walks slowly down the aisle with hopes of closing a sale. A man went through with a pushcart, calling out, *"Piroshki, piroshki, piroshki,"* like John Belushi would cheeseburgers, while paperboys peddled the latest edition of *Moskovskii Komsomolets*. On that particular train, a smarmy man made a killing selling chandeliers. His customers could choose from any one of a wide selection of laminated photographs in a scrapbook and then follow him back to his seat to pick up their purchase, which came disassembled in a re-usable cardboard box, lightbulbs not included.

A couple of hours into the journey, I happened to glance over at the blonde slumbering on the bunk across from me just as a cockroach crawled out from under her pillow and ran across her pretty face. The *devushka*, the beer-guzzling lady, and I seemed to notice it at exactly the same moment. We screamed. The blonde awoke with a jolt and wiped the roach off her face. It landed on the table from which I had been writing letters and scrambled toward me. We continued to scream. Then, from across the aisle, a boy of about seven ran up to the table and smashed it dead with his bare fist.

That was a hell of an icebreaker: The four of us chattered nonstop for the remainder of the trip. I even pulled out my pocket-size photo album to show them scenes from my life back home: my sister's wedding, high school graduation, a Christmas dinner, little cousins swinging at a *piñata* at Easter, belly dancers swarming around the drum circle at an Eeyore's Birthday celebration (which, for the uninitiated, is Austin's grandest crunchy hippie fest).

There can't be many audiences more attentive than Russian women. "And who is this *devushka* with you?" "Where does she work?" "How much money does she make?" "Is she married?" "No? Why not?" "So, she lives with her parents?" "No? Why not?" "Does she speak Russian?" "No?! Why not?" "She sure is smiling big. Why is she so happy?"

When that *devushka* resurfaced a few photos later, they noticed right away. "Oh, here's Joy again! She looks much better in this photograph, did she lose weight?" That prompted a serious discussion in which I had to pull out all my photos of Joy so they could decipher if in fact she had lost weight, and if so—in which picture.

As we reached the end of my album, I remembered that I had seen the blonde sifting through photographs while we were still at the depot in Moscow and asked if we could take a look.

"Oh, they are not very nice photographs," she stammered, her face reddening.

Mistaking her reticence for embarrassment over the quality of her photos, I cooed: "That's okay; I would love to see them."

Reluctantly, she pulled out her own album. They turned out to be the photographs her son sent from Chechnya, where he had been serving as a soldier for the past eight months. When Boris Yeltsin dispatched troops to the southern Caucasus region in December 1994 to extinguish the fiery independence movement of the largely Muslim people, he thought it would be an easy victory. He got a Vietnam instead. Not only were Chechen fighters far more impassioned and skilled than he'd anticipated, but the once mighty Red Army was poorly trained and badly equipped and had a rock-bottom morale. By July 1996, some eighty thousand people had been killed, many of them civilians, and the capital, Grozny, leveled.

No one said a word as the photographs made their way around our now solemn circle. Frame after frame depicted dead bodies, ransacked villages, and cities in rubble. The last one was a group shot of her son's platoon. Dressed in fatigues with Kalashnikovs clenched at their sides, the soldiers—many of whom were younger than me—stared stoically into the camera as a street fire blazed in the background. I looked closely at their eyes, trying to fathom the atrocities they'd seen. That's when I noticed that one of the soldiers was making bunny ears on another.

"OUR DREAM HAS come true!" Elena cried when I stepped off the train and into her arms. "You're in Russia! You've finally made it to Russia!"

We held hands all the way back to her uncle's car, as Russian friends sometimes do, and made the hour-long drive to Balakhna, where she lived in a two-bedroom wooden house with her parents and husband, Valera. They had married just a few months before Elena left for Austin; though I'd heard a great deal about him, we'd never actually met. He easily could have passed for Elena's twin brother: They had the same high cheekbones, white blond hair, and radiant blue eyes. A staunch supporter of his wife's ambitions, Valera had cheerfully committed himself to following her career track long ago (a rarity in any nation, but especially in Russia). Whenever I am with the two of them, Valera becomes husband to us both—helping us on and off buses, carrying our bags, pouring our tea, making our dinner, washing our dishes, and buying us cognac at the theater.

Supper was waiting on the table when we arrived: pork chops, stewed potatoes, marinated tomatoes, homemade pickles, and black bread, with tea and chocolates for dessert. I had just about given up on Russian cuisine until I met Elena's mother, Irina Vasilyevna. "She spends half her life teaching in the classroom and the other half cooking in the kitchen," Elena said. It hadn't been time in vain: Irina Vasilyevna's recipes included rich *borscht* and hearty cabbage stews, raviolis called *pelmeni* doused in sour cream, and crepes called *blini* smothered with preserves. There was something inherently comforting about this food, like the homemade macaroni and cheese my paternal grandmother used to bake when we visited her in Minneapolis, Kansas. In fact, there were moments watching Irina Vasilyevna mash a big pot of potatoes in that Russian kitchen when I felt temporarily transported to my grandmother's side. I was eight years old and barefoot again, begging for stories about my great-great-uncle Jake, the traveling hobo, or Scurvy Irv, the hermit who sold iron out of his ramshackle cabin and spat tobacco into a potbellied stove.

Instead of sending me down to the basement for an extra potato as Grandma used to, though, Irina Vasilyevna dispatched me to her garden, where onions, potatoes, carrots, and beets lurked beneath the earth and cabbages, peppers, and dill above it. The trees, patches, vines, and bushes would soon burst with apples, cherries, currants, and berries, while the greenhouse kept the temperature-sensitive produce, like tomatoes and cucumbers. "Stesha, if you bury a potato in May, you'll have ten by August!" she'd say, and laugh as my eyes grew big.

Elena's father, Oleg Anatolyevitch, had two passions in life: physics and painting. He quenched the former through his job as head engineer at the local military plant and the latter at night in front of an easel. His artwork was nailed to every room of the house, alongside hanging Persian-style rugs. The in-house favorite was a portrait of Elena in pigtails tied with big red bows, age five. Others were of tranquil, wooded landscapes; the gallant onion domes of cathedrals; peasant women wearing shawls; and religious icons outlined in gold glitter.

After supper, Elena and Valera invited me to *gulyat'*, or go for a stroll. I'd actually taken up late night jogging in college but hadn't had any deliberate exercise since I'd been in Moscow. In a place where life itself was a workout, people never seemed to run without reason (someone chasing them, for instance). So I slid into sweats and Adidas and went outside to stretch in their garden. Elena and Valera soon joined me, having also changed—into even nicer clothes than they were wearing before. Too polite to tell me the whole town would be out strolling and this was a time to see and be seen, they asked if I was ready. I said *da* and we walked through the front gate. I sprinted forth, reached the far end of the block, and turned around to see that Elena and Valera had just made it to the second house.

"*Vcyo normalno, Stesha?*" Valera shouted out, concerned. Is everything all right?

Feeling rather silly, I circled back and joined them. "*Vcyo khorosho*," I assured him as I slowed down to their leisurely pace. I tried to remember the last time I had taken a walk with neither a destination nor an intention to burn calories and could not.

As we strolled through the sleepy town of fifty thousand, I counted statues of Lenin. One crested a column in a courtyard; another sat pensively in a schoolyard; still another stood importantly before an official-looking building. I was under the impression that such statues had been ceremonially knocked off their pedestals the day the Soviet Union disintegrated, as in Erevan, Armenia, where a Lenin was lifted onto a truck and driven round and round the central square like a funeral procession, or in Warsaw, where Poles toppled their towering statue of Felix Dzerzhinsky (head of the first configuration of the Soviet secret police) with the ritual of a public execution. But thousands of these statues remain in Russia for the practical reason that towns like Balakhna can't afford to haul them away. Elena and Valera didn't seem to mind, though. They said that the statues simply melted in with the scenery, along with the linden trees and the hand-carved wooden fences.

"It's part of our history." Elena shrugged. "What's the point in denying it?"

IT WAS ONLY 6:20 A.M. but Elena and I were already running late. She had recently gotten a job with a British clothing firm in Nizhnii Novgorod. To get there by 9:00, we needed to catch the 6:45 town bus to make it to Balakhna's depot in time for the 7:00 bus to Nizhnii, where we would transfer to a trolley and then a tram. Elena spent some twenty hours a week commuting to and from work but felt that the prestige of Nizhnii—which at 1.7 million is a major Russian city—was worth it. There she might be able to establish the sorts of contacts needed to find a job in Moscow that could grant her a *propiska*.

Elena made the most of her long commute, reading and rereading the English and German books she bought in Austin, underlining unfamiliar words, looking them up in her pocket dictionary, and committing them to memory. When that grew tiresome, she gazed at the scenery. The bus to Nizhnii passed through dozens of villages of wooden homes lustrously painted in cherry reds, mint greens, polar blues, and golds and purples, with decoratively carved window frames and roofs that looked like doilies from a distance. And when that got old, she could contemplate the inner decor of the buses themselves. On our way up, the walls were plastered with posters of kittens, puppies, and cottontail rabbits; on the way back, there were buxom blond and redheaded playmates in soft-porn poses.

Eventually we rolled into Nizhnii Novgorod, a city with two claims to fame: the birthplace of Maksim Gorky, the father of socialist realism and darling of Soviet literature, and the home of exile for Andrei Sakharov, hydrogen bomb inventor turned Nobel Prize–winning dissenter. Gorky probably enjoyed his stay in Nizhnii, but the KGB kept Sakharov under twenty-four-hour surveillance for seven years there, screening his mail and phone calls, tormenting his family members, and stealing the nearly completed manuscript of his memoirs three times. When Sakharov protested these human rights violations by hunger striking, they force-fed him. He died three years after his release and has since been called the "tidal wave" that wiped out totalitarianism in the Soviet Union and paved the path to democracy. Ironically, the city where he rose to international fame was one of the last in Russia to open up to foreigners.

We made it to Elena's office, a small room located on the top floor of a garment factory, with two minutes to spare. It seemed minimalist—three telephones, two typewriters (one Cyrillic and one Roman), a fax machine, an enormous portrait of Lenin, and an orange polka-dotted teapot—until Elena headed to the ringing phones and proceeded to carry out her duties in perfectly accented British English, German, and Russian. After confirming the day's shipments, she took me to her alma mater, Nizhnii Novgorod State Linguistic University. As soon as we passed through security, we were surrounded. Having achieved what would have been impossible only a few years before (pursuing an education on former enemy turf), Elena had become the resident rock star. A dozen different students offered us cigarettes, pastries, and invitations to *prikhodi v gosti*—come over for a visit—as Elena gave me a tour of the campus that culminated at the American Culture Center, where she spent three years poring over *National Geographic* magazines preserved in homemade book covers.

We returned to Balakhna in time for dinner. After I gorged on potato *piroshki* and two bowls of *borscht*, Valera announced we were going to his *babushka*'s for dessert. The seventy-five-year-old had never met a foreigner before and wanted a good look at me. As we drove deep into the countryside in their uncle's Lada, we seemed to transcend a year a mile, from the cold war to the world wars and civil wars to the Revolution itself. The paved road devolved from gravel into dirt; bathrooms reverted to outhouses. Kerchiefed women carried sloshing buckets to and from wells while brawny men retired from the fields with sickles slung over their shoulders. Freely roaming cows, pigs, goats, and chickens outnumbered the people ten to one.

"Look at their faces," Elena whispered into my ear. "This is real Russia."

When we pulled up to the front door of the log house Valera's grandparents built with their hands, a spunky old woman dashed out with six kittens, three dogs, and a cat at her heels. Her slender figure and lively blue eyes masking at least a decade of her age, *Babushka* threw her arms around me for a lift-you-off-your-feet hug and announced that Americans weren't so bad, after all. Gripping my hand, she led me through two doorways to a giant pen, tossed some corn at the colossal hogs scruffing inside, and opened a third door to a bountiful garden that would yield pumpkins, zucchinis, squashes, radishes, turnips, peas, and beans and dozens of different apples and berries that spring. The big shed had cabbages, cucumbers, and mushrooms pickling in glass jars in one corner; currants, cherries, and berries preserving in another; and a dozen jugs of *samogon* (moonshine) brewing in a third. The little shed housed a thousand honeybees and their drippy, sticky hive. *Babushka* boasted that they ate nothing they didn't plant, pick, raise, or kill themselves. Their cows were milked four times a day for their cheese, butter, and sour cream; their pigs yielded their pork and lard; their bees provided their natural sweeteners. Their medicines came from the garden, and their water came from the well.

Back inside the house, the table was set with a thickly frosted cake, bowls of black currants, slices of honeycomb, and milk fresh from the udder. Two kittens jumped in my lap as I sat down, and a third curled up on my boots as *Babushka* demonstrated how to eat honeycomb: Shove it whole in your mouth and then suck it husk-dry.

Feeling the need to entertain, I whipped out my scrapbook of photos.

"Where do you keep your pigs?" *Babushka* inquired when I showed her my home in the South Texas suburbs.

We didn't have any pigs, I said.

"Oh, they're with your *babushka*." She nodded knowingly.

None there, either.

"Then where?" she asked, puzzled.

I admitted that our pigs came from the market.

The old woman clicked her tongue against the roof of her mouth and frowned. Pigs from a market? *Bozhe moi!*

A FEW HOURS before I headed back to Moscow, Elena and I decided to accept one of the invitations we'd received to *prikhodi v gosti* back at her university. Mae was a beautiful Belorussian with thick ebony hair and tan eyes who lived in a concrete sky-rise on the outskirts of Balakhna. Every member of her family greeted us at the doorway and escorted us to the comfiest seat in the house—a sofa covered with a zebra-patterned blanket and purple pillows. The exact same Persian-style rugs that hung in Elena's home were nailed there, too, along with ceiling-to-floor bookshelves similarly lined with leather-bound volumes of Turgenev and Dostoevsky. (In fact, every Russian home I visited that year looked that way. It was kind of like being back in the South Texas *barrio*, where every Mexican family has the *Last Supper* hanging in the living room and plastic covers on the couches. But with Russians, it was a matter of supply; we demand our decor.)

Since we had been invited for tea, I had polished off an extra-big lunch back at Elena's to please Irina Vasilyevna. But Mae's mother laid out a full-scale spread before us: potato pancakes topped with sour cream, plates of cold ham, black bread, and slices of cucumbers. Every time I cleaned my plate, she served me another—until I deduced that Russians leave a little food behind to signify their fill. Then she started firing off questions.

"So what do you study in school, Stesha?"

"Journalism and Russian."

"And what do you plan to do with that?"

"Write about Russians."

"Write about Russians . . ." She mulled this over as she bit into a lemon slice. "Why do you think you can write about Russians?"

"Well, I've studied the language a few years and, um, I am in Moscow now, and . . . I've read Pushkin . . ."

"And how do you plan on writing about us?"

"By talking with you and sharing your stories."

"And how do you know we are not telling you what we think you want to hear?"

"I . . . well, I suppose I wouldn't exactly . . ."

"Then how will you write about us?"

Uncertainty churning in my belly, I looked from the inquisitor to her daughter to my friend. How *would* I know if they weren't telling me what they thought I wanted to hear? I didn't even know enough Spanish to gather family secrets from my own blood relatives. That was the follow-up question I've often wished I had asked that CNN correspondent at that journalism convention so long ago. Learn Russian . . . and then what? How can any foreign correspondent accurately cover a society not their own?

As I wrestled for an answer, Mae's little sister emerged from the kitchen with a cake called *chuda* (miracle cake), consisting of ten pita-width layers coated with honey and nuts. Her mother poured a small amount of concentrated black tea into each of our cups from an orange polka-dotted teapot and then diluted the leaves with boiling water from a kettle. After passing around a bowl filled to the brim with sugar—which Elena and Mae nearly emptied—she showed me a little jar.

"This is a very special jar of preserves, Stesha," she said as she plopped a spoonful onto the rim of my saucer. It was made from wild berries that grew only a few weeks a year in patches protected by thorny brambles. "You have to get down on your hands and knees and crawl through the brambles to get these berries, and it takes several kilos just to make this one little jar of preserves."

The preserves were so intensely sweet, my lips puckered on contact, but thinking it the proper thing to do, I called it delicious: *"Ochen' vkusno! Tak vkusno!"*

She smiled, capped the jar, and handed it to me. "A present for you."

"Thank you! But I can't take this! These are your special preserves!"

Elena leaned over and whispered in English, "When a Russian offers you a gift, you must accept it."

I did, fiercely regretting that I had nothing to give in return.

By that point, my time in Balakhna was running thin. Elena and I had only an hour to run back to her house, pack my bags, and catch the bus. Overwhelmed by their hospitality, I thanked Mae and her mother profusely. They walked us to the staircase and extended an open invitation for future visits.

"The next time you come, I will make you dinner!" the mother shouted down the stairwell. "Forgive me for only serving pancakes! Next time I will make a real Russian meal!"

With two full meals gurgling in our bellies, Elena and I staggered home, cutting through back alleys and side streets to make up time. We dashed through the front door to find her entire family waiting at the table, neatly set with another meal.

"Maaaa," Elena gasped. "We just ate!"

"Nonsense!" Irina Vasilyevna chirped. "Stesha has a big trip ahead of her. She must eat."

I sat down to my third meal in as many hours and forced down some soup while everyone else rushed about, gathering my things. Irina Vasilyevna wrapped an entire lemon pie in a towel and stuffed it in my backpack along with a biography of Anna Akhmatova and a book of poetry.

"Stesha, do you have a good scarf back in Moscow?" Irina Vasilyevna asked anxiously. "I have a nice woolen one, brand new. I'll go get it!"

"Maaaa! We need to go!" Elena insisted.

Amid the bustle, I managed to slurp three-quarters of my soup and slip a roll into my pocket after scattering its crumbs atop my plate. I stealthily unbuttoned my bursting jeans beneath my sweater and waddled from the table. Irina Vasilyevna pulled me to her billowy breast and stroked my hair. "Oh, Stesha! Promise me you'll return for our harvest!"

"Maaaa!" Elena cried as she and Valera tried to pull me away. After a brief tug-of-war, they prevailed. Valera hiked my heavy pack upon his back and we darted toward the door.

"Wait!" Irina Vasilyevna and Oleg Anatolyevitch bellowed, then motioned for us to sit. Surprisingly obedient, Elena and Valera squatted in front of the door and bowed their heads. I looked around me, bewildered, before joining the family on the floor. A moment of silence ensued. I looked over at Elena, who smiled and winked before closing her eyes to reflect on the upcoming journey, as per Russian tradition.

"*Davai*," Valera said softly, calling us out of the quiet. I tearfully hugged Irina Vasilyevna and Oleg Anatolyevitch once more before scrambling out the door. At last, we had reason to run and did so, laughing manically as we chased each other through the Lenin-lined streets to the bus that would take us to the train station in Nizhnii, where they would wave from a platform as I rolled into the night back to Moscow.

6. THE VODKA CHRONICLES

PIT' BUDEM, GULYAT' BUDEM,
A PORA PRIDYET, POMIRAT' BUDEM!

WE WILL DRINK, WE WILL HAVE A GOOD TIME,
AND THEN THE TIME WILL COME WHEN WE DIE!
—*Russian toast*

IT DIDN'T TAKE long to discover that everything I'd ever heard about Russians' drinking capabilities was grossly under-exaggerated. Twelve-year-olds could drink me under the table. The average Russian (man, woman, or child) consumes about 4.2 gallons of vodka a year—35 percent proof, without so much as an ice cube to dilute it. Dr. Alexander Nemtsov, one of the nation's leading authorities on alcoholism, has estimated that vodka claims about half a million lives there annually, not only from things like cirrhosis of the liver and car crashes, but from causing its abusers to leap out of windows or pass out in the snow. He also blamed vodka for the drastic decline in life expectancy for Russian males, down to fifty-seven years and three months in 1994 (the lowest in the developed world).

Russian leaders have been trying to ban alcohol for at least four centuries—including a short-lived attempt by Gorbachev in the mid-1980s—but they succeeded only in strengthening the pastime of brewing *samogon*, or moonshine. Ever resourceful, Russians have always devised other ways to drown their sorrows when the real thing isn't available, from rubbing alcohol and paint thinner to fingernail polish remover, gasoline, antifreeze, and brake fluid.

But then, Russians don't generally drink for taste. It's the effect they are pursuing.

"The best thing about vodka? It makes you so hung over, you don't remember why you started drinking in the first place," was how one vendor explained it to me.

Prior to Russia, my drinking experience consisted of standing around a keg and pumping lukewarm beer into a plastic mug emblazoned with some fraternity's logo. When I first got to Moscow, I could stomach three shots of vodka before I started puking. By the time I left, I lost count after about a dozen. This skill was honed primarily during the great Russian pastime of the dinner party, where the rule of thumb was to buy a bottle for every guest plus one. Apparently this tradition started back in Former Times, when vodka bottles couldn't be recapped. If one was opened, it had to be fully consumed. The technology may have changed since then, but the mentality has not: My friends never reshelved bottles or served half-full ones.

So when Nadezhda invited me to an overnight dinner party at her family's spare apartment in the nearby town of Nara, I knew it would be raucous just by looking at the guest list: five guys and five *devushki*, or eleven bottles of vodka. We met at a train station early that Friday evening. The others had studied together at MLI, taking the exact same classes with the exact same teachers for four years. A good-looking bunch, the guys wore pressed trousers, sweaters, and leather jackets; the girls wore figure-flattering coats and riding boots. They all carried bulging *sumki*, the hefty plastic shopping bags Russians carried around when stores didn't furnish them. *Sumki* could be a status symbol of sorts, especially if they had foreign languages printed on them. People admired the Gap and Banana Republic bags that Nadezhda brought home from America as though they were Coco Chanel purses.

Inside these *sumki* were enough provisions to party for a month. The boys brought the booze (eleven bottles of Stolichnaya vodka; one of Sovietskoe Shampanskoe, Soviet Champagne; and twenty of Baltika, a Scandinavian beer venture in St. Petersburg), while the girls toted the food (hunks of cheeses named for their regions of origin, like Moskovskii, Latviskii, Yaroslavskii, and plain old Russkii; cans of pickled beets; smoked sausages; an assortment of potatoes, cucumbers, and tomatoes; and a big box of chocolates).

We settled onto a clump of wooden benches on a sparsely filled outbound train. Alexei, an ash blond with dazzling eyes, popped open the first bottle of Stolichnaya of the night, took a swig, and passed it to Nadezhda. Then he jumped into the center aisle and announced that he had a joke. Everyone in the train car looked up as he launched into something like this:

> During Clinton's trip to Moscow, Yeltsin shows him how Russia has developed the technology to telephone hell. Impressed, Clinton calls the Devil for a chat and is stunned to find the transaction costs only 32 cents.
>
> When he returns to Washington, Clinton learns the Pentagon has a similar phone service. He calls the Devil again and talks a long while. A month later, he receives the bill and is shocked to find he has been charged $14,000.

"How could this phone call have cost so much?!" he complains to the operator. "The same call cost only thirty-two cents in Russia!"

"That's because it's a local call over there," the operator says.

Nadezhda leaned over and whispered that that joke had been around since Brezhnev and Carter, but everyone laughed as though hearing it for the first time. Alexei triumphantly took his seat as Misha, a dark-eyed ladies' man, stepped into the aisle.

A *Novie Russkie*—New Russian—is cruising around Moscow in his Mercedes-Benz and nearly gets killed in a car crash. He crawls out to the side of the road and begins to cry. A crowd quickly gathers around him.

"Oh, my Mercedes!" he wails. "I just lost my Mercedes!"

Someone in the crowd realizes the Mercedes is not all the *Novie Russkie* has lost.

"How can you cry over your car when you have also lost your hand?" he asks.

The *Novie Russkie* looks down at his missing hand, and even more tears stream down his face.

"Oh, my Rolex! I just lost my Rolex!"

Sergei hopped up after Misha and was followed by Marina, Larissa, and Olga. Then a few of the other passengers on the train joined in. Meanwhile, the bottle of Stoli worked its way up and down the aisle, followed by a package of cookies someone contributed for communal consumption. Everyone in our group told a joke, and before long, eyes turned to me. So I took a deep breath, moved into the aisle, and attempted my first joke in Russian, with help from Nadezhda. It was actually more of a story than a joke; my ex-boyfriend, a Colombian, used to tell it a lot. (He always swore it was true, but in 2003 a really bad movie named *Kangaroo Jack* came out with the same plot, so who knows?)

"So there was this guy named Jorge from Cali, Colombia," I started, then pretended to sniff a line of cocaine to catch everyone's attention. "Jorge wanted to see the world, so he saved up four thousand dollars, quit his job, and bought a one-way ticket to Australia.

"He joined an old Aussie truck driver heading across the Outback. Neither knew the other's language, so they just waved at each other across the rig and exchanged cigarettes." I mimicked this; everyone guffawed.

"Then, late the third night, the truck hit a kangaroo!" I got down on all fours, rolled over, and stuck out my tongue.

"Jorge was sad they killed it, but thought it would make a good souvenir photo. So he pulled the kangaroo up to its floppy feet and wrapped his coat around him, along with his glasses and baseball cap. The Aussie snapped their picture—and the flash brought the kangaroo back from the dead! It bolted away in Jorge's coat." To illustrate this, I hopped down the aisles of the train. My audience erupted in laughter.

"But Jorge's passport and four thousand dollars were still in that coat pocket! So poor Jorge had to head back home to Colombia." I pretended to sniff another line of coke, everyone cheered, I bowed, returned to my seat, and took a big bite of pickle.

Soon after, our train rolled into the station and we stepped into the cool Nara night. Nadezhda's apartment was a good two miles away, but everyone agreed it was the perfect weather to *gulyat'*, so we did, joining the families and lovers lingering in the moonlight.

The tenth invited guest—Nadezhda's childhood friend Oksana—was waiting for us in the courtyard of an apartment complex, blowing smoke rings at the stars. She was quite a sight. Her chin-length ebony hair contrasted starkly with her translucent white skin; her lipstick was so purple, it was nearly black. With her black coat, black pants, black sweater, and black shoes, Oksana could have blended with many crowds in this world—a Depeche Mode concert, an Anne Rice book signing, New York City—but the citizens of Nara weren't among them. Like Elena, Oksana wanted very much to nab a Moscow *propiska*, but she had a different strategy. A local bachelor named Anton actually owned one of the coveted resident permits, and Oksana had spent the past two years scheming on how to share it with him. Anton may have drunk like a fish, had a miserable temper, and—by Oksana's own admission—been a stumbling idiot, but as another Russian saying goes, *Bez bumazhki, miy kakashki*—Without papers, we are shit. In Oksana's eyes, Anton's *bumazhki* made up for the fact that he was a *kakashki*. So she seduced and married him and bore his child. Then she sent him off to Moscow to find an apartment and a job. Too unskilled for professional work, too proud for manual labor, and too intimidated by the black market, Anton repeatedly returned empty-handed. In time, he tired of searching for work altogether and announced he was perfectly happy in Nara. Infuriated, Oksana moved back to her parents' one-bedroom flat with their six-month-old daughter. The couple had not spoken since.

To be sure, Oksana once had better plans for her life. She had studied sociology in college—a promising field in Former

Times. But when the Soviet Union collapsed, it took many of its job prospects with it. Unless a woman spoke excellent English like Elena and Nadezhda or had solid business contacts, she often had to rely on men to make her way in the new world. (That is what leads so many *devushki* to either mingle with the *Mafiya* or sign up to be somebody's mail-order bride.)

Oksana didn't know what to do about her future, but her objectives for that evening were clear. She sought some comforting.

The genders split as soon as we entered Nadezhda's flat. The *devushki* went straight to the kitchen, where they industriously peeled potatoes, chopped cucumbers, and sliced cheese with a set of meat cleavers that looked straight out of a horror flick, while the guys headed into the living room to drink and listen to music. I spent fifteen minutes trying to pry the top off a can of beets with a rusted manual can opener before Oksana swiped the can from me, bludgeoned it with a cleaver, and handed me a towel to mop up the bloodred juice. Taking advantage of the way foreigners can either transcend social orders or be forgiven for breaking them, I then grabbed a Baltika from the fridge and joined the guys on the sofa.

Eventually the food was ready and we sat down at the table that had been pushed to the center of the living room. Igor, the evening's *tamada*—toastmaster—lined the vodka bottles in a long row beside his plate and our evening began. Half a century ago, the first toast always went to Comrade Stalin; today it goes to the guest of honor. Igor smiled broadly and led everyone in a toast to me, the kangaroo *devushka*.

"Za zdarovie," they drawled as they raised their glasses, clinked them midair, tossed back the vodka, and chased it with an appetizer.

I was the only one who didn't drain their glass. Everyone noticed.

"*Pei do dnya!*" they shouted in unison. Drink to the bottom! So I did. It singed my tongue and scorched my throat like fire. I held it down a couple of seconds before choking and gasping for air.

"*Nyet, Stesha! Ne tak,*" Igor chided. He demonstrated how to drink by taking a deep breath, chugging fast, and exhaling immediately, so that the fumes didn't reach my nose—the philosophy being that if I couldn't actually smell what I was drinking, it wouldn't make me drunk. Then, Igor urged, I needed to follow each shot by eating something smelly, like a sausage or a pickle.

"And if there is nothing to eat," he said earnestly, "sniff *voloci.*"

"*Voloci?*" I asked incredulously. Hair?

"*Da, da.*" Everyone laughed.

That bewildered me, but after a few more toasts, I forgot all about hair sniffing. Igor was quite the *tamada*, delivering toasts both witty and poetic (though they grew a tad long as the night drew on). No one drank between toasts, and every drink was drunk like a shot. As soon as we polished off one bottle, Igor hid it beneath the table and uncapped another.

Five bottles into the evening, Oksana walked over to the tape deck, cranked it as high as the speakers could handle, and began to dance as though she were fending off her demons— Anton, *bumazhki*, parental responsibility, entrapment. Misha allowed her two songs of solitude before joining her on the well-worn strip of pea green carpeting. Their bodies snapped into place like a puzzle—her head fitting into the hollow of his neck, breasts beneath pecs, pelvises clenched together. After grinding for a song or two, they disappeared into a back room somewhere, never to return, while the rest of us danced in the living room, smoked in the kitchen, and drank at the table until the sun rose seven hours later.

When I groggily awoke late the next afternoon, I discovered all eleven of our vodka bottles standing beneath the table.

Every last one was empty.

One by one, the rest of the gang stirred awake and the *devushki* trickled into the kitchen to fix up the leftovers for breakfast. Misha eventually strolled into the living room, zipping his pants like a stud, and put a U2 tape in the cassette deck.

"Do you like them?" I asked excitedly. My sister had brought home *Under a Blood Red Sky* when I was eleven and I'd been a huge fan ever since. Bono put words like *imperialism* and *apartheid* in my vocabulary and inspired me to join Amnesty International and Greenpeace in high school. Had I found a fellow politicized fan?

"*Da*," Misha said. "They are the only American group I can stand."

Letting his mistake slide, I asked what he had against American music.

"It's crap, just like everything else from that country," he said brusquely, rolling up the sleeves of his Polo sweater.

"Have you ever been there?"

"*Nyet.*"

"Do you know anyone from there?"

"*Nyet.*"

"Then how do you know that?"

"TV. The movies, too. I know all about American culture."

I'm the first to criticize my country's cultural exports, but, somehow, hearing it from him ticked me off. "You don't know shit about my country!" I shouted so loud, one of the *devushki* in the kitchen poked out her head.

"I know enough to know I'd never want to go there," he snapped back.

"Good! We wouldn't want you!"

"Just like we don't want you, either," he said, glowering.

That remark couldn't have stung more if it had been delivered with a nail gun. Before I could react, Nadezhda bolted out of the kitchen, eyes blazing. She told Misha something in a sharp Russian I didn't catch, and he rose to leave.

Determined to have the last word, I screamed: "And U2 are Irish, not American, you idiot!" as he headed out the door.

"That explains why I like them so much," he said with a laugh as he slammed it shut.

The *devushki* surrounded me to apologize for Misha's behavior.

"He's just hung over."

"He's just pissed off that he never got to study in America."

"He's just a jerk."

It didn't really bother me when that Metro *babushka* told me to get out of her country. Anti-Americanism was ingrained into her psyche more than half a century ago. But Misha was only twenty-two—just one year older than me. Hadn't our generation learned how dangerous it was to mistake people for governments?

7. FROM *DEVUSHKA* TO *ZHENSHINA*: FROM GIRL TO WOMAN

LONG IN HAIR, SHORT IN BRAINS.

I THOUGHT I SAW TWO PEOPLE, BUT IT
WAS ONLY A MAN AND HIS WIFE.

TO BEAT HER IS TO LOVE HER.

A CHICKEN IS NOT A BIRD AND A
BABA IS NOT A HUMAN BEING.
—*Russian proverbs*

"ALL RUSSIAN WOMEN do is try to look good for men," Nadezhda lamented one morning as she wrestled with an unwieldy pair of panty hose (nude). After testing an iron with a dabble of spit, she meticulously pressed a skirt (paisley) and blouse (silky) and added: "That's what I really miss about Austin. I could wear jeans anywhere there."

I glanced down at my Levi's (lived in) and nodded.

"All my friends ever spend their money on is clothes and makeup and shoes," she continued as she fiddled with the packaging of her brand-new Cover Girl compact. "It's terrible." She outlined her lips with a freshly sharpened pencil.

I stifled a yawn and checked Nadezhda's alarm clock. It was 8:03 A.M. Nadezhda had been primping for the past forty-five minutes and had yet to get to her hair (which she planned to curl) or her riding boots (which she wanted to polish). Fortunately, I was accustomed to my friend's morning routine. Back in America, we spent two weeks traveling the West Coast by train. My backpack yielded two pairs of jeans and shoes, one skirt, four tops, a pocketknife, a map, a couple of books, and a journal. Nadezhda, meanwhile, crammed hair rollers, a curling iron, a pound of cosmetics, half a dozen pairs of shoes, and three-quarters of her wardrobe into a suitcase, an enormous knapsack, and a backpack. When men failed to offer their assistance at the Amtrak station, she was incensed.

"If we were in Russia, we wouldn't have to carry this," she hissed as she struggled with her luggage.

"Why not?"

"Because we're women! It doesn't look right."

Every night of that trip, Nadezhda set her shoulder-length auburn hair in rollers and spent an additional hour and a half getting ready in the morning. I didn't even bother stepping into the shower until Nadezhda was satisfied with both her hair *and* makeup and was digging through her luggage for that day's co-ordinated outfit. We were equally amazed and repulsed by each other's rituals, but by the end of our journey, she had seen the virtue of fast primping. Our last night in Seattle, she got ready in just under half an hour—and even considered it progress. Nadezhda eventually returned to Moscow a markedly different *devushka:* She had pierced her nose, grown out her dye, trashed her rollers and half of her cosmetics, and traded in her frilly skirts for faded blue jeans. She was, as she put it, ready to take on her Motherland as a liberated woman.

Yet here we were a year later, back to hours-long primping sessions and strategic wardrobe planning. Peer pressure must have had something to do with it. Moscow felt a lot like Dallas: No respectable woman would dare run down to the neighborhood kiosk without base, concealer, blush, eyeliner, eye shadow, mascara, and lipstick. And their scrutiny was inescapable. I was in a car accident at age seven that left a scar on my lip that plastic surgery reduced to a minuscule mark. Americans hardly ever notice it, but I have yet to meet the Russian woman who hasn't asked about it upon first acquaintance and then tried to cover it up with her lipstick. Friends also kept me informed of how much weight I had lost or gained since we last saw one another and how much farther the ends of my hair had split.

Dozens of theories have been offered for these idiosyncrasies. Journalist and author Francine du Plessix Gray once suggested that such scrutiny generates from centuries of political terror, where citizens learned as a survival technique to quickly size up strangers and determine whether or not they were trustable. She rationalized women's fashion obsession as an extension of Russia's *pokazukha*—false show—tradition, à la the Potemkin villages set up for Catherine the Great's countryside tours to shield her from the misery of her people. Given the dearth of color during the Soviet years, it is understandable why women went out of their way to sparkle themselves up. Women have always used fashion to express individuality during times of repression. Even at the height of the Taliban, Afghan women dared to wear makeup beneath their *burqa*. But the pressure for Russian women to dress up did not cease after the collapse of their regime. Rather, it has intensified with the availability of products. In 1996, Russia boasted some fifteen thousand Avon ladies who could be seen selling their wares everywhere from factories to beauty salons to park benches (but never door-to-door—partly out of security concern and partly from good old-fashioned Soviet etiquette).

Being a foreigner allowed me to circumvent the fashion burden to a certain extent, but between my jet-puffed down coat, mud brown corduroys, bulky sweaters, and hiking boots, I admittedly felt like an androgynous pauper among the high-heeled *devushki*. I brought one black miniskirt with me to Moscow and by the end of my stay was wearing it practically every day, along with contact lenses and those little black shoes that barely kept me out of the clutches of those drunk men that night. Once again, a Russian proverb puts it best: Beauty demands victims.

YOU CAN TELL by the smell when March 8—aka International Women's Day—has arrived. Buckets of tea roses, carnations, tulips, gladiolas, birds of paradise, daisies, chrysanthemums, and tiger lilies are flown in from Holland and Central America and sold on every street corner. Milk chocolates come in shiny wrappings tied with ribbons; kiosk vendors shove aside their boxed juices and beer to make shelf space for perfumes and scented soaps and creams. Women parade about in their feminine finest while men commit random acts of chivalry. A perfect stranger actually stopped me in the middle of the street to hand me two pink carnations. Russians first celebrated this holiday as part of the peace movement against World War I in 1913. The Bolsheviks appropriated it as a socialist holiday, but it has since evolved from a day of feminism to one of femininity.

On the morning of March 8, my suitemates and I were breakfasting in the *stolovaya* when we overheard someone mention a Take Back the Night march that would be held that afternoon in Pushkin Square. We looked at one another with excitement. People taking to the streets and demanding social change?! The only march I'd ever been to was a counter–Ku Klux Klan protest at the Texas State Capitol on Martin Luther King Jr. Day my sophomore year in college. I had looked forward to it for weeks, but only half a dozen Klansmen and fifty Birkenstock-clad hippies showed up. We booed at them, they hissed at us, and then we all went home.

But this was Russia. If anybody knew how to march, it would be a people who had been forced to for seventy years! My suitemates and I wolfed down our bread and cheese, raced to the Metro, and ascended the stairwell at Pushkinskaya Ploshad' into a thick crowd that included men and children as well as women. Whole families had shown up to Take Back the Night! We maneuvered into a clearing and saw that the line of protesters stretched for nearly two city blocks.

"Just look at the solidarity," I marveled as we bounded over to join the tail end.

After a few minutes of standing still, Katie moved up to the front to see what was the holdup—a counterdemonstration? a police blockade?—and returned rather sheepishly. "Uh, guys? This is the line for McDonald's."

Moscow Mickey D's had chosen that day to premiere the McChicken. We backed away from the crowd as though it were contaminated.

Just then, off in the distance, I noticed a small group of women being followed by a clump of news cameras and photographers.

"There they are!" Karen cried.

We sprinted across the street, scaled a fence, and pushed our way through the reporters, who outnumbered the demonstrators two to one, to join our Russian sisters. The women directly in front of us turned around and smiled. Delighted to make such an instant connection, I bade them *zdravstvuite*. The pretty blonde in the Gore-Tex jacket blushed. "Sorry, I don't speak Russian," she said in a suspiciously familiar drawl.

"Where are you from?" Karen asked cordially.

"Houston. Where y'all from?"

Karen upheld our end of the conversation while I stole ahead to get a feel for the rest of the demonstrators. Judging by the languages, Russian women seemed to be outnumbered not only by journalists, but by foreigners as well. Among the liberties they had gained with the collapse of communism was the right not to march, and they utilized it in awesome numbers.

We Took Back the Night at a small park surrounded by empty benches and a wrought-iron gate. The organizer, a middle-aged brunette named Natalia Gaidarenko, called us into a circle, gave us each a candle, and spoke about the state of women in her country. She became one of Russia's most outspoken feminist activists after writing a newspaper article about a young girl who was raped by a stranger and then ditched by her family after becoming pregnant. More than nine hundred women responded, many with stories of their own. Gaidarenko sent them all a notebook for rape survivors that she had translated from English into Russian and then established the Moscow Sexual Assault Recovery Center, the nation's first rape crisis center. After sharing some grisly statistics—like how 60 percent of the women murdered in Russia each year are killed by their husbands and how domestic violence occurred in one of every four Russian families—she led us in a moment of silence for victims of domestic violence.

A woman in hiking boots and jeans broke us out of the quiet. "Men think they can treat us like animals for three hundred sixty-four days a year and then appease us on March eighth with flowers and candy!" she yelled as she waved her fist in the air, her curls bobbing with every thrust. "We have to let them know we aren't going to take it anymore! Tell your brothers and fathers and boyfriends and husbands that we are no longer docile, feminine objects! That time has passed!"

Everyone in our circle cheered, but I couldn't help noticing the McChicken crowd that had gathered around the fence to listen. When the curly-haired woman called on her sisters to give back the gifts they'd received that day, the *devushki* snickered. Return their flowers and fries? No way. This was their one day out of the year.

ON THE ORDER of Ivan the Terrible, a monk wrote a *domostroi*—law of the home—in the sixteenth century that set the tone for the treatment of women for generations to come. The text gave men pointers on how to beat their wives—"privately and politely"—and instructed women to hush about their domestic quibbles. *Russkie zhenshini* could not work outside the house, get an education, apply for a passport, or execute a bill of exchange without their husband's consent until 1914.

Then came the Bolsheviks, who promised—among other things—to legalize abortion, relax divorce laws, and implement a child care system in the workplace. Deeming housework the "most unproductive, most savage, and the most arduous work a woman can do," Lenin called for the establishment of public laundries and communal dining facilities across the nation. Then he tackled the family unit. Writing off marriage as superfluous, the Bolsheviks allowed men and women to merge and disperse as freely as they wished. Any offspring that came from these unions would then be raised by public employees of the state, thus vanquishing the concept of illegitimacy. As Soviet sociologist S. Vol'fson put it in 1929: "[The family] will be sent to a museum of antiquities so that it can rest next to the spinning wheel and the bronze ax, by the horse-drawn carriage, the steam engine, and the wired telephone."

The problem with this utopia was that women invariably got stuck with the most physically demanding and lowest-paid labor, as men were rarely if ever assigned to the communal kitchens, laundries, or child care centers. Women found themselves cooking, cleaning, and caring not only for their own families, but for hundreds of others as well. When the socialized kitchens and laundries eventually shut down, women were shuffled into mines and factories alongside the men during the day and were then expected to rush home to cook, clean, sew, raise the kids, and tend to their husbands at night.

The collapse of the Soviet Union in 1991 has alleviated some of women's burdens by expanding their freedoms, cutting down their wait time at stores, and remarkably increasing the quality and quantity of goods. Other problems have intensified, however, such as inflation, delayed wages, mass unemployment, deteriorating health care and public services, and a steep rise in crime and corruption. Russian women also have to contend with the inequalities known to women the world over, like earning 71 percent of a man's average hourly rate for the exact same work and having fewer opportunities for promotion. Some employers stipulate quite openly that their female workers be *bez kompleksov*, or without complexes (that is, willing to sleep with the boss), in order to climb the career ladder; others ask female applicants to send in photos with their measurements. Nadezhda often remarked that she would have to change her profession soon, as no firm kept female translators past the age of twenty-six (that is, when they lost their *svezhest'*, or freshness).

Yet not a single sexual harassment case went to court in the Russian Federation between 1993 and 1996. At least in Former Times, women could complain to their local Party organization or trade union representatives about unfair practices. Today they either have to accept them or quit.

I PLAYED INTERNATIONAL courier for a number of people that year in Russia, transporting letters and packages in both directions. One evening, I dropped off a present at the apartment of Karina and Vova, a happily married couple in their late twenties. The children of intellectuals, they'd grown up listening to the BBC and reading *samizdat* (underground dissident publications) when it was still "counterrevolutionary activity." Karina, a striking brunette with shiny black eyes, had studied abroad in Germany; Vova once spent a few weeks wandering around New York City. Their bookshelves showcased just as many volumes of Flaubert, Twain, and Goethe as Blok, Nabokov, and Tolstoy. Both were radio journalists who took pride in their "Western ways"—Vova even wore little round John Lennon glasses.

As Karina prepared a meal of beets and fried potatoes, Vova fixed Russian margaritas (Sprite on ice with a few shots of tequila) and joined me at their folding table propped between a dark green sofa bed and two folding chairs. Slipping into journalist mode, he asked me to describe myself. Having gone from kindergarten to high school with the same people, I had developed an identity before I was even cognizant of it, and I'd been trying to shake it ever since. So I really loved questions like that, responding not with who I actually was, but with the labels I hoped someday to acquire. And back then, it was a militant-vegetarian-Chicana-feminist. The first part baffled Vova and

Karina (*Kak?*), the second confused them (*Shto?*), but when I got to the *feministka* part, they laughed so hard, their margaritas fizzled out their noses.

"Is it true that American feminists get mad if a man opens the door for them?" Karina choked out between snorts and giggles.

"Well, I guess some might, but that is really not a major point of—"

"Really?" Vova asked incredulously. "They get mad if men act chivalrous?"

"One or two might, but that isn't the—"

"Do you get mad?" he wanted to know.

Before I could answer, Karina rattled off another question. "And I heard you burn your bras. Why would you do that?"

"We don't! I mean, some of us did in the sixties, but we got over that once we—"

"So, Stesha, I have a question for you. Why do feminists hate men?" Vova asked.

"We don't! Lots of us are married with children and—"

"But you have girlfriends on the side, right?" he asked with a lascivious grin.

"I think you two are missing the point," I said, somewhat flustered. "Feminists simply believe that men and women should have equal rights and opp—"

"You American feminists are always fighting for the right to work, but we're sick of it!" Karina interjected. "Can you imagine what it's like for women to run a household, do all the family's laundry by hand, buy groceries, care for parents, husband, and children, and maintain a career on top of that? If that's equality, we don't want it."

Vova rubbed his wife's back sympathetically as she spoke, but I wasn't about to let him off the hook. They had both worked just as many hours that day, but Karina was the one who had spent the bulk of the evening tidying up their one-room apartment and peeling the potatoes and boiling the beets while Vova sat on his ass with me.

"Why does it always have to be women who do the house-work?" I asked, staring pointedly at Vova.

"Because men are incapable," Karina answered for him. "Haven't you heard the saying *Ya i loshad, ya i bik, ya i baba, i muzhik*? I'm the horse, I'm the ox, I'm the woman, and the man!"

With a self-satisfied smile, she reached for her husband's plate and served him the last of the potatoes.

TO HEAR A Russian describe it, the *banya* is Eden: a steamy, womblike place where you take off all your clothes and snack on caviar and smoked herring. I'd been told since I started studying Russian that it was a cultural tradition in which I had to partake. So before Kandy and our friend Heidi headed back to the States at the end of the semester, we visited the *banya* near the 1905 Street Metro to dip into the fountain of Slavic vitality. A *babushka* took our rubles at the front door and pointed us to a brown vinyl booth with a shower curtain for privacy. We crowded in and kicked off our hiking boots and ripped off our socks, chatting all the while. When we realized what needed to come off next, though, we grew strangely quiet and started staring at the fuzz between our toes.

"So!" Heidi broke the silence. "Guess it's time to get naked, huh?"

"Yeah," Kandy said in a faraway voice.

"Guess so," I murmured.

"This is going to be great," said Heidi, a former Deadhead, as she pulled her shirt up and over her shoulders. At the first sight of her bra, Kandy and I averted our gaze from her to each other to our toes again. We each removed a strand of fuzz.

"Come on, ladies, the *banya* is waiting," Heidi quipped as she unclipped her bra and her breasts spilled forth.

Ex-boyfriend aside, I hadn't disrobed completely in front of anyone since about the second grade. Dread churning in my belly, I stood up, turned to face the wall, and began peeling off my layers with as much nonchalance as I could muster. Jeans, long-sleeved T-shirt, tank top. That left just the bras and panties. Carefully sucking in my stomach, I turned around to see how the others were progressing. Heidi was completely naked, but Kandy had stripped down only to her black bikini. *Dios mío*, why hadn't I thought to bring along a bathing suit? Taking a deep breath, I slipped out of my final layer and covered myself with a towel.

Together we flip-flopped out of the booth, through the dressing area, and into a room lined with communal showers crowded with stitchless Russian women of all ages, shapes, and sizes. Some were washing, others drying, still more rubbing their bodies with ointments and oils.

"This is it? This is the *banya*?" I asked, disappointed. I had waited all these years for a glorified shower? Where was the caviar? What about the vodka?

"There's got to be more. Where does this go?" Heidi asked as she pushed on a heavy wooden door that was hot to the touch. I followed her through and was immediately engulfed by a sweltering steam that burned my eyes and nose and pierced every pore of my skin. This, it turned out, was the *banya* part of the *banya*—a wooden construction with a large furnace stove at one end. Twenty women were perched at different levels on the bleachers before us, each one red, naked, and sweating profusely. They all started shouting at once.

"*Devushki!* Close the door! You're letting out all the steam! Are you coming in or aren't you?!"

As I quickly closed the fiery door, a *babushka* with more wrinkles than a shar-pei marched over and seized Kandy by a bikini strap.

"Take it off! Off!" she scolded.

"Back in a second," Kandy called over her shoulder as the bellicose *babushka* dragged her outside and yanked the offending bikini right off her body. According to folklore, *banya* are inhabited by an evil spirit called the *bannik* that bewitches clothes worn inside. Good thing *babushki* are around to protect us.

Cowering behind Heidi, I flip-flopped to the bleachers. We spread our towels on the first row and cautiously lowered our buns upon them. The wood was hot as blazes. I shifted my weight from one cheek to the other, positive both would be blistered within seconds. Sweat flowed down my limbs in rivers; a pool formed in my belly button. I tried to talk to Heidi, but it burned my lungs too badly. When Kandy returned, I could only wave a greeting. By the end of the third minute, I could take the heat no longer.

Gotta go, I motioned as I rose to my melting flip-flops and made a beeline for the door. Kandy and Heidi were right behind me. The outside air splashed against me like a glass of cool water, and I breathed in deeply.

"This way, *devushki,*" a middle-aged woman called out, and led us down a corridor and through another unmarked door. This one opened up to a swimming pool filled with half a dozen skinny-dippers laughing and dunking one another beneath the water. An enormous disco ball suspended overhead bounced colors off the walls; Russian pop music blasted from hidden speakers.

"Davai!" our guide cried as she held her nose with her fingers and did a cannonball into the pool.

The three of us obediently jumped in after her, unaware the water was as balmy as an ice bucket. The screech that ripped through my lips ricocheted off the walls like the colors from the disco ball. My fingers turned white; my nipples grew blue.

"Cold! *Kholodno! Frrrríííííí-o!*" I cried as I frantically climbed up the side of the pool. It was so slippery, I fell back inside and convulsed in shivers. "Who are these people? Sadists?" I thrashed my limbs about to ward off hypothermia. I thought the *banya* was supposed to prolong one's life—not end it.

"Khorosho, da?" a lady asked as she calmly bobbed up and down in the water like an apple. Isn't this nice?

I swam—quickly—to a ladder and climbed out. The others weren't far behind.

"Let's do it again!" Heidi exclaimed.

Cursing her silently, I followed her back into the sweat house.

As it turns out, one-thousand-degree steam is slightly less painful when breathed through the mouth instead of the nose. A bit more at ease, I turned my attention to my surroundings. These were Russian women as I'd never seen them before. Gone were their pretensions of appearing dignified or regal: They were massaging packets of salt into each other's pores, examining one another's cellulite, swapping beauty secrets, gossiping about jobs, kids, and lovers. Naked as they were, not a one sucked in her stomach, electing instead to let them spill out with freedom. I managed to give up makeup and hair dryers in college, but that was one level of emancipation I hadn't yet achieved. I *always* sucked in. As I gazed at the room full of round, extended bellies, I thought about the heavy helpings of butter, jams, honey, and creams that Elena and Nadezhda shamelessly smeared on their food while I allowed myself only the paltriest smidgen and decided that being at peace with one's naked body must be the highest degree of self-liberation. I looked around another minute or so, gathering up the courage, before cautiously letting out my stomach, too.

Just then, a stout *babushka* walked in carrying two buckets of birch branches soaked in water. She pulled one out and proceeded to swat herself with it. As little red welts sprang up across her thick body, the other women started climbing off the bleachers and crowding around her. They each selected a branch and all began to thrash themselves, too, as in some ancient, tribal Slavic dance.

Meanwhile, a second *babushka* created more steam by scooping cool water out of a pail and splashing it against the heated stones inside the stove. It erupted like a volcano, spewing out thick, sizzling steam. Coughing furiously, I scrambled for the exit. The birch leaf *babushka*, mistaking my presence as a sign of consent, reached out and grabbed my wrist. *"Davai!"* she cried as she smacked me with a bundle of twigs.

"Owwww! Owwwowwowwww!" I yelped as I tried to cover my more sensitive parts with my hands.

Kandy laughed so hysterically that the *babushka* reached over and swatted her, too. Then we each grabbed a branch and slapped the old woman back—to her delight—and then each other, and then ourselves. Nothing breaks down barriers like nudity. In the *banya*, even *Russkie zhenshini* are equals.

A FEW WEEKS before I departed for Moscow, I got dumped by the love of my life: a sultry *colombiano* named Mario. Eight years my senior, he'd combed South America and Cuba by motorcycle and North America by thumb and spun stories that rivaled those of my father and that CNN correspondent from long ago. Mario could have won me over with his adventures alone, but he also had an aquiline nose, Che Guevara hair, disarmingly blue eyes, and hands that stayed warm even when it was cold outside (from milking so many cows as a kid, he said). Those hands were the first to ever undress me, to touch, stroke, palm, caress me. I used to imagine those beautiful hands slipping a ruby ring onto my finger at an altar someday. Holding our thick-haired, olive-skinned children.

But then those very same hands reached deep inside my chest, yanked out my heart, slam-dunked it into a trash can, and incinerated it.

I put up with far more grief than any woman ever should from Mario, and only in retrospect do I realize I did so because he was exactly the person I aspired to be: a traveler and a story-teller with a deep sense of home and family and culture. Mario wasn't a half-breed trying to fit in with one group or another. No, he was a full-blooded, soccer-playing, coffee-picking, sign-of-the-crossing Latino. That's probably what made his rejection of me so devastating. I felt pushed away not by a man, but by a people. My people—or at least the people I wanted so badly to claim.

When I related this sad tale to Nadezhda and Elena, they insisted there was a cure for my still-smoldering heart. They prescribed me a *Nastayashii Russkii Muzhik*.

Now, there is a lot of talk about what quantifies a Real Russian Man. Cunning, guile, and wit are a part of the equation, as is an appetite for vodka (it should be hearty). A *muzhik* also has an earthiness about him, an ability to connect with his people. Leo Tolstoy once defined him as "not the man who defeated Napoleon, and who conquered other peoples. . . . No, he is the humble, hardworking, God-loving, gentle, and patient man who grew and now carries on his shoulders all that plagues and depraves him."

But while there was no shortage of *muzhiki* in Moscow, the *nastayashie* ones seemed rationed. My first suitor was a sailor named Boris. Kandy and I were slamming down screwdrivers at a table for two in an Irish pub one night when he and his buddy Nikita dragged over some stools and joined us. Boris was short and stocky; Nikita was tall and lanky. Both reeked so heavily of vodka, they made my eyes water. A cocktail waitress brought us a round of shots, which the boys balanced atop their elbows and then attempted to catch with those same hands. Instead, the vodka splashed across the table and the shot glasses shattered on the floor. They shouted for another round. Before long, we were doused, they were soused, and the bar was covered with shards of glass. Seven rounds into the night, Kandy and I excused ourselves to the ladies' room, never to return.

Next came the smartly dressed man who claimed to be a direct descendant of Tolstoy himself (and carried the papers to prove it). We met at a café near the Taganka Theatre, one of the few places in Moscow that let me write for an hour on a single cup of coffee. (Most kicked me out after six sips.) Writing in a journal is, incidentally, a great way to meet Russians, who are immensely curious about literary endeavors. (Being young, single, and female probably also helps.) When Tolstoy walked through the door, he beelined to the seat directly across from me, even though the café was empty. If that had happened in America, I would have assumed he was a pervert, gathered my things, and left. Russians, however, are a social bunch who tend to equate aloneness with loneliness. People often assumed that if I was sitting solo, I wanted company.

Within minutes, Tolstoy's neck had stretched clear across the table as his gray blue eyes strained to read my writing. When I looked up, he turned my journal around so he could better see it. "Oh, it's in English. No wonder I was having such a hard time," he muttered. Then he ordered us both a beer.

Halfway through our Heinekens, Tolstoy invited me to his great-great-great-uncle's estate at Yasnaya Polyana that weekend, where he had access to the summer cottage. "My wife and kids will stay with their *babushka;* it will just be the two of us," he said enthusiastically. When I declined his offer to commune with literary spirits, he shrugged good-naturedly and called for more beer.

Then came May 9, or Victory Day, the holiday honoring the twenty million Soviets who died defeating Nazi Germany. I passed the afternoon on a hilltop on Kutuzovskaya Square, watching throngs of decorated veterans mill around the World War II memorial while drinking *kvass* (a poor man's beer made of black bread and yeast served out of a blimplike contraption).

I didn't notice suitor number three until he cast a shadow over the patch of dandelions I was lying in.

"Excuse me, *devushka*, do you speak English?" he asked politely.

Russians who approached me with that question usually either wanted a language tutor or needed a recruit to drag to church. *"Nyet,"* I said flatly without even turning around.

"Forgive me for disturbing you. Enjoy the festival," he said smoothly.

His was a classical Russian, highly educated and somewhat appealing. So I rolled over to see whom I'd just blown off—and there he was, stretched out beside me. Late twenties, well built, and rugged, he was clad in black from head to boot. Seeing he'd captured my interest, he picked a yellow dandelion, placed it in my palm, and clasped it shut with his own. His touch was callused but gentle.

"I'm Andrei." He smiled, revealing perfect, pearly teeth.

"I'm Stesha," I said, somewhat dazed.

I had met my *Nastayashii Russkii Muzhik*. I was smitten.

AS FAR AS dramatic life stories go, I never thought I'd top Mario's. (A few years before we met, he was kidnapped by guerrillas in southern Colombia and held for ransom in the Andes mountains for nearly a month before his captors released him. Or so he said.) But Andrei's was practically lifted off the pages of a Dostoevsky novel. He was forced into manhood at thirteen when his father died and took odd jobs to help out his mother and little brother, Oleg. Andrei was conscripted to the army straight out of school, but while his friends weaseled their way out with bribes and fabricated illnesses, he looked upon his two years of service as a patriotic obligation. So in March 1986, he handed Oleg the keys to their father's Lada and reported to duty.

One month later, a faulty nuclear reactor in Chernobyl, Ukraine, exploded with such force, it blew off its own cover. Its graphite moderator burst into flames and burned for nine days, releasing two hundred times as much radiation as Hiroshima and Nagasaki combined. Party officials quickly evacuated their families but dawdled over instructing the hundreds of thousands of nearby residents to leave. It was history's worst nuclear disaster—and Andrei's platoon was sent in to clean it. Each soldier was given a choice: He could either work furiously in the "hot spot" for a carefully clocked ninety seconds and be permanently released from military duty, or he could toil indefinitely at the fringes.

Andrei's father had been a scientist, so Andrei knew the dangers of cesium. The thought of exposing himself to even a minute and a half of such raw radiation horrified him, but so did the idea of potentially spending the next two years in Chernobyl. He opted for another route. He lagged behind in the barracks when his platoon went to the makeshift cafeteria for lunch one day and, five minutes before they were due back, slit his wrists with a razor blade. When he awoke, he was strapped to a cot in the mental ward of a state hospital.

For the next half year, Andrei lived little better than a prisoner. His daily rations—bread, tea, and the occasional pat of butter—dropped ten pounds off his frame that first month alone. Each morning, a nurse dumped a mound of slipper-making materials at the foot of his bed. Since he was the only capable man on the ward, he was expected to fill the entire labor quota himself. He once asked the head nurse for a day off, and she gave him an inoculation that caused him to vomit repeatedly over a seventy-two-hour period. He never asked again.

Andrei tried to keep his sanity intact by writing epic poems and letters to his family, but they always went unanswered. He later learned that his mail had been confiscated, but at the time, he thought his actions so disgraced his family, they'd abandoned him. That left him with only his bedside "neighbors" for company: Anton, who beat his head against the metal bedposts, and Petya, who chewed his own fingers into pulp.

Never once did Andrei regret leaving Chernobyl. Yet there were many times he wished he had cut himself deeper.

Meanwhile, back in Moscow, Andrei's mother was bribing every bureaucrat in sight to get her firstborn an honorable discharge. When her rubles finally greased the right palm, she flew out to the Ukraine and retrieved her emaciated son. After a few weeks' recovery, Andrei started applying to colleges and was eventually accepted to Moscow State University, the Harvard of the Soviet Union. In 1991, he graduated with top marks in topography, assured of lifelong employment and a respectable pension. Yet just a few months into his new job, his employer—the Soviet state—went under.

"The capitalist system has no need for topographers," he explained to me, "but it does let you travel."

So Andrei joined the mass exodus of Russians who left the country once the borders opened. Some friends of his family had been living in exile in New Zealand for years and invited him to make a fresh start there. He tried, but within a year, news began trickling out about the overnight fortunes that entrepreneurs were making back home. Friends called to brag about their latest purchases: cell phones, CD players, leather coats, Mercedes. Auckland was a gorgeous place, granted, but it didn't hold much promise for a Soviet-trained topographer who spoke almost no English. Andrei also had a girl back home he missed.

"She wrote to say she'd marry me if I returned. So I did."

Moscow had undergone sweeping changes in Andrei's absence. Stores that had been barren his entire life now sold Italian shoes, French wines, and American music. Bookshelves featured dissident writers as well as controversial works from abroad. Monks and nuns, recently released from prison, renovated churches and reopened them for services. Foreigners abounded—and it was permissible to talk to them. But the main difference Andrei noticed was in his people's psyche: Everyone had grown obsessed with money.

Initially, Andrei was excited about these changes. He and a couple of buddies decided to pool their resources and start a small-scale furniture factory. They rented a room of an abandoned steel plant on the outskirts of Moscow and within a few weeks were churning out sofas, tables, and chairs. People liked their handiwork, and they were just beginning to turn a profit when three beefy men in Nike tracksuits and gold chains paid them a visit. After surveying their carpentry, one said, "Don't forget, boys. We get forty percent of the profit."

"Or what?" sneered one of Andrei's pals.

"Or you stop making profit," he said as he cracked his gold-encrusted knuckles.

What with rent and overhead, there was no way they could afford to pay off a *krisha*, or roof, too. They closed shop that same day, and Andrei had been drifting ever since. Most of his friends had opted for the *Mafiya* and were reaping in the rubles, but Andrei refused to engage in what he called "black *biznes*." Anyone who did was a "sellout," including his former fiancée. (Soon after he shut down the furniture business, she left him for a sixty-year-old with a shiny new sports car.)

Looking back, I question my attraction to Andrei. Did the writer in me romanticize his struggle, as I had with Mario? To be sure, Andrei had his share of "material." In the three months we were together, he was beaten up by the police for not having his *dokumenti* (or a decent bribe). He lost one friend to thugs and another to a drug overdose.

Maybe I felt that if I unraveled his turmoil, I would finally "get" Russia—the country that had mystified me since childhood. If that was the case, what separated me from those beer-bellied expats who chased after taut young *devushki* at every bar and nightclub in town? They exploited Russians for sex; did I for understanding? Which was worse? (The mental, after all, can be just as invasive as the physical.)

Yet Andrei was charming, outgoing, tenacious, and sincere. Even idealistic, which was rare in post-Soviet Moscow. He was also enormously affectionate. The first thing he did after kissing me hello was remove the backpack from my shoulders and slip it onto his own. Initially, this worried me (Is he going to run off with it?); then it angered me (I can carry my own damn bag!); but eventually, admittedly, it pleased me (It's nice not having backaches). He also ripped off his jacket whenever mine didn't appear warm enough and wrapped it around my shoulders. Painted me landscapes with watercolors. Read me excerpts from his family's extensive library. Took me down to Red Square to hear the Kremlin bells strike midnight. Called me his *golubka* (little pigeon), his *lapachka* (cat's paw), his *dusha moya* (soul). Mario used to treat me to sumptuous five-course meals, but that didn't mean nearly as much as when Andrei brought me half his supper in a Tupperware dish that his cat had chewed on.

I guess that's what made him a *Nastayashii Russkii Muzhik*.

AS FAR AS girlfriends go, I'm pretty low maintenance, but I do like to go out now and then. Problem was, my new boyfriend made the equivalent of $10 a week as a freelance welder. Dinner and a movie could easily eat up his entire month's salary. I am of the philosophy that the check should go to whoever can afford it—which, in this case, would be me—but for me to foot even a beverage bill mortified Andrei.

"I can't believe you just spent ten thousand rubles for this cup of coffee! I could have made us two pots for that amount!" he hissed the time I treated us to cappuccino at a café. I had some vague romantic notion of us lounging there together all afternoon, but he downed his cup in one gulp.

"Why are we just sitting here? It's boring. There is far more to see in the street than in this café. Aren't you done yet? Come on. *Poidyom gulyat'*."

So I polished off my cappuccino and we went for a stroll down the Arbat, the pedestrian arcade that was the birthplace of *glasnost* in the 1980s. Political radicals used to gather there along with poets and street performers, writers and artists, Hare Krishnas and punk rockers, each one eager to explore the boundaries of "openness." A sort of Russian Haight-Ashbury, circa 1969. But by the mid-1990s, the arcade had become a capitalist showcase housing a marble-pillared McDonald's and a spit-polished Baskin-Robbins (also like Haight-Ashbury). The only remnant of the Arbat's gritty past was a graffiti wall memorializing Viktor Tsoi, the beloved Soviet rocker who cried for *Peremen* (Change) but got killed in a dubious car crash in 1990 at age twenty-eight.

Regardless, the Arbat was a place to see and be seen—and roaming photographers could even document your experience. For a nominal fee, you could pose for Polaroids with the exotic pet of your choice: an eagle with a broken wing, a defanged python, a monkey with a bad case of mange. I once watched an attractive young woman in a blue silk suit cuddle seductively with a bear cub in front of the camera—only to drop-kick him seconds later when he began to pee. The photographer lifted up the cub by the collar and shook him senseless, cursing all the while. When I pointed this out to a passing policeman, hoping he would ticket them for cruelty to animals, he ambled over and lent the soiled woman his handkerchief.

Andrei and I slowly wove our way through the Arbat, side-stepping panhandlers, nomadic bands of Romani, and clumps of those ubiquitous woodwind musicians from Peru. A short bus ride later, we stood at the base of his gargantuan alma mater, Moscow State University—thirty-two stories of red and gray granite that paid tribute to the Soviet architecture style known as "Stalin Gothic." It was as decorative as a wedding cake—only with hammers and sickles instead of tea roses and ivy—and a ruby red star blinked from its central spire. We stole past the security guards and slipped into the labyrinths of cavernous hallways and dimly lit stairwells. On our way to his old dormitory, we bumped into his friend Kari, a petite *devushka* with rich olive skin and black, almond-shaped eyes. She invited us over for tea in a tiny room with hardwood floors, a window overlooking Lenin Hills, and a load of laundry drip-drying from a rope strung between two corners. Andrei and I sat on her cot and watched her flit between the desk and the bureau, peeking into drawers and tin containers. Finally, she joined us on her bed with a sigh: *"Chai—nyetu."* There is no tea.

I assumed Kari simply ran out, but as we were leaving, I noticed Andrei slip her 20,000 rubles, or $4. That being twice as much as he had ever spent on me, I asked about it once we'd left the titanic building.

"She's from Tajikistan," he replied.

I stared at him blankly.

"You're an American. You don't understand anything." Andrei rolled his eyes and shook his head. "If I don't give Kari money, she'll starve."

Plucking a note from my bank of optimism, I reasoned: "Well, she's studying in Moscow's best university. Maybe after she graduates she'll get a good—"

"Stesha," he said sharply, "she's from Tajikistan, don't you get it? She is not a pure Russian. They call her 'Yellow Monkey' everywhere she goes. And she doesn't have a *propiska*, so when she graduates, they'll send her back home."

Russians don't apologize for their prejudices. The most popular street performers on the Arbat back then were three long-haired guys in their late twenties who sang a cappella. Judging by their crowd's reactions, they seemed immensely funny, and I often stopped and strained to listen. One word I heard them sing time and again was *Evrei*, which I assumed to be an insult by the adjectives that surrounded it (greedy, dishonest, scheming, and the like). But I looked it up in a dictionary and saw it meant Jew. Even acquaintances who studied in the West and "knew better" referred to natives of Central Asia as "yellow monkeys" and the southern Caucasus as "black asses." The *propiska* was basically a government-sanctioned method of keeping out these "undesirables" altogether. White Russians like Elena and Oksana had trouble enough securing those documents, but for people from the former Soviet republics like Kari, it was nearly impossible. For starters, who could afford it? In 1994, a Moscow *propiska* cost the equivalent of five hundred times the minimum monthly salary for Russian citizens, or about $7,000, and many times *that* for noncitizens. Without one, Kari couldn't legally work, rent an apartment or hotel room, vote, obtain a driver's license, or receive social or medical services in the capital. In fact, she couldn't even be buried without it.

Andrei lit a cigarette, took a long drag, and laughed bitterly. "Kari is studying geography, understand? This country needs a geographer about as much as it needs a topographer."

Like Andrei, Kari had chosen a field of study rendered useless by the destruction of the state. Her job prospects were as grim as his.

"There is only one way you can make it here nowadays, and do you know what it is?" Andrei asked, then answered for me. "*Biznes.* Black *biznes.*"

With that, he flicked a few ashes.

ANDREI'S CHILDHOOD BEST friend was a good-looking twenty-nine-year-old with an impish grin named Kirill. He lived in the same concrete slab of apartments as Andrei, but his flat was filled with imported leather couches, Japanese stereo equipment, three cordless telephones, and alphabetized stacks of CDs and videocassettes. I couldn't contain my surprise the first time I visited. "How did you get all of this?" I asked.

Kirill flashed his puckish grin. *"Biznes."*

"What kind of business?"

The grin broadened. *"Biiiiiizzzzznes."*

One thing endeared me to Kirill, and that was his heart. A few years prior, he was walking home in a midwinter storm and noticed someone lying facedown in the snow. The body appeared young and feminine, so he turned it over. Sure enough, it was an eighteen-year-old girl—blond, forlorn, and nearly dead from drink. He scooped her up and carried her home with him, where she slept on the couch for two days straight. When she awoke from her stupor, she took a long shower and emerged breathtakingly beautiful. Kirill invited her to stay with him as long as she wanted. Within three months, they were married.

Kisa quickly bored of housewifery and soon found a job at a cosmetics counter in GUM, a shopping mall adjacent to Red Square. A photographer noticed her in passing and asked if she ever modeled. She lied, he hired her, one shoot led to another, and she soon became a fashion model. Her purple-blue eyes and pouty red mouth were plastered to Metro placards, billboards, and covers of magazines. Men began offering her thousands of dollars to sleep with them and—once she developed a drug habit—she started accepting. When Kirill confronted her, she walked out.

The night I met Kirill, he hadn't seen his wife in two and a half months. Beneath that perpetual smirk was a broken man. Andrei said that when Kirill came home from "work," he pulled down the shades, stared at photos of Kisa, and cried.

Having recently been swept off my feet and dropped on my head, I could relate to Kirill's pain. When he showed me pictures of his glamorous wife, I imparted the wisdom gleaned from my relationship with Mario: "You can't trust anyone that good-looking."

Kirill groaned and hit himself with a black leather pillow.

ANDREI AND I were hanging at Kirill's one evening when he asked if I'd like to call home—for free. He'd just acquired a phone that was rigged to charge hotels at random for his international calls. When I questioned its legality, he and Andrei laughed and said I still had a lot to learn about Russia. I eagerly took the phone out to the balcony and dialed every number I knew from memory. The whole time I chatted with my housemates back in Austin—"Guess where *I'm* calling from?!"—the guys talked in the living room. They usually cracked jokes when they were together, but the conversation seemed serious that night. By the time I hung up, they were arguing. Their street slang was hard to decipher, but I distinctly heard the figure $10,000 used several times. Andrei kept shaking his head over and over until he finally shouted, *"Nyet!"* Then he grabbed my hand and pulled me out of the apartment. Bewildered, I waved good-bye to Kirill, but he didn't notice. He was flipping through a stack of magazines to gaze at Kisa some more.

"What was the yelling about?" I asked Andrei as we hurried down the stairwell.

"I don't want to talk about it."

"I do."

"You're American. You wouldn't understand."

I waited until we were outside before letting loose. "Don't give me that! Tell me about those ten thousand dollars—*now!*"

Andrei sighed, slung his arm across my shoulders, and whispered that Kisa had given Kirill an ultimatum. She needed $10,000. If Kirill provided it, she'd move back in with him. If not, he'd never see her again. Then she hung up.

The quickest way to make cash back then was a contract killing, so Kirill called around and found himself a job. He was blindfolded and driven to an apartment complex in an unfamiliar area of town. The thugs gave him a gun and told him to bump off the guy who lived in the ninth-floor suite. Then they drove away. With Kisa on his mind, Kirill climbed to the top of the stairwell.

"That guy was supposed to return at ten, but ten came and went, and he didn't show up. And then it was ten-thirty, then eleven, then eleven-thirty. Kirill started thinking about what he was doing, and it messed with his mind. You know"—Andrei drew little circles around his temple with his hand—"it made him kind of crazy."

By midnight, Kirill was soaked in his own anxiety. His hands were quivering; his teeth were trembling. Cold spasms followed hot flashes followed chills. He had just made up his mind to leave when he heard footsteps ascending the stairwell. He tried to stay calm, but as soon as he made out a man's figure at the end of the landing, he bolted past him, raced down nine flights of stairs, burst through the door, flew into the street, flagged down a cab, and went home to bed.

"The next day, he returned the gun," Andrei concluded.

The story slowly sank in. "And you were mad because . . . ?"

"He asked if I'd go with him next time."

A FEW WEEKS later, I convinced Andrei to let me treat us to a movie one afternoon and arranged to meet him at the cinema just outside Krasnopresnenskaya Metro. As I exited the station, I could see him leaning against the banister of a stairwell in the distance, shoulders shaking, head hung low. I ran to him and found his face streaked with tears.

"Andrei, what's wrong?" I gasped.

He shook his head. For once, I didn't insist.

"I don't know if I can sit through a movie right now," he said softly.

I nodded.

"Poidyom gulyat'." Let's go for a stroll.

Catercorner to the cinema was the zoo, which had free admission that day. We walked among the steel cages in silence until we got to the wildcats. Then I remembered it was Parents' Day, when Russians pay respects to their elders. Maybe Andrei was mourning the death of his father.

"Did you visit the cemetery today?" I asked, not yet having mastered the art of subtlety in a foreign language.

As I watched the color ebb from his face, I saw I was not mistaken. "You must miss your father," I whispered as I pulled him close and stroked his tousled hair.

"*Nyet*. That's not it." He pushed me away.

"Andrei! Please tell me wh— Oh, my God. Is it Kirill? Did something happen to Kirill?"

"*Nyet*, not Kirill, but another friend, a really good friend. He'd been missing for two weeks, but they found him this morning, full of bullets, in the middle of a forest. . . ."

"What happened?" I breathed.

Andrei slammed his fist into the chain-link fence of the tiger cage before us. "What do you *think* happened?" he yelled.

At that, a haggard tiger began to pace back and forth in the cage that was at least three sizes too small. Andrei watched him a long time before turning to me, face contorted, voice trembling.

"You know, Stesha . . . I'm afraid to continue living in Moscow. . . ."

9. THE WILD EAST

IF THE RUSSIAN prototype of the 1970s dressed in gray and languished in breadlines, the *Novie Russkie* of the mid-1990s sported Versace and drove a bulletproof BMW. Their molls were leggy; their bodyguards were beefy. Widely considered a by-product of capitalism, the *Mafiya* was the buzzword of the times—the premier cliché of the post-Soviet era.

Russian *Mafiozi* were generally classified into four strata. First were the grunt boys, the small-scale smugglers and swindlers. The second layer consisted of thick-necked hit men who extorted payoffs from *biznesmeni* for "protection" and, in turn, bumped off their competition. Tattoos divulged their ex-con pasts. Next were the sleekly dressed thugs who claimed *biznes* for a profession. White-collar crime was their vice. And the undisputed chiefs were the former KGB agents and Party bureaucrats whose *vlast' i svyazi*—power and connections—accorded them Godfatherlike status.

Collectively, *Mafiozi* were known as *krisha*—roofs—for the protection they "provided." An effective *Mafiozi* could bully a businessman into handing over as much as three-quarters of his profits, but rates typically ran between 20 and 40 percent. It was nearly impossible to pursue any form of entrepreneurship in Russia without one. By the mid-1990s, the underworld controlled about half of Russia's stock exchanges, 60 percent of its banks, and 40 percent of the nation's economy—and their *vlast'* was constantly growing. By 1996, there were nearly eight thousand documented organized crime groups, and when one came calling, you either had to pay up, close down, or skip town. Any act of resistance was sure to be met with beatings, kidnappings, attacks on family members, or cold-blooded killings. Unlike Kirill, the bulk of contract assassins fulfilled their duties: There were more than five hundred contract killings that year alone, and Russia's murder rate was roughly double that of the United States and many times that of European cities. As Mikhail Zhvanetsky, the famous Russian satirist, once put it: "If a man comes home from work beaten up, that's called small *biznes*. If he comes home killed, that's big *biznes*."

My introduction to the underworld occurred in an underpass a few blocks from my dormitory, long before I met Andrei. Crossing major streets in Moscow was roughly akin to slathering oneself in chum and swimming in a shark tank: mobsters' convertibles roared through traffic lights while onslaughts of Ladas, taxis, buses, trolleys, and trams terrorized pedestrians from every direction. Underpasses—called *perekhod*—were thus the saving grace of the pedestrian population. Some featured nomadic salespeople who peddled everything from cookware to lingerie on folding tables that could be quickly disassembled in the event of a police raid; others lodged Romani families, gangs of street kids, or drunks.

Three ancient *babushki* inhabited my neighborhood *perekhod*. One, who always wore a black cloak, sat on her hands and knees behind a crescent of religious icons and bobbed her head up and down as she made the sign of the cross at passersby. Another condensed her autobiography to three piteous sentences scrawled on a piece of cardboard that hung around her neck: "I lost my apartment, daughter, and husband to fire, illness, and drink. I suffer from diabetes and arthritis and need a new pair of glasses. I haven't eaten in two days." The third *babushka* intermittently wailed, *"Pomogi mne!"*—Help me!—and slept.

I ventured down the *perekhod* after morning traffic thinned one day and caught the *babushki* on break. They were seated upright, lively and laughing. When they noticed me, however, they resumed their woeful postures and rattled their bowls. I walked the length of the underpass and climbed the stairwell out of their view. Then I crept down a few steps, peeked around the corner, and—as I suspected—saw they'd become their chatty selves again.

Just then, a bedraggled *dedushka*—the male counterpart to *babushka*—climbed down the stairwell at the far end of the underpass. After glancing over his shoulder to ensure no one was looking, he slowly made his way from woman to woman. Each one reached into the folds of her layers of clothing and handed him a wad of rubles. He pocketed their money, walked up the stairwell opposite me, and hobbled away.

Who was that geriatric man? The arthritic leader of a *perekhod* cartel?

Soon after, I awoke one morning to discover a new kiosk plopped in my backyard. Business boomed for a week or two, and it rapidly evolved into a spacious walk-in store with four walls and a sturdy ceiling. Then it doubled its dimensions and posted a neon sign. But when I paid a visit one morning, its doors had been bolted and chained. A week later it was gone. Literally.

By midsummer, I didn't even have to cross the street to see a little *Mafiya* action: A gang moved in right down the hall (which had long been vacated for the summer). Initially, I thought the dorm's newest residents were simply a rowdy pack of Georgian students with a curiously developed taste for double-breasted suit jackets, wing-tipped shoes, unruly parties, and half-naked hookers. They were fine neighbors otherwise. The dark and handsome one always doffed his cap at me. I found this charming. Andrei did not. "You can't get any worse than a Georgian," he spat. "They must be *Mafiozi*."

Deeming that comment racist, I shot back that any respectable *Mafiya* would put its boys in more glamorous housing than a dingy old dorm. But I soon heard rumors that my new neighbors didn't pay rent. When I mentioned this to Andrei, he gloated.

"Of course they don't! And the *komandanka* knows better than to do anything about it. She's too afraid even to crash their parties."

That much was true. The Poison Dwarf came knocking if Andrei stayed in my room a minute past curfew but didn't say a word to the Georgians, who chased women up and down the stairwell all hours of the night. So who were these guys? Mobsters? Wealthier-than-average bachelors who somehow talked the *komandanka* into free room and board? According to Andrei, Western cars and stylish clothes were telltale marks of a *Mafiozi*. He often dismissed people as gangsters with a single glance.

"But maybe they just have money," I once countered.

"And how do you think they got that money?" he shot back.

How did anyone ever make money? "They earned it?" I asked in a small voice.

"No one in this country has ever gotten rich ethically," he said sharply. "You only get money from *biznes*. Black *biznes*."

But "black *biznes*" is hardly new. Landlords conducted

"black *biznes*" when they extorted payoffs from peasants in Imperial Times, just as Party officials and bureaucrats did from the proletariat in Former Times. The *Mafiya* isn't a by-product of capitalism: It thrived throughout the entire twentieth century. Journalist and author David Remnick once called the Soviet's old Party apparatus "the most gigantic mafia the world has ever known." Capitalism has simply been a continuation of the system instituted by the czars and refined by the Communists. Even under "democracy," honest people like Andrei suffer.

LIKE MOST MUSCOVITES, Nadezhda lived with her family in an anonymous concrete sky-rise in the suburbs of the city. We arrived after dark one evening and discovered the elevator out of order. She looked at me apologetically, and we began the long climb up to the fourteenth floor. From the second floor onward, the light fixtures had no bulbs, so we gripped the railing and felt around for each succeeding step. Halfway up, we passed an elderly man whose cabbage white face was illuminated by a candle. His shadow stretched up three flights of stairs, making our journey easier but eerier. A bloodhound's guttural bark ricocheted off the walls; a baby wailed from a faraway crib.

As soon as we crossed the threshold of Nadezhda's apartment, however, warmth and coziness enveloped us. Nadezhda shut and locked the three steel doors—the last one padded to keep out the cold—and we sat upon stools to exchange our street shoes for the *tapochki* on the rack, signifying our transition from the public sphere to the private. The foyer led into a small area that simultaneously served as living room, dining room, guest bedroom, and study and was covered with the same Persian-style rugs that hung in Andrei's and Vova and Karina's flats in Moscow as well as in Elena's and Mae's homes in

Balakhna. Ivy coiled around bookshelves crammed with Russian classics, geraniums and begonias covered the table, and rubber trees tickled the backs of the chairs. The connecting balcony served as the requisite garden, its floor covered with jars of jellies and pickled vegetables and its railing lined with dill and tomato seedlings.

Nadezhda's mother, who had just returned home from work, whirled out of the kitchen to promise a hot meal within the hour. Nadezhda rolled her eyes and brushed right past her. She despised her mother's constant catering, but I relished it. (My own mother, a corporate businesswoman who grew up on beans and tortillas three times a day, seven days a week, despised the kitchen and always told us to cook our own dinner.) We chatted a few minutes before I followed Nadezhda down a hallway the width of two skinny people or a single pudgy one.

Nadezhda's room consisted of a writing table, a wall of coordinated cabinets, a dark green sofa that doubled as a bed, and just enough room to stand between the three. We flopped atop the sofa and pored over the piles of photographs she took during our travels together in America. Mingled in with the images of Disneyland and the Statue of Liberty was a sepia-toned photo of Nadezhda from her Young Pioneer days, her long hair in plaits, her neck in a kerchief, a badge of Lenin's boyhood silhouette gleaming from her chest.

"I lost that badge once." She giggled at the memory. "I was so hysterical, my family spent the whole day on their hands and knees searching around for it. Dad finally found it lodged in the drain."

"You all look so . . . serious." I stared at a class photograph of impossibly glum seven-year-olds framed by a border of hammers and sickles.

"You mean Soviet." She rolled her eyes again.

Mesmerized, I sorted through the photographs. The full-colored glossies seemed so familiar—Barton Springs, the Drag, Quackenbush's Coffee House, the co-ops back in Austin—while the black-and-whites depicted a world that ceased to exist only five years before. Of all my Russian friends who studied abroad in America, Nadezhda had the hardest transition home. "I was given freedom only for a year, and then it was stripped away," she described it. She wanted her own apartment, but her traditional parents refused to let her move out until she married. Some of her childhood friends had eloped for the sake of being independent, but Nadezhda didn't want anyone or anything to prevent her from going overseas, should that opportunity arise again.

After a time, I came upon a picture of a pint-size Nadezhda happily picking strawberries at her *dacha*, or countryside cottage. Her father stood in the background, his arm resting upon the shoulder of a teenage boy who bore a striking resemblance to him. When I asked about the boy, Nadezhda hesitated a moment before identifying him as her older brother, Vlad.

"I didn't know you had a brother! Where is he?"

"I don't know," she said quietly.

Something in her voice halted my usual prying. We stared at each other for a long, quiet moment before her mother called us to dinner. *"Kushai, kushai,"* she urged before retiring to her bedroom for the night. Eat, eat.

Upon the table were two plates piled high with steaming *vareniki*, tasty raviolis stuffed with cottagelike cheese and dunked in sour cream. As Nadezhda prepared our tea by mixing boiling water from a kettle with a strong infusion from an orange polka-dotted teapot, I tried to think of something to say. Over the past two and a half years, I had come to think of her as one of my closest friends. How had I not known of a brother?

Nadezhda pulled out a stool from beneath the kitchen table and sat across from me. "Vlad was like a wall to me, always protecting me," she said quietly. "I know if he were still here, we'd be in America now."

Vlad was twelve years Nadezhda's senior. Although he lived in that tiny dining room/living room/nursery until age thirty-two, the family knew little about him. He was particularly secretive about his work and only acknowledged that he ran some sort of *biznes*. Their phone rang constantly back then and it was always for him, Nadezhda remembered. Vlad sometimes took off for days and even weeks at a time, though he always called home to let them know he was all right. Whatever his business, it was profitable: He drove a BMW, remodeled the family's *dacha*, and kept his little sister *modnaya*—in fashion.

But nearly three years ago, Vlad stopped coming home at night. Nadezhda didn't think it unusual until several weeks passed and her twenty-first birthday drew near. She knew her brother wouldn't miss the occasion, so when the date approached without a letter or phone call, she began to worry. The night of her birthday, her mother admitted to the rest of the family that Vlad once predicted he might someday disappear—and warned her not to tell a soul if he did. But after a long discussion, they decided to report him missing to the police. Soon after, the police called to say they found a corpse that had been held under a river by weights for weeks and asked if a member of their family wished to examine it.

"My father went, but he didn't know—he couldn't tell if it was Vlad or not. Maybe my mother should have gone instead. A mother always knows. We buried the body, had a funeral, everything. But I feel in my heart that it wasn't him. I think he's still out there, maybe in America, waiting until it's safe to come back again. Of course, it's been three years now."

When Nadezhda lived in Austin, I thought of her as my Russian alter ego. We seemed to come from equivalent socioeconomic backgrounds and share similar interests and dreams back then. I felt that I could relate to her, that the difference between being a Young Pioneer and a Brownie was purely semantics, that we were one and the same. But as she told me this story, I understood that her reality was far, far removed from my own. I thought of my own older sibling, a poet with a master's in classical literature who married a member of San Antonio's SWAT team. Barbara would never just "disappear"—and if she did, Alex and his buddies would fan out to find her. But Nadezhda couldn't launch a full investigation for Vlad because of the promise her mother once made. She didn't even know if the body they buried was his.

Nadezhda took a meditative sip of tea and focused her hazel eyes on me. "You know something?" she asked quietly. "It is only a coincidence you were born you and I myself."

NADEZHDA TURNED TWENTY-FOUR a few weeks later. She invited Andrei and me to celebrate her birthday at the Hungry Duck, a Canadian-owned bar fast becoming a Moscow institution. In 1996, it was still relatively tame: Only a few hundred people violated the fire codes, and the *devushki* who danced atop the oval-shaped bar just got partially naked. But over the years, it evolved into one of the lustiest joints in the city (if not the free world), with a record 920 *devushki* once cramming in for the infamous ladies' night. The concept was brilliant: Feed girls free beer for two hours, hire some male strippers to rile them up, then bring in the boys eagerly waiting outside. I would later hear vivid accounts of male expats barely getting through the bar's front door before swarms of topless, sodden *devushki* attacked them.

Then members of the Duma—Russia's parliament—caught wind of the pub's debauchery and paid a visit. As the legend goes, at the precise moment they walked in, an ivory-skinned *devushka* went down on a Nigerian male stripper atop the bar as the Soviet national anthem blasted from the speakers. According to former owner Doug Steele, the Hungry Duck was denounced on the floor of the Duma thirty times (one charge being the promotion of miscegenation) and declared an "enemy of the people." Things went downhill from there. Within three years, the Duck racked up 256 criminal cases, eight police raids, and two bomb threats, and four of its original owners died. Steele himself received five death threats and paid hundreds of thousands of dollars in bribes. The Hungry Duck was finally shut down in 1999 by its landlady, an eighty-two-year-old prima ballerina who used to dance solo for Stalin. It eventually reopened under new ownership, but I hear it lost its zing.

Regardless, I didn't have to twist Andrei's arm too much to be my date. We squirmed through the throngs of beastly bouncers, drunken *devushki,* and inebriated expats and nabbed a booth next to a party of Brazilians. I ordered some *pivo,* Andrei lit an unfiltered cigarette, and we watched the reverie for an hour as we waited for Nadezhda. When she finally showed up with her boyfriend Lev and some of their friends from work, I knew something was wrong. Nadezhda had recently quit her job as a translator for a government-run television station in order to work for a privately owned time-share company. Judging by the stylish new clothes she had been wearing lately, it seemed to pay well. (Her previous employer—the state—was sometimes four months late with her paychecks.) I was leery of her new profession, however. Her work phone number changed constantly, and her company had switched office locations at least twice in the month she'd been there. Nadezhda never said much about it, though, even when pressed.

This was my first meeting with Lev. Blond and broad shouldered with pale green eyes, he wore Calvin Kleins and a black Polo shirt. Nadezhda once described him as gregarious and fun, but he seemed reserved that night. After a quick round of introductions, their friends headed over to the bar—now covered with a chorus line of *devushki*—and Nadezhda and Lev squeezed into our booth. As the guys delved into conversation, I asked Nadezhda what was wrong. She looked at me for a long time before replying in a low voice that a close friend of Lev's had just been found—dead.

I closed my eyes and leaned back into the booth. First Kirill and Andrei, now Vlad and Lev. This was lunacy, madness, insanity. How had the *Mafiya*, a bad cliché a short time ago, suddenly merged with my own reality?

"Lev doesn't want to be here right now, but he didn't want to spoil my—"

"I thought you said Lev was getting out!" I interrupted. Nadezhda told me about Lev's dealings with *Mafiozi*—two of his cousins recently got jumped for being in the wrong place at the wrong time—but Lev supposedly promised he would leave.

"He *is* getting out, but these things take time," she started.

"Well, he needs to hurry up! In the meantime, you can't be involved. My God, Nadezhda, just think about . . ." I stopped before saying her brother's name aloud.

"The *Mafiya* is everywhere; you can't escape it. Everyone in Russia has some sort of tie to it," she said coolly. "Besides, you don't choose who you love. You can't make orders to your heart."

With that, Nadezhda grabbed Lev's arm and headed toward the bar, where their friends awaited. After I collected my thoughts, Andrei and I joined them. Lev soon left, but the rest of us had a surprisingly good time that night at the Duck, dancing atop the infamous bar, drinking lousy beer, and singing Smokie's "Living Next Door to Alice" at the top of our lungs.

I am grateful for this memory, as it is one of the last I have of Nadezhda. I would see her only once more.

10. FREE LOVE, RUBLE BEER

IT IS A CURIOUS FACT THAT WITH EVERY GREAT
REVOLUTIONARY MOVEMENT THE QUESTION OF "FREE
LOVE" COMES INTO THE FOREGROUND.
—*Frederick Engels, 1883*

ON LAZY AFTERNOONS, I liked to catch up my journal in the tranquil Novodevichi Monastery. Built as a fortress in the bend of the Moscow River in the sixteenth century, the monastery is stunningly beautiful, enclosed by a brick wall so high that only its regal onion domes and towers are visible from the outside. The tombstones in its cemetery read like a *Who's Who* of Russia, with literary masters like Gogol, Chekhov, Bulgakov, and Mayakovsky and politicos who fell from favor like Khrushchev and Stalin's wife, Nadezhda (who shot herself—or so they say—in 1932). I arrived one day to find an artist replicating the landscape with watercolors.

"I've been coming here for years and I still can't capture the way the light reflects off that dome over there," she remarked, pointing at the glittery gold with a dripping brush.

She looked to me as if she were doing it justice, and when I said as much, she smiled and patted the bench beside her. My mother's age, she seemed wise and kind. As I slid in next to her, she asked if I'd heard about Gogol.

"They say he was buried alive, right behind those walls," she said, her blue eyes widening. "When the caretakers dug up his grave, they discovered claw marks all over the inside of his coffin."

I shivered in the heat, and she laughed. "You're not married, are you?"

When I shook my head, she launched into another story. "This is where they would have sent you, then!" she exclaimed, throwing out her arms as if to wrap them around the monastery. "All the royalty who couldn't find husbands got dumped off here. They say you can still hear them at night. Some say they're crying, but others say they're having a ball."

Next she told me about Sofia, Peter the Great's half-sister, who ruled as the empire's regent until young Peter came of age—and promptly got banished to Novodevichi after he snatched away the throne. Incensed, Sofia spent the next decade plotting her revenge and, when Peter returned to Russia from his travels in Europe, attempted a coup.

"But it failed, and do you know what her little brother did? He hung every last one of her supporters from the trees right outside her window," she said, pointing wildly at a tower in the distance. "They hung there all winter long, their legs dangling in the breeze. They say it drove her mad."

Story after story the artist told, each one steeped in legend and history. This was what mesmerized me about Russia. I loved how locals crammed into art museums and jotted thoughts or sketches into their notebooks as they contemplated pieces. I loved that every Russian I ever asked—including some of the children at the *priyut*—could recite at least one nineteenth-century poem from memory and usually a great many more. I loved how people exclaimed, "Why, that's Pushkin's birthday!" when they learned I was born on June 6. That families' bookshelves were stacked with masters like Bulgakov and Dostoevsky and that they said with complete conviction that between those covers was the finest literature the world had ever known. That an amateur painter came to Novodevichi each week to attempt to capture the way the sun glistened off the four-hundred-year-old domes.

Before we parted company, she urged me to call her twenty-four-year-old daughter, Natasha. "She's a concert pianist. Her Rachmaninov could make a deaf man weep." When I did a few nights later, Natasha greeted me like a long-lost friend and instructed me to meet her at the Park Kulturii Metro that Friday night.

She described herself as a "Russian Marilyn Monroe," which would have been more accurate if she'd added a date, like 1983. Natasha had bleached her shoulder-length hair platinum blond, outlined her purple blue eyes with turquoise shadow, and swathed her curvaceous body in acid-washed denim and dozens of sterling silver necklaces, bracelets, rings, and earrings. A beauty mark kissed her pink-frosted lips, and she had a fruity fragrance. She enveloped me in a bear hug and, linking her arm in mine, led me to a café to meet her two closest friends, who were also named Natasha. After so much drama with Andrei and Nadezhda, it felt refreshing to giggle about clothes and makeup and boys over milkshakes and fries. Then we bought some Baltika at a kiosk and headed over to Red Square. After toasting beneath St. Basil's Cathedral, we rambled over to a Tex-Mex bar called the Armadillo, where the Natashas' dates awaited. I felt awkward being the seventh wheel, but Natasha number one spent the evening dancing and laughing with me instead of Anton, her date. "One of the Natashas set me up with him; I don't even know the guy," she said, dismissing him with a wave of her hand.

Natasha and I bonded that evening, making plans for the upcoming months—art exhibits, plays, her musical concerts—and telling each other secrets. When she asked if I planned on marrying and I declared, "Not for another decade," she gave me a high five and we drank to being single. Around 3:00 A.M., she asked Anton—who'd spent the entire night at the bar with the guys—to drive us home. I got dropped off first, and Natasha and I promised to see each other soon.

The following week, Natasha invited me to *gulyat'* around the Garden Ring surrounding Moscow's historic region. She bought us a bag of *ponchiki,* or hot doughnuts dipped in sugar, and we chatted about that night at the Armadillo. When I asked about Anton, she made a face, spat on the ground, and let loose a string of Russian that would have made a sailor blush.

"Tell me, tell me—what what what?! Did you kiss?" I jumped up and down, playing along with our junior high school skit.

"Kiss? He made me sleep with him that night after we dropped you off—and then he never called again," she said indignantly.

My jaw dropped. Anton and Natasha hardly exchanged a word that night. They didn't even seem to like each other. What did she mean by "made me"? Did Anton rape her? My perception of that night, which had seemed so fun and carefree, tarnished. Before I could inquire any further, she skipped to another subject.

"The guy I really liked that night is Sasha, you know, the one with the long hair. Actually, all of us *devushki* like Sasha, so he always gets to choose who he wants to be with. He chose another Natasha that night instead of me," she explained.

Something caught her eye in a passing window. "Oh, look at those boots! They're on sale!" She grabbed hold of my elbow and steered me inside. Not another word was said about Anton again.

NATASHA AND I didn't see each other for a couple of months after that, as her music conservatory selected her and a few other students to tour around the country and hold concerts. When she finally returned to Moscow that summer, tanned and vivacious, she had big news for me. "I'm pregnant!" she squealed.

"Congratulations," I murmured as I pecked her cheeks. "Who is the father?"

"His name is Jan! He's Belgian!" she crowed. "I'm going to have a European baby!"

They met on the Black Sea—the Russian Bahamas—where she vacationed after her concert tour. Her eyes shining brightly, Natasha confided that she agreed not to use a condom after Jan promised to marry her and bring her to Brussels. The very thought made me cringe, but Natasha looked so happy, I sucked up my skepticism and treated her to a chocolate milkshake as she rattled off possible names for the baby. Then she dragged me over to Dyetskii Mir, a children's department store adjacent to the KGB's old headquarters. Admittedly, her excitement was contagious: By the end of our day, she had me squealing over baby bonnets, too. When we finally parted, she promised to invite me over for dinner before she moved to Brussels.

Three weeks passed. I was considering checking up on Natasha when I happened to run into her on the street. She greeted me so sullenly, I had the feeling things hadn't worked out as planned. I took her out for pizza for the details.

"He never returned any of my calls," she said, more to her pepperonis than to me. "So I had an abortion. My second one in two years. It's really terrible, you know?"

She focused her purple blue, turquoise-shadowed eyes on me. "Why do men always say they'll call and never do?"

IT WAS THE Bolsheviks who introduced "free love" into the Russian psyche. During the early days of the Revolution, intellectuals made lots of it as they passed around sex surveys and dissected Freud. Feminist Alexandra Kollontai, the first woman ever elected to the Communist Party's Central Committee, summed up the new mood of the nation with the oft quoted "The sexual act should be recognized as neither shameful nor sinful, but natural and legal, as much a manifestation of a healthy organism as the quenching of hunger or thirst."

But Lenin tended to be more on the prudish side, as illustrated by his famous retort: "To be sure, thirst has to be quenched. But would a normal person lie down in the gutter and drink from a puddle?"

A few years later, Stalin halted the licentiousness altogether by mandating that sex occur between two married adults of the opposite sex for procreational purposes only. (He also recommended the act last no longer than two minutes.) Words like "menstruation" and "prostitution" became taboo in the Soviet press, while the once popular academic disciplines of sociology and social psychology were removed from university curricula altogether. Before long, the Communist Politburo had created a society that Jerry Falwell and John Ashcroft would envy: They eradicated sex education from schools, advised parents to teach morality instead of the birds and the bees, outlawed erotica, and censored art (thus the depiction of Soviet women as a breastless proletariat). But while the bigwigs preached purity and chastity, they didn't exactly abstain from their own pursuits of carnal pleasures. Brothels, massage parlors, porn flicks, and "blue film" showings were purportedly always at their leaders' disposal. It has been widely rumored that Brezhnev, Khrushchev, and Stalin kept leggy concubines in secret apartments, and some have referred to Stalin's police chief, Lavrenty Beria, as a sadist. While the Masses were deprived, their leaders clearly were not.

So when Gorbachev introduced *glasnost* (openness) in the 1980s, the first thing to fly was the collective zipper. The pornography that had been banned by Soviet law suddenly proliferated. *Moskovskii Komsomolets*, long a Party mouthpiece, got so salacious that it was nicknamed *Moskovskii Sexomolets*. I used to count images of naked people on my way to school every morning. The elevator in the dormitory (when it worked) always revealed a couple of bubblegum stickers of buxom ladies. When I exited the doorway, I'd see housewives and *babushki* carrying *sumki* bags that, like the buses of Balakhna, were covered with either kittens or busty women. A bit farther down the street, media kiosks openly displayed pinups, sex manuals, and videos. Peddlers who couldn't afford kiosks clipped titillating magazines and periodicals to a long rope, hung it around their necks, and became walking peep shows. Even respectable publications tucked a little nudity between their broadsheets, particularly in the advertisements. One brand of paint was promoted by a *devushka* straining to finish a high wall in a miniskirt; in another ad, a woman performed fellatio on a chocolate bar. Just outside my university stood an enormous billboard exhibiting bountiful breasts supported by two jugs of beer; the caption read, "A hundred years ago, entertainment looked like this [re: breasts]. Now, it's this [re: breasts + beer]." I once counted twenty images of naked women before my 9:00 A.M. class.

Another by-product of *glasnost* was the myth of the *inter-devochka,* or high-class prostitute. Russian women had been sleeping for hard currency and tough-to-find items like cologne, lingerie, and chocolates almost since communism's inception, but the world's oldest profession wasn't formally acknowledged until newspapers started running stories about the alluring lives of the glamorous *interdevochki* who escorted foreign clientele in the mid-1980s. Prostitution became one of the nation's biggest growth industries, offering women such status that polls soon showed one out of every eight schoolgirls wanting to be a hard-currency *interdevochka* when she grew up.

The vast majority of prostitutes, however, worked for the ruble, entertained in the bathrooms of train stations or back-street alleyways, and hovered above the poverty line. When the Soviet Union dissolved, Russian and Ukrainian women became—and are today—some of the most heavily trafficked sex workers in the world. Lured into cartels with promises of lucrative careers overseas, young women are drugged, raped, and held against their will until they have either paid off their debts, escaped, been arrested and deported, or committed sui-cide.

But the free love factor that has affected more Russian women than any other is birth control—or lack thereof. The So-viet Health Ministry never included contraception on its list of priority drugs, producing only enough condoms for each adult male to buy three a year. Women who took the pill, meanwhile, risked the social stigma of being associated with the moral de-generation and sexual promiscuity of the West. (Even today, few of my Russian friends use it, claiming it has too many bad side effects.) This left many women resorting to the rhythm method, withdrawal, and—particularly in the countryside—home remedies throughout the twentieth century. I heard and read multiple accounts of Soviet women drinking solutions of stewed tansy, roasting in steaming *banya*, taking hot baths with mustard, and injecting themselves with iodine or urine to ward off unwanted pregnancies. Miscarriages were often induced by jumping off refrigerators or lifting heavy objects.

The Bolsheviks were a progressive bunch, legalizing abortion soon after the 1917 Revolution and making it available free of charge. Within eight years, the number of abortions surpassed the number of births. This enraged Stalin, who feared a decrease in labor and production a generation down the road. So in 1936 he called for a ban on the procedure altogether. Women who couldn't bribe doctors to perform clandestine abortions turned to midwives, who used instruments ranging from knitting needles and spindles to crochet hooks, goose feathers, and carrots. Others simply had tons of kids—and were awarded shiny medals for their "contribution" to the state.

The abortion ban was lifted soon after Stalin's death in 1953, and Russian women have been undergoing the medical procedure at staggering rates ever since. Some reports claim the average sexually active female has between two and three abortions in her lifetime; others show the rate between seven and eight. In the mid-1990s, they rarely received consultation before an abortion, anesthesia during it, or a place to rest afterward. In some cities, the procedure was performed only if a friend or relative donated blood, and women had to bribe for sedatives. Natasha described her clinic as an "assembly line."

All of this has taken a serious toll on Russia's demographics. In 1920, the average woman gave birth to 7.5 children; by the early 1990s, that number had fallen to 1.4. There are currently more deaths than births in Russia—a phenomenon that has not occurred in that nation's history since World War II.

THE EPICENTER OF Moscow's gay community in the mid-1990s was a discotheque called *Shans'*, or Chance. My friend Ira, another Russian I met through the co-ops in Austin, invited me there one night with a group of her friends. None of us were gay, but everyone seemed eager to go, including the guys (and not one whispered, "Pretend you're my girlfriend," as we walked through the door). Homosexuality was actually fairly accepted in Russia throughout much of her history. Some aristocratic and imperial family members led fairly open gay or bisexual lifestyles, and homosexuality was often the subject of bawdy jokes, shocking many a European diplomat during the sixteenth and seventeenth centuries. The closet door shut under the influence of Western missionaries in the eighteenth century, but the Bolsheviks opened it back up—only to have it slammed again by Stalin. He recriminalized consensual sex between men soon after taking power and sentenced thousands of gay men to prison terms of five to eight years apiece. (I never found much research on the historical plight of lesbians, though—perhaps because, as my lesbian friend Laima joked, the thought of two women choosing each other over a *muzhik* was too unfathomable to Stalin to make a policy about it.)

Homosexuality was finally decriminalized in 1993, and by 1996, gays and lesbians had a few known hangouts, including the park in front of the Bolshoi Theatre and the Aleksandrovsky garden by the Kremlin Wall. While I heard that gay men were occasionally jumped walking to and from *Shans'*, the club seemed immensely popular with gays and straights alike.

Nearly every hipster in line had a cigarette dangling from their sexy, pouted lips, and their noses were pierced, hair was dyed, and platforms ranged between four and six inches high. Drag queens abounded, including a Debbie Gibson impersonator.

The first floor of *Shans'* pulsed with London's latest techno raves, while the second blared Russian pop. We danced for hours, then crashed upon the plush black couches beneath the huge aquariums filled with punk-rock fish and rainbow-colored gravel along the back wall. When the clock struck 2:00 A.M., the strobe lights dimmed and a spotlight appeared in the largest tank directly behind us. Tchaikovsky resounded through the speakers as three sculpted men in goggles and Speedos dove in. Their performance started off as a graceful synchronized swim, but by the end . . . well, suffice to say Stalin would have had his work cut out for him.

With this underwater *ménage à trois* as a backdrop, I started contemplating my own sex life—or, more accurately, my lack thereof. Although my twenty-second birthday was right around the corner, my virginity remained intact. This wasn't entirely by choice: Back in high school, my friends used to brag about having to push their guys away, but my Good Catholic Boyfriend was more interested in "talking" than exploring, and nobody asked me out my first three years in college. Mario was so taken with my novelty, he wanted to preserve it—no matter how much I protested.

It's hard being a virgin at twenty-one. I certainly didn't want to hold out for a husband who might or might not materialize years down the road, but if you've waited that long, you can't give it to just *anyone*. And your standards rise with each passing month. You want romance and passion and seduction. Flickering candles beneath full yellow moons. Promises whispered above the sound of running water.

In other words, you set yourself up for some serious disappointment, because who could possibly meet the expectations of twenty-one highly anticipative years?

My relationship with Andrei had been growing in intensity, however, and I was beginning to wonder if he should be the One. He seemed to think so. "You're still a *devochka* [little girl]?!" he—who didn't bat an eyelash over nuclear radiation or Ukrainian mental wards—had gasped in shock/befuddlement/opportunism when I confessed why I always held back.

Did I want to share this fairly momentous experience with Andrei? In my Post-Soviet Youth Culture class at UT, I learned they had a "sexual revolution" during glasnost: Whatever came of that (besides public underwater trysts)? Feeling strangely brazen, I turned to Oleg, the good-looking twenty-eight-year-old sitting beside me on the couch at *Shans'*, and asked point-blank how many *devushki* he'd slept with. Taking the question in stride, he tore his eyes away from the fish tank and spent the next few minutes in thought. But even after wiggling both sets of fingers a few times, he admitted that he didn't know.

"What do you mean, you don't know? Don't you keep track?" I asked. Wasn't carving notches into a belt or headboard a universal male ritual? "How many *devushki*? Ten? Twenty?"

"*Nyet, nyet,*" he said, shaking his head. "More like eighty. Maybe one hundred."

"You mean, one hundred times?"

"*Nyet.* One hundred women."

"One hundred women!" I shrieked.

Embarrassed by my outburst, he recanted. "No, it couldn't have been one hundred. You're right. It probably was only eighty. Maybe even seventy-five. Why?"

"Oh, just wondering," I said, then quickly started up a conversation with the person to my left. Later, when everyone headed back out to the dance floor, I gathered some of the *devushki* together for a conference call.

"Hmm. One hundred. I guess that's about right," one decided.

"What do you mean, 'about right'?! How many people have *you* slept with?"

"Oh, I'm just a *devushka*—only about twenty," said the twenty-four-year-old. "Guys have a lot more experience than we do. Just ask my boyfriend."

Turns out, at age twenty-six, he had slept with sixty-five women, *bolee menee*.

"But—how?"

"There's a forest on the edge of Moscow." He shrugged. "I used to go there a lot."

That certainly gave me pause. From then on, I started analyzing every move Andrei made. He'd bring me tea and toast in the morning. Yes, I'd think—maybe he could do. Then he'd light up a stinky, unfiltered cigarette and I'd think, No way.

I thought about how it would sound: "I lost my virginity to a *Nastayashii Russkii Muzhik* who cleaned radioactive waste in Chernobyl."

Did that beat "I lost my virginity to a Colombian who was held hostage in the Andes"?

I really had wanted Mario to be the one, not only because I was in love with him, but because all those clichés about "Latin lovers"—in this case, anyway—were pretty damn true. But he was gone, off in a coffee field in Colombia somewhere, fending off guerrillas. The last time we spoke on the telephone, days before I left for Moscow, he yelled, "It's over, don't you get it? We're through!" before slamming down the receiver. So he no longer seemed a candidate.

A few weeks after my twenty-second birthday, I flew out to Prague to visit a friend from college for ten days. I was surprised by how much I had missed Andrei when I saw him standing in the concourse of Sheremetyevo Airport back in Moscow. He took me back to the flat he shared with his mother and surprised me with gifts: a candelabra burning six red candles alongside two bottles of Sovietskoe Shampanskoe (Soviet Champagne) chilling in ice on the bedside table. A pirated Sinéad O'Connor CD crooned on the stereo.

And then he began to kiss me.

We did as we'd done many times before—clothes came off, a condom rolled on. But when we got to the point we'd always stopped at before, he kept on going. I soon said *nyet* and nudged him away, but then he forced his way inside. I freaked out. Slapped, pushed, screamed. Mario, Mario, I'd wanted this to be Mario—to have a brown body caressing my body instead of a white one digging into it. To hear something salty and sweet in my ear: the roll of an *r*—not the slur of a *kh*.

But my fight didn't last long. What else could I have done? If I'd grabbed my things and left, I would have been stuck in a run-down apartment complex in northwest Moscow, hours after the subway had closed, miles away from home, with an armload of luggage and purchases from Prague. Somehow, that scenario seemed worse than staying.

"Forgive me, Stesha," Andrei mumbled afterward, pointing at the empty bottle of Shampanskoe on the table. "I had too much to drink."

He curled up beside me and held me the rest of the night, as I wept for a man that wasn't him.

When I think of why I stayed with Andrei after that awful night, practical reasons come to mind. Except for those Georgian *Mafioẓi*, the dormitory had emptied by that point in the summer. I hated living alone in that creepy, unlit hallway in a fly-infested room with no air-conditioning and frankly saw no alternative. Nadezhda and Ira barely had enough room for themselves in their cramped apartments. The *komandanka* had made me pay the entire summer's rent up front, and I didn't have the means or the money to move elsewhere.

Moreover, while I felt strong and fiercely *feministka* in Moscow, I had grown strangely dependent on Andrei. Though I had been instructing girlfriends to "dump his ass" for years, I couldn't imagine doing the same myself. As with Mario, being with Andrei was too interesting to let go. I held on to those men, no matter how they mistreated me, because they brought me closer to worlds I wanted to become a part of.

Women have been sleeping with men for the wrong reasons since the beginning of time: for money, for promotion, for shelter, for protection, for confidence, for company. I guess I did it for the story. What amazes me is how well we can convince ourselves it is for love.

11. DEMOCRACY 101

EVEN NOW, LENIN IS MORE ALIVE THAN THE LIVING.
—V. V. Mayakovsky

VLADIMIR ILYICH ULYANOV LENIN had one dying wish: to be buried by his mama in St. Petersburg. When he succumbed to a massive stroke in January 1924, his Politburo planned to lay him in state at the Kremlin for a few days before granting his request. But all winter long, waves of delegations kept crashing by. As Soviet expert John Collee recorded it: "They came from Siberia, Central Asia, and the Far East, men with gold teeth and impressive fur hats, stamping the snow off their boots. They came from the shores of Lake Baikal and the Caspian Sea, from Arkangel to the north and Magagdan to the east. From Irkutsk and Alma-Ata they came, from Novosibirsk and Samarkand, Khiva and Kiev." Just when the Politburo thought they had seen the last of them, another telegram came from a distant land: "Don't bury him yet! The roads are blocked but we're on our way."

Ever the leader, Lenin was the one who finally halted these processions. As spring rolled around, his thawing carcass emitted such a bad odor, no one could stand to be around him anymore. By that point, however, successor Stalin had decided the

pseudoreligious ardor that Lenin's corpse had created could ensure the survival of the Communist state. Why bury a carcass
that can serve a higher purpose? As Felix Dzerzhinsky, founder
of the KGB, put it: "Kings are embalmed because they are
kings. In my opinion, the question is not so much if we should
preserve Vladimir Ilyich's body but how."

So two renowned scientists immersed Lenin's decomposing
body into a tub of balsamic liquid based on glycerin and potas-
sium acetate and then put his remains on display in a neocubist
mausoleum for generations of socialists to contemplate—some
sixteen million between 1924 and 1940 alone. Reds across the
world met similar fates, including Mao Zedong of China,
Georgi Dimitrov of Bulgaria, Klement Gottwald of Czecho-
slovakia, Ho Chi Minh of Vietnam, Linden Forbes Sampson
Burnham of Guyana, Agostinho Neto of Angola, and Kim Il
Sung of North Korea.

Mausoleums around the Bloc began handing out eviction
notices to their in-house icons in the early 1990s, but Lenin
managed to hold on to his prime real estate throughout the
twentieth century—though not without a battle. President Boris
Yeltsin was a particularly fervent advocate of kicking out Red
Square's most notorious tenant and got the church to back him
up. (Russian Orthodoxy preaches that only evil can arise of improper burials—and Lenin had been without for three-quarters
of a century and counting.) But when it comes to prophecy,
Communists can hold their own. Whenever the controversy
started brewing (usually around Lenin's birthday), they were
quick to remind the nation of the time Russian archaeologists
ignored the omens and dug up Tamerlane in 1941. "And look
what happened—the Nazis invaded!"

Who wants to tempt that kind of fate?

Save for the occasional busload of tourists or schoolkids,

Lenin doesn't receive many visitors nowadays—not like he used to, anyway. In addition to ideological reservations, there are logistical problems: Lenin's visitation hours seem to fluctuate at the whim of his surly guards. Science must be honored as well: Lenin's embalmers sometimes shut down the mausoleum to conduct studies or bathe him in a special solution that prevents tissue decay. (Old man that he is, Lenin also leaks from time to time.) I made dozens of trips to Red Square with hopes of catching a glimpse of the revolutionary who saw Russia's power "lying in the street" and snatched it up—the act that birthed the Soviet Union—but the tomb was always closed.

Then came the morning I doglegged through the square to get to the central telegraph office and noticed a queue of Russians wrapped around Lenin's tomb. At last—it was open! I bounded over to the end of the line. A man well into his seventies turned to greet me with a hearty *"Tovarish!"* (Comrade!). I returned his salutation and asked about the rows and rows of spit-polished medals gleaming across his chest. He beamed as he displayed his favorite: a silver bust of Lenin encircled with a bloodred banner, a five-pointed star, and a tiny hammer and sickle. He got that one for helping defeat German troops at the Battle of Stalingrad, the turning point of World War II.

"It was too cold for the Germans!" the old man crowed. "They couldn't take it! Only a Russian can survive a Russian winter! We Russians endure!"

When I nodded, he gave me one of the crimson carnations he held in his hands. Accepting this as a token of friendship, I thanked him. As our line crept forward, however, I noticed that just about everyone was carrying flowers. Moreover, the queue consisted almost entirely of septuagenarian Russian men. Was it *Dedushki* Day at Lenin's tomb?

After a forty-minute wait, a guard counted me into the next

group of fifteen to enter the black and red granite mausoleum. The old men in front of me hobbled forth, removed their furry caps, and—in a rheumatic ripple—laid their flowers upon the grounds of Lenin's resting place. Igor, the decorated veteran, turned to me. "It's our comrade's birthday," he explained before adding a carnation to the floral display and nodding at me to do the same. A lump festering in my throat, I tried not to think of death squads or dissidents as I tossed the red flower into the pile.

The mausoleum was so dark inside, I could barely make out my hands, much less my surroundings. Gripping a railing, I teetered down the stairwell. My eyes were just adjusting to the darkness when Lenin suddenly appeared on a bed of scarlet velvet. His fingertips were purplish blue, and his goatee was long and straggly. A black business suit accentuated his pasty face; his bald head shone like chrome. Not bad for a 126-year-old, although his expression seemed more peevish than peaceful.

There was much to contemplate in that dark, clammy room, but the guards didn't stand for dawdlers. The *dedushki* and I were ushered around Lenin's glass case as though he were the Hope diamond, and we were on the other side of the door moments later. Just behind the mausoleum was the old Party cemetery, which contained the likes of Leonid Brezhnev, astronaut Yuri Gagarin, and American journalist turned Soviet sympathizer turned Warren Beatty motion picture character John Reed. As I flitted about from one tomb to the next, scanning the headstones for familiar names, a lavish one caught my eye: Josef Stalin. For nearly a decade, the beady-eyed dictator slumbered with Lenin in the indoor tomb, but he eventually fell from favor during Khrushchev's tenure. As the story goes, a Party Congress delegate reported that Lenin appeared to her in a dream and said: "It is unpleasant being beside Stalin, who brought such misfortune to the Party." The Politburo promptly banished Stalin's corpse to the humbler outdoor quarters, inspiring the Soviet proverb "Don't sleep in a mausoleum that doesn't belong to you." In recent years, there's even been talk of shipping him back home to his native Georgia.

Yet the freshly cut flowers and standing wreaths showed that Stalin still had a few admirers out there. Among the offerings was a sepia-toned photograph of Stalin tickling a little girl. Her fair hair was combed into plump braids; a badge of Lenin twinkled from her jumper. As I examined the disconcerting image, Igor passed by. "Ah, *Tovarish* Stalin," he murmured as he peeked over my shoulder. With some effort, he lowered his body into a squatting position, bowed his head, and laid a carnation on Stalin's grave.

I found Igor's actions touching and repulsive, fascinating and horrifying. Lenin and Stalin may have taken the Soviet Union from an undeveloped country to one of the world's greatest industrial and military powers in the miraculously short span of twenty-five years, but surely Igor didn't think those ends justified their means. Lenin utilized famine as a political weapon, waged war on independent thought, and banished dissenters to labor camps—paving the way for future dictators like Adolf Hitler, Mao Zedong, and Pol Pot. Then he was succeeded by a man who subjected the minority nationalities of the Soviet Union to brutal Russification, empowered the secret police, forced neighbors to spy on one another, and executed anyone who questioned or opposed him. True, Stalin may have—as Churchill once said—taken Russia from "wooden ploughs to nuclear heads," but dissident Aleksandr Solzhenitsyn, author of *The Gulag Archipelago*, has estimated that sixty million of his own people perished in the process.

Yet Igor—a decorated soldier who doubtlessly suffered under their regimes—was bringing them flowers. Why? For the same reason my own country revered Christopher Columbus, a man who obliterated entire populations of indigenous people so that his own kind could steal their land and riches? Do human beings inherently need to make heroes out of their nation's "founders"?

After a long, silent moment, Igor straightened up—knees cracking, medals jingling—looked at me with spry blue eyes, and shook his *shapka*-covered head. "The road to hell is always paved with good intentions, isn't it?" he asked. Chuckling aloud, he continued down the trail to pay respects to the other masterminds of the fallen regime.

AMERICAN MEDIA TOUTED the 1996 presidential election as Russia's Verdict on Democracy. Would she continue down the uncertain path of political and economic liberalization? Would she turn back to the legacy of seven decades of communism? Or would she travel another road altogether?

Whichever the route, plenty of men seemed eager to pave the way. There was the virulently anti-Semitic nationalist Vladimir Zhirinovsky, whose campaign promises included returning Alaska to the Motherland. Military general Aleksandr Lebed looked upon Pinochet as a personal role model for restoring Chile's economy while killing "no more than three thousand people." Communist Gennady Zyuganov assured voters they need not worry about his proposed return to the Soviet past. After all, he claimed, *Party members* were the hardest hit during those years of purges and repression—not doctors, lawyers, artists, professors, priests, or dissidents. Businessman Vladimir

Brintsalov was vague about his political agenda, but he did have a sexy young wife who once pulled down her pants to display a sculpted, spandexed ass on national TV for his campaign.

The "Democratic" candidates weren't quite that crazy but had serious strikes against them as well. A hero in the eyes of the West for terminating the cold war, Mikhail Gorbachev was largely disdained by his countrymen. Communists berated him for collapsing their empire; pro-democracy advocates blamed him for the mayhem that befell the country's transition to a market economy. Grigory Yavlinsky was young, well educated, and popular among intellectual circles, but too many Russians despised his considerable ego and Jewish heritage. As for the incumbent Boris Yeltsin: The raging war in Chechnya had wreaked havoc on his popularity, his reforms were in shambles, his health was in the dumps. In the early months of the campaign, it was questionable whether he could resuscitate his image as the golden reformer who rode atop tanks and conquered coups.

Whoever the voters picked faced quite a task, what with the fallen economy, rampant crime and corruption, and the devastating war. All the leftover benefits of living under a controlled state—free education, assured employment, socialized housing, health care, and pensions—had just about dried up, and "democracy" had yet to replenish them with anything tangible. Instead of worrying about the KGB knocking on their door at midnight, Russians now feared *huligani* kicking it down or—if they were *biznesmeni*—*Mafiozi* gunning it down. True, they could now read great writers who had once been banned, like Bulgakov, Solzhenitsyn, and Mandelstam—but who had the time? Yes, they could buy Nikes at their neighborhood kiosk— but who, nouveaux riches aside, had the money? Sure, they could traverse the world without restriction, but who had the time or the money? Metro stations and underpasses teemed with pensioners forced by the rapidly inflating ruble to clean out their closets and hawk their pets, shoes, orange polka-dotted teapots, and thimbles so they could buy potatoes. Few sights are more sobering than a *babushka* shuffling between subway cars selling a rusty pair of scissors in one hand and an opened package of birthday candles in the other.

So it was understandable why many Russians felt nostalgic for their Soviet past. What befuddled me were the inconsistencies.

"We used to have good Russian sausage and Russian sauerkraut and Russian cheese," Andrei grumbled one afternoon as we strolled past a kiosk selling Doritos and Snickers. "Now it's just American bullshit."

When I asked why he took Lipton Cup-a-Soup to work every day for lunch if he hated our exports so much, he made a face. "What else am I supposed to bring? You shop here—you tell me. What else is there?"

Not much. Moscow's state stores (that is, the affordable ones) sold some of the finest breads and dairy I'd ever tasted, but most other products left so much to be desired, you really had to question the nation's priorities. Russia had designed the world's most efficient Metro but not a decent broom with which to clean it. They put a dog in orbit, but their pens leaked. But while Andrei complained about the influx of American goods and culture, he rarely supported what little his country actually did produce. And it wasn't just him. When *Four Rooms* premiered in Moscow cinemas, tickets sold out days in advance. Several of my friends saw it twice. When a new Russian film opened a few weeks afterward, however, I couldn't drag anyone with me. I went alone and was literally the only one who showed up. The lady at the *kassa* refused to sell me a ticket. "We won't roll the projector for just one person," she snapped. "Try back later."

Since it had taken over an hour to get there, I decided to try my luck at the next screening. Adjacent to the theater was a small gated park; I sat on its dilapidated bench and opened my journal. Before I had written half a page, three guys strolled by and, seeing a single young female, joined me. Anton, a twenty-two-year-old with tobacco-stained teeth, hospitably offered me a swig from their bottles of Fanta and vodka. When I asked if they had come to see the Russian flick, he laughed. "*Nyet!* We're saving up for *Four Rooms*!"

"Wouldn't you rather support your own film industry?" I asked, hoping to cajole them into buying tickets so that I could see it.

"*Pochemu?* It's crap," Anton spat as he tossed the emptied Fanta bottle over his shoulder.

"What are you talking about? You've got Kira Muratova, Andrei Tarkovsky . . ." I ticked off the directors I'd admired in my Russian film class at UT.

"We'd rather see *The Terminator*," Dima and Misha chimed in with not bad Schwarzenegger accents. They then proceeded to reenact scenes from the movie, using the Fanta bottle as a machine gun and my bench as a military target.

I probably could have connected better with the average Muscovite if I'd invested more time absorbing my own pop culture than their highbrow one. The "most Russian" thing to do after a night at the ballet, for instance, was eat a Big Mac at McDonald's. You could actually follow the high-heeled crowd to the nearest Golden Arches as soon as the curtain fell. Hip-hop from the South Bronx had become the anthem of an entire subgroup of Russian youth; rave and techno, another; Metallica, a third. I was once invited to the home of an educated middle-class couple in their early fifties. Over dinner, the husband tried to talk to me about American sports cars while the wife wanted to gossip about the latest episode of *Dynasty* (which was insanely popular there at that time). I, meanwhile, tried to engage them in a discussion about their impending presidential election. It was a pretty silent dinner.

After an hour of reenacting scenes and dialogue from *Terminator II*, I said *hasta la vista* to Dima, Misha, and Anton and went back inside the cinema. Apparently someone else had shown up: the *kassa* lady sold me a ticket. Sure enough, there was a young couple snuggling beneath the gargantuan chandelier of the massive, barren theater. Curious as to who they were, I stole past fifty empty rows to the one across from them. I was about to say *"Privyet"* when I noticed a copy of the English-language daily the *Moscow Times* peeking out of their Jansport backpack. They were foreigners, just like me.

LOOKING BACK ON the 1996 election, we can at least be grateful that Zhirinovsky—the neofascist nationalist—didn't win. He threatened Japan with "more Hiroshimas." He bullied the Baltics with radioactive waste. He pledged to extend Russia's borders south to the Mediterranean and west into Europe. His rallying cry was "Cheap vodka for everyone." Yet his promises to restore the Motherland to her former glory struck a chord in a startling number of Russians. Even liberals could relate to some of his chief concerns, such as the eastern expansion of NATO and the treatment of ethnic Russians in the Baltics. Disgruntled workers, the unemployed, the police, and the military elected him to Parliament, where he once slapped a female deputy for being "unfeminine." He became the heralded spokesman for the disenchanted, and people took him disturbingly seriously.

So when I heard Zhirinovsky was staging a rally near the Bolshoi Theatre one cloudless summer day, I hurried over. As I exited the Metro and trotted toward the theater, I counted a whopping crowd of thirty that included twenty-six members of the foreign press corps setting up their cameras. The other four, sitting in the back of an army truck, were the hired entertainment. An aging blonde in a black-and-silver sequined dress belted out ballads while her cohorts droned on some badly tuned accordions. Two purple-and-blue balloons swayed in the wind.

A chorus of "Zhir-i-nov-sky! Zhir-i-nov-sky!" gradually became audible as several hundred ralliers turned a corner and headed our way. Nearly all were young, buff, crew-cut, acne prone, and male. Zhirinovsky strode in the center in a canary yellow suit coat and black trousers, surrounded by adoring young men who took turns holding a blue umbrella flecked with yellow stars above his head. The quartet hastily jumped off the army truck to make room for their grand pooh-bah, who hopped aboard to great fanfare and launched into his usual rant and rave, reiterating his ideas of burying radioactive waste along the Baltic border and blowing it across with gigantic fans, seizing the country's lost land (including that renegade province of Alaska) so that Russian soldiers could "wash their feet in the Indian Ocean," and giving every woman free flowers. All the while, members of the foreign media crept closer and closer until photographers from *Newsweek* and *The Washington Post* climbed right inside the truck with their Nikons and Leicas. Without skipping a beat, Zhirinovsky began to slam America and its media. The photographers—who probably spoke little Russian—snapped away as the presidential candidate bashed them and their livelihood. The crowd went wild.

—

IN THE EARLY DAYS of the campaign, it really did seem that Zyuganov had a fighting chance at leading Russia into the twenty-first century. His Communist Party of the Russian Federation had just taken an astounding majority in Parliament. He had a well-organized, loyal following and a defined ideology— both of which every other candidate lacked. He could also capitalize on the Soviet nostalgia that even *I* was starting to feel.

I was hunting for something—anything—green and leafy on Tverskaya (Moscow's Fifth Avenue) one afternoon when the sound of shouting became audible. I tossed the $13 package of frozen broccoli I'd just found back into its bin and went outside to investigate. There were five hundred Communists marching in a row, brandishing portraits of Lenin and homemade signs emblazoned with socialist rhetoric. Psyched to see people taking to the streets—whatever the cause—I joined in. The crowd consisted primarily of pensioners, impoverished conservatives, and workers who hadn't received a paycheck in months. The bulk were either homely looking in their shabby clothing or maladjusted and kooky seeming, but for the first time since my arrival, my mud brown corduroys fit right in. I trotted alongside them for a mile or so, until we reached the rallying point: a bust of Karl Marx. Zyuganov got behind a wooden podium, adjusted a loudspeaker, and blasted "The Internationale." Everyone swiped off their *shapki* and sang:

> *Eto est' nash poslednij*
> *I reshitel'nyj boj,*
> *S Internacionalom*
> *Vosprjanet rod ljudskoj!*

> Then, comrades, come rally
> And the last fight let us face
> The Internationale
> Unites the human race!

With the removal of their caps, I realized something else about the demonstrators: Nearly all were balding or gray. But as I moved through the crowd, I noticed a dozen teenagers standing on the fringes as well. Swathed in black leather and chains, they wore steel-toed combat boots and hardened looks. One waved a poster of Stalin over her head, a pin of Lenin's silhouette gleaming from her silver-studded jacket. What was she doing? Making some sort of anarchist statement? Or was there an underground punk-rock Commie scene I hadn't heard of? I walked over. "Excuse me."

"Yes?" She fixed her pale blue eyes on me.

Not knowing how to begin, I stated the obvious. "I see you have a picture of Stalin there."

"Of course. He was our greatest leader."

"Even though he killed millions of your people?"

"Who told you that?" she asked, her eyes narrowing.

Who hadn't? I was conjugating verbs for my response when her posse began to gather around me in a circle. Uh-oh.

"History books . . ." I hesitated.

"Whose history books?" asked a guy with dyed black hair.

"Where are you from?" demanded another with no hair at all.

I was tempted to say, "The workers have no country!" but didn't think they'd see the humor in it. Was it wise to debate the merits of Stalinism with someone who brandished his portrait? Admit you were an American at a Communist rally?

"Mexico," I replied coolly. As their brows crumpled in

geopolitical contemplation, I bade them well and hurried off, praying they wouldn't call out in Spanish.

That was the first time I lied about my nationality in the Bloc. It would not be the last.

BORIS YELTSIN HAD been shirking his presidential duties for years. He all but ignored the rapidly declining state of his country, possibly because his own health was similarly deteriorating. His clogged arteries, high blood pressure, and pickled liver gave him the sparkle of a week-old corpse. But once his aides got it through his sodden head that he could very well lose the presidency to the Communists in the first round of voting, Yeltsin agreed to (temporarily) put down the bottle and entered the campaign trail with a roar. He crisscrossed the country, taking thirty-three trips in four months. He granted thousands of workers billions of rubles in back pay. He issued tax breaks to fallen industries. Predicting that Lebed would do well in the polls, he pumped money into the Pinochet-loving general's coffers so he could later steal his votes. But I would argue that things really got cooking when he did the twist at a rock concert in Rostov-na-Donu.

Yeltsin captured the youth vote by holding a series of mega-rallies that showcased the nation's hottest entertainers—and himself. Nearly one hundred thousand gathered for his show on Red Square that used the Kremlin and an enormous white, blue, and red arc as a backdrop. I arrived just as the wildly popular Mashina Vremeni, Time Machine, took the stage. The crowd, consisting primarily of Muscovites under thirty, went nuts, singing and dancing almost spastically. For many, it was the biggest staged event they'd ever attended that wasn't some stodgy political parade. (In Former Times, any unofficial gathering larger than a dozen was bound to be broken up by police.) Even the soldiers were stamping their boots in time. Teenagers shinnied up the lampposts to wave gigantic flags of the Russian Federation. At that moment, I knew the election belonged to Boris.

My hunch was confirmed the next morning when I ventured outdoors to scrounge for breakfast and discovered that my neighborhood had been transformed into Yeltsin's campaign headquarters. Gone were the billboards that once advertised boobs and beer. Colossal posters of Yeltsin shaking hands with Yuri Luzhkov, the incumbent mayor of Moscow, had been plastered to every streetlight, kiosk, store, and residence in sight. And it wasn't limited to my backyard; wherever I went, Yeltsin beamed: "Muscovites, your choice has been made."

Indeed it had. Yeltsin alone had the formula for victory: money, power, and the media. Soon after the Soviet Union's demise, a small circle of bankers and industrialists who came to be known as "the oligarchs" snatched up the nation's state properties at rock-bottom prices and became overnight billionaires. Correctly equating media with power, one of the most notorious oligarchs—Boris Berezovsky—bought a string of newspapers, radio stations, and a large interest in the most respected TV channel, ORT. Fearing they'd lose their fortunes if Communist contender Zyuganov triumphed, Berezovsky and his fellow oligarchs put up more than $100 million and instigated a fierce media war to keep their man in office. To be sure, Russian journalists didn't need much persuading to heap praise on Yeltsin. Worried they would lose their jobs if the censorship-happy Communists returned to power, many chucked objectivity out the window. National newspapers threw their unabashed support behind the incumbent, while the same man who ran the day-to-day operations at another major TV station—NTV—simultaneously ran the Yeltsin ad campaign. (Dan Quayle, who was visiting Russia at the time, likened that to Dan Rather running an American presidential campaign.) Newspapers reminded readers of collectivization, deportation, and purges. The TV broadcast chilling documentaries of Stalin's reign of terror. Media simplified the presidential election: It was a choice between good and evil.

Zyuganov, meanwhile, continued his grassroots campaign of knocking on doors and leading marches through town. His supporters stood atop milk crates and called out to their *tovarishi* through megaphones or cupped hands. Their perseverance was admirable. If you turned on the television or flipped through a newspaper, it seemed the election had already been won.

ON JUNE 16, I dragged Andrei out of bed at the crack of dawn and marched him to the nearest polling station, located on the second floor of a government building. I'd gotten it in my head that election day would be my chance to witness Democracy In Action, but perhaps because we were so early, the line at the poll consisted of four people above the age of sixty-five. While Andrei registered, I walked across the empty room and sat at a table. A Russian flag hung on one wall; full-color posters of photographs and biographies of the presidential and mayoral candidates were tacked on another. Andrei soon joined me at the table, clutching his empty ballot. No way could I pass an opportunity to cast a Verdict on Democracy: I swiped the sheet of paper away from him, checked off Yeltsin for president and Luzhkov for mayor, and dropped it in the ballot box myself.

(Only in retrospect did this disturb me. If *I* was able to vote in place of a Russian citizen at a polling station, it isn't hard to imagine others doing it, too.)

Yeltsin ended up beating Communist Zyuganov by about three points, for approximately 35 percent of the vote. General Lebed surprised everyone with his strong 14 percent showing. Yavlinsky—the Jewish reformer—came in fourth place; the anti-Semitic nationalist Zhirinovsky placed fifth. Gorbachev, at 1.5 million votes, just barely beat Brintsalov and his spandexed wife. Since no one earned more than 50 percent of the votes, runoffs would be held in July. Luzhkov, meanwhile, made a clean sweep in Moscow's mayoral race.

In the weeks that followed, Yeltsin's men did three visible things to secure his reelection. First they lured Lebed into the Security Council to capture his voters' support. Then they slapped gigantic ONLY TOGETHER! stickers on the thousands of billboards, banners, and posters that featured the presidential hopeful and mayor-elect. Finally, they beefed up their scare tactics, running documentaries of Communist atrocities back-to-back on the television networks. The man of the hour, however, was nowhere to be seen. Yeltsin's aides contended he had a cold and was tired; the press suspected another heart attack (which turned out to be true). Regardless, Yeltsin didn't give the media that boosted him into office so much as a press statement when he won the July runoff by fourteen points. The oligarchs who made his victory possible were paid in kind with even larger media holdings and privatization deals for refineries, oil wells, and factories, but not a word of thanks was uttered to the voters who elected him to office.

Back in America, however, the election was triumphantly summarized: Democracy Prevailed.

12. *MOSKVA CLYEZI NE VERIT:*
MOSCOW DOESN'T BELIEVE IN TEARS

NADEZHDA AND I formed a pact the night we met: If I showed her my country, she'd show me hers. While she lived in the United States, we explored the West Coast by train, the Mexican border towns by Buick, and D.C. and New York City by foot, and she promised the highlights of Eastern Europe in return. But that was before she became overburdened with concepts I'd either shunned (like Responsibility, Relationships, Career) or couldn't relate to (like Political, Economic, and Social Instability). When Nadezhda hinted that she might not be able to take the whole summer off as we'd been planning, I balked. How could she choose obligation over adventure, commitment over autonomy? It all seemed so simple to me: Ditch your job, dump your man, and hop on a train and be free. But when I said as much, she snapped: "Our problem is that I have changed and you have not."

After that night at the Hungry Duck, she started flaking a lot, either rescheduling our dates or canceling altogether. I tried to be understanding until the night she kept me waiting under a giant mosaic of Stalin in the Arbatskaya Metro for two hours and never showed up.

"This never would have happened before," Andrei offered as consolation when I showed up, fuming, on his doorstep.

"Before what?"

"Before now. In Former Times, we respected our promises and friendships. Now we care only about materialism." He looked at me closely. "She's probably doing black *biznes*, too, you know."

"No, she's not!" I snapped. "She's just . . . busy."

But I was actually wondering myself. When I returned home the next morning, however, there was a four-page letter from Nadezhda wedged beneath my door. In it, she announced her breakup with Lev and resignation from her time-share company and invited me to her *dacha* that weekend to plan our summer journey.

The *dacha* is a tradition that keeps many an urbanite sane. Most Russians I met had a little wooden cottage tucked somewhere in the countryside that they escaped to now and then to soak in the sun and till the land. At Nadezhda's, stems and stalks hung heavily with tomatoes and cucumbers, lettuce and spinach, and scallions and celery, with brilliant roses blooming in between. Nadezhda and I spent hours on our hands and knees foraging through the strawberry patches, marveling how their seed-studded skins could be so warm from the sun while their flesh stayed so cool. Never had I known fruits and vegetables to have such full-bodied flavors and scents. I almost felt cheated somehow, like a retired pianist who just realized her piano had always been badly out of tune.

We pored over my *Let's Go: Eastern Europe* that evening, eventually deciding to visit Nadezhda's friends in Odessa before hitting the Crimea and Sochi along the Black Sea. She would take care of the tickets and arrangements; I need only call upon my return from my upcoming trip to St. Petersburg so that she could tell me when to be at the station. But when I did so a week later, her mother informed me that Nadezhda no longer lived there. She'd just moved to Turkey.

"*Kuda?*" I asked incredulously.

"Turkey. She wrote you a letter, Stesha. Won't you come by and get it?"

"I don't want it," I said faintly, then hung up.

Fleeing your apartment in the middle of the night without saying good-bye is another bad Russian cliché. In Former Times, you did it to escape political persecution; today you did it either to dodge a *biznes* deal or—in Nadezhda's case—to seal one. When a job opened up in her time-share company in Istanbul, she snatched it. Looking back, I should have understood how the overprotectiveness of her parents, the ghost of her brother, and the madness of living in a world where the bodies of overly ambitious young men got pumped with bullets and dumped in forests might have driven my friend to break a promise or two. But my world was far more black and white at twenty-two. When she didn't uphold her end of the bargain, I concluded that our friendship was finished.

I've since heard that Nadezhda moved on to Spain to work in the hotel industry. I like to think of her there with a rose in her hair, learning to dance flamenco. But we haven't spoken since.

AFTER NADEZHDA'S HASTY departure, I realized my own days in Moscow were dwindling. I'd reached that awkward point in traveling where you've surpassed tourism but haven't committed to building a "Real Life" yet—mainly because you can't figure out what that life should be. Was I a student? A volunteer? An expat? Or a drifter?

People like Vova and Karina kept me from any delusions about being a "local." That same night we crowded around their folding table drinking Russian margaritas, they asked how I had spent Easter. I recounted my excursion to the partially reconstructed Cathedral of Christ the Savior at midnight to hear its bells chime for the first time in half a century. Stalin dynamited the Napoleonic-era structure in 1931 with plans to erect a gargantuan statue of Lenin in its place, but World War II intervened. A crew of 2,500 had been working in twelve-hour shifts to finish the church by Moscow's 850th birthday bash in 1997. To my outsider's eyes, the sight of that bearded monk ringing those glorious bells represented another victory over the dictator who tried to stifle spirituality, but when I said so, my friends laughed even harder than when I declared myself a *feministka*.

"That is exactly the propaganda bullshit they want you to believe!" Vova slapped his knee.

Karina patted my hand sympathetically. "Really, Stesha, it is. Moscow has dozens of beautiful churches that were closed and condemned in Former Times. If the government truly cared about religion and spreading the word of God, they could have renovated them all for the same price it took to rebuild Christ the Savior and those ridiculous domes."

Indeed, I would later learn that a bank had donated 110 pounds of gold for the ostentatious domes. A good many miners could have been paid their backlogged rubles with that kind of money.

"There used to be a swimming pool in that spot. It was heated and open year-round, the biggest in the world. I guarantee if they asked us Muscovites what we wanted, we would have voted for the pool, not the church," Vova opined.

I sighed. My greatest obstacle in understanding Russia was neither cultural nor linguistic. It was my own naiveté. Something in me just wanted to believe that the sound of monks ringing church bells was inherently *good*. And that people with money *earned* it honestly. And that protest *could bring* social change.

"Even now, propaganda is at the root of everything here— religion, politics, even history. We were always taught that World War Two was between Russia and the Nazis, and we won the battle over fascism for our Motherland. But you probably learned that the victors were America and the Allied powers, right? In our textbooks, America barely gets a footnote, and neither does Russia in yours. Every country has its own perspective generated through its own propaganda," Karina explained.

"The thing is, we finally caught on that all that ideology stuff is bullshit," Vova said as he took a juicy bite of beet. Then he wiped his mouth and looked straight at me. "When will you?"

AT LAST, ALL those years of conjugating verbs on the backs of buses paid off: Elena landed a job with a company that issued her a *propiska*. Late that summer, she and Valera moved into a one-bedroom apartment in eastern Moscow, having achieved the Provincial Dream at age twenty-four. Three years later, Elena would chalk up another accolade by winning a full scholarship to business school in England.

How did Elena rise above the system that had stumped Nadezhda, Andrei, Natasha, Oksana, and so many of the other young people I'd met, without mingling with the *Mafiya* or marrying a foreigner? She was ambitious, of course, but not in the materialistic way that had destroyed so many of her peers. Valera once defined success like this: "Say you inherit a pig farm. Success would mean passing it along to your children with one more pig than you started with."

Somehow Elena had adopted the greatest traits her countries of influence had to offer—resourcefulness and ingenuity from the Soviet Union; opportunism and optimism from the United States—and warded off the corresponding greed and corruption. She could have gone corporate in Germany, the United Kingdom, or America but chose instead to make her difference working in her native Russia. And when it came time to retire, she planned on returning to Balakhna to keep up the land so many generations of her family had sown.

On my second-to-last night in Moscow, Elena and Valera invited me over for dinner in their new apartment. We were just finishing our tea and chocolates when Valera pulled a bottle of Sovietskoe Shampanskoe out of the refrigerator. Even champagne was making me nostalgic; tears sprang to my eyes as Valera twisted off its hood.

"Stesha," Valera said softly, "soon you are going to be home in Corpus, near the ocean. *Vcyo budet klassno.*" Everything will be cool. He popped the top off the champagne and poured a tasting into three flutes. "Here, it is very difficult to live."

"That's the difference between America and Russia, isn't it? There, it is easy; here it is hard," I summed up what people had told me since the day I arrived.

"*Legche znachit luchshe,*" he said as he raised his flute. Easier means better.

"*Ne vsegda,*" I ventured as I clinked his flute. Not always.

"You know, Stesha, it took me a whole year to get over the transition from America back to Russia," Elena offered in her quiet, nonimposing way. "But I can't tell you how strong I feel inside now."

"What caused that, do you think?"

Elena looked out the window a few moments before responding in a steady voice that swelled with pride.

"Wisdom." She smiled, then downed her flute.

ON MY LAST full day in Russia, my *Nastayashii Russkii Muzhik* took the afternoon off so we could visit Kolomenskoe, a grand stretch of crumbling buildings that once served as the Czars' summer estate. As we lay in a dandelion field along the Moscow River, Andrei pointed at a distant crop of hulky apartment blocks and said: "A television station once had a contest where they showed a photograph just like that—apartments surrounded by a river—and viewers had to guess where it had been taken. They received thousands of entries, each one naming a different city!"

"America is like this, too, only the apartments are tract houses surrounded by strip malls."

He shook his head in dismay. "Why did they have to paint them all gray? Couldn't they have made some of them yellow or blue?"

"They wanted you all to be equal."

"Equally miserable, maybe. It's like this in America, too?"

"*Da*. We call it Suburbia."

"I wish I could paint my apartment block purple. Then if anyone took a picture of it, I'd recognize it. And my kids would never get lost on their way home from school."

As the sun sank into the horizon, Andrei and I headed back to my neighborhood for one last meal at Guria's, the local Georgian hangout. We dined on hot cheese bread, stewed eggplant, and a bottle of red wine as a unibrowed lady in a fringed floral shawl strolled about, serenading the chain-smoking, pistol-toting patrons. Then we walked to Red Square, a sight that always quieted me. St. Basil's Cathedral anchored one end as a towering symbol of the nation's spirituality—a structure so majestic, Ivan the Terrible gouged out the eyes of its architect so he couldn't duplicate its beauty. The Kremlin marked the spot where Czars issued edicts, Stalin orchestrated his reign of terror, the Congress of People's Deputies dissolved their Soviet Empire, and Yeltsin hyped his New Democracy. Across the way loomed GUM, the shopping arcade that had yielded little more than orange polka-dotted teapots and the same-size shoes in Former Times but now sold Nike, Estée Lauder, and Christian Dior. And squatting amid it all was the nation's last remaining bastion of Soviet chic: Lenin's tomb. Would he be there when I returned—or would he have been placed by his mother's side, as per his dying wish?

Andrei and I kissed in the shadows of the cathedral and then headed back to his flat, where he put Vladimir Visotsky on the tape deck, lit some candles, and made love to me. After he closed his eyes for a few hours' rest, I watched the wax ooze into a puddle on the bedside table and reflected over the past eight months of my life. I felt different, somehow. More confident. Independent. Self-assured. When I finally nodded off to sleep, I felt certain I'd done everything a woman should before leaving someplace special.

Except confirm the next day's flight.

Andrei's brother dropped us off at Sheremetyevo Airport at 5:30 A.M. sharp so I could catch my 8:30 plane. When I searched the arrival/departure screen for the gate assignment, however, my flight wasn't listed. The clerk behind the desk glanced at my ticket and announced smugly: "*Devushka*, that flight was canceled two months ago."

Panic shot through my body as I thrust my backpack into

Andrei's arms, raced over to the phone office, and called my parents collect. When Mom's voice came over the wire, all the self-reliance I'd cultivated that year vaporized. I pressed three and shrieked: "My flight got canceled! Do something!"

I had allotted only three days to reenter my old life in Texas: the first for family bonding, the second for laundry, and the third for packing up and moving back to Austin for my last year of college. I couldn't possibly pare it down more than that. I paced up and down the office until my mother called back half an hour later. "There's a flight to New York that leaves at two-thirty P.M., but it's overbooked by forty-five passengers. Get on it."

Andrei and I pushed and shoved my seventy pounds of luggage to the airline booth and—with respects to my ovaries—made a sofa out of the suitcases and plopped upon them. Andrei kept us nourished over the next seven hours with cucumber pizzas and iced vodka.

"Of course," he'd say when I thanked him for waiting, "you're my *devushka*."

Amazingly, I finagled a ticket on the flight and got in the two-hour queue through security, customs, luggage check, and passport control. Andrei was allowed to accompany me only to a point before we had to say our good-byes. Though I would—after gaining a few points of comparison—come to resent many things about Andrei, the thought of leaving him just then devastated me. I cried so hard, the two guys behind me in line had to carry my luggage. Moved by my outpouring of emotion, Andrei shouted that I would forever be his *golubka* (pigeon) as I crawled down the concourse toward my gate.

But of course, the tears I shed that day weren't for Andrei. I wept for the same reason runners do when they finish their first marathon or mothers after giving birth. In the previous half year, I had confronted linguistic barriers, mobsters, bomb threats, drunks, Poison Dwarves, beets, and flies. And I had fallen so hard for Russia in the process, I ached when it came time to leave her.

北京

A REVOLUTION IS NOT A DINNER PARTY,
OR WRITING AN ESSAY, OR PAINTING
A PICTURE, OR DOING EMBROIDERY;
IT CANNOT BE SO REFINED, SO LEISURELY
AND GENTLE, SO TEMPERATE, KIND,
COURTEOUS, RESTRAINED, AND
MAGNANIMOUS. A REVOLUTION IS AN
INSURRECTION, AN ACT OF VIOLENCE BY
WHICH ONE CLASS OVERTHROWS ANOTHER.

—Mao Zedong

13 . THE CULINARY REVOLUTION

ANYTHING THAT FLIES IN THE SKY BUT KITES
ANYTHING THAT HAS FOUR LEGS BUT STOOLS
—*Preamble to a Chinese menu*

THOUGH I LOVED my experience in Russia, I couldn't help feeling that I'd missed out on something by arriving there five years after communism's collapse. It could just be me, but Slavophiles really did seem to describe their pre-1991 travels with the same smugness of fans who caught their band years before they turned platinum ("Sure, U2's *Joshua Tree* stadium tour was great and all, but nothing like when they used to play punk clubs for *War*"). I wanted to go where the Revolution prospered and Former Times was the present. So when the Henry Luce Foundation invited me to live and work as a journalist in an Asian country for ten months as part of their Luce Scholars Program, I chose the big Red one. However, when the representatives in charge of securing my job placement started making inquiries at Chinese publications, none wanted an American cub reporter on staff—even one whose labor came free.

"It looks like China only brings foreigners on board as editors, not journalists. How about we send you somewhere you can actually write, like Thailand or Japan?"

"I'm happy to edit."

"But China's English media is nothing but propaganda. You'll be bored to tears. How about Taiwan or Hong Kong? They're part of China, technically."

How could I explain that I actually *wanted* to spend a year editing a mouthpiece of the Chinese Communist Party, in all of its "Long Live the Party of the People" glory? First of all, I was dying to know who worked there: Maoists, Marxists, tried-and-true believers? Or idealists trying to beat the system from within? Either way, it would be a prime opportunity to experience censorship firsthand and observe a state propaganda machine at its source. And once I gained my colleagues' trust (which I guessed would take a week or two), they might invite me on secret interviews with dissidents (which happened on a regular basis, I figured). This was, after all, the nation where millions of citizens took to the streets and faced down tanks in the name of freedom in 1989. Surely some of that fiery spirit smoldered. I envisioned late-night heated debates that halted the presses. Watching my colleagues put their livelihoods—and their lives—on the line to print their discoveries.

I wrote the representatives a letter explaining my strange request and, after a few more rounds of "If you're *sure* this is what you want," they called back to say they'd found a taker. As long as I promised not to write while affiliated with their publication, a weekly English-language newsmagazine agreed to let me "polish" their copy. So in August 1997, after an inspiring week of orientation with the Luce Foundation and bonding with the other scholarship recipients, I departed for China with a head full of fantasies about slipping subversive messages through the iron bars of prison cells and witnessing dissidence in action.

IT WAS A HOT, muggy night when I arrived at Beijing International Airport and followed the throngs of short, slender people through corridors emanating wan green light to customs, passport control, and baggage claim. People's Liberation Army (PLA) soldiers stood stiffly at attention in every corner. Though they looked eighteen if a day, they reminded me of those hardened soldiers who mowed down protesters during the Tiananmen crackdown eight years earlier. I glowered at them.

Just outside the gate was a barricaded walkway, behind which thrashed a mob of rubbernecking Beijingers. It was startling to see so many people who—at first glance—seemed so strikingly similar, from their iron-straight hair and small, flat noses to their rolled-up trousers and thin cotton shirts. As I approached them, what would become my new nickname sounded in waves: *laowai*. Literally, it means "foreigner," but when shouted repeatedly and accompanied with finger pointing, it seemed to insinuate "freak" as well: *"Laowai, laowai, laowai!"* I walked down the aisle and caught my first whiff of Beijing: cigarette smoke, sweat, and soy sauce.

Off in a corner of the concourse stood a man in starched khaki pants holding a sign with my name on it. This was one of the many advantages of being affiliated with a foreign foundation instead of a local university: When the former sends drivers, they show up.

"Hen re!" he greeted me. It's hot.

I felt a jolt of excitement: A Chinese spoke to me and I actually understood! After studying Russian for five years and achieving only a childlike coherency, I worried how I'd get by in Beijing on only a summer's worth of private tutoring. But compared to Russian's grammatical monstrosities, spoken Mandarin is a breeze—as long as you can hear (and hit) the tones, which are sacrosanct. Basically, every syllable can be pronounced five different ways for at least five totally different meanings. *Ma*, for instance, can either mean mother, marijuana, horse, or a curse word or serve as a vocalized question mark, depending on the intonation. If you get the tones down and have a decent memory for applying them to thousands of monosyllabic words, Mandarin isn't as intimidating as it seems. Nothing declines, nothing conjugates, every word is neuter. Written Chinese, of course, is another story—but even Chinese who can't speak English can sometimes transcribe simple words into Pinyin, the Latin transliteration.

The driver helped carry my luggage—which I'd pared down to a manageable fifty pounds—to a little white van parked outside, and I hopped in. As we rolled into the night, I pressed my face against the window for my initial glimpse of Beijing. After miles of darkness, the headlights began to reveal open-air markets featuring silvery wok hills and glittering cleaver rivers. Families gathered around low-to-the-ground tables alongside their fruit and vegetable stands and slurped noodles with chopsticks. The elderly had wise, ancient faces but moved around spryly; the men were shirtless and hadn't a chest hair among them. Ponytailed girls in flip-flops chased barefoot boys with bowl cuts. Lone cyclists rode beneath the street lamps, some pedaling cartfuls of produce or coal behind them. Rows and rows of bicycles had been parked for the night.

We soon pulled up to a six-story compound in the northeast quadrant of the city. Expats were barred from renting flats in

Chinese apartment buildings back then, so lawfully minded *laowai* had to fork over big bucks to live in segregated housing. My one-bedroom apartment—enormous by Chinese standards but modest by a Texan's—would run about $1,400 a month, and that was considered "low end." (Expats living closer to downtown paid upward of $3,000.) I would later meet *laowai* who bribed Chinese landlords to rent them cheap flats among locals, but they had to be prepared to evacuate at a moment's notice during police raids.

I walked around my new home in wonder, opening and closing the refrigerator, turning on the stove, testing the water faucets. I had suddenly acquired more furniture than I'd ever owned: a bed, a writing desk, a dining table and chairs, a sitting area—even a screened-in porch balcony, which I stepped onto. Through a part between the cascading limbs of willow trees, I caught fleeting images of the street below. Of red-and-yellow taxis breezing by in search of fares. Of dumpling stalls closing for the night. Of vendors discounting the last of their produce by candlelight.

WHEN MY EYES opened the following morning, I jumped out of bed and darted over to the window, eager to see Beijing by sunlight. I could barely make out the high-rise building across the street. A billowy grayness hung so heavily, the throngs of cars and cyclists disappeared in either direction after a few yards of visibility. Was it misting, fogging, smoking, snowing? As I stepped onto the balcony, my lungs filled with such foulness, I started coughing. This, I'd soon learn, was why Beijingers hacked like six-pack-a-day smokers and spat like Major League baseball players: The pollution was so dense, you could almost hang a hat on it.

That afternoon, I visited my work placement. An editor whose name immediately escaped me gave me a tour of the building, which housed several different English-language publications. As we ascended a staircase, a sudden burst of Mandarin ricocheted off the walls. It grew louder and angrier as we neared an open doorway at the far end of a hall, and I could soon make out a pudgy, middle-aged man tearing into a reporter who looked fresh out of college. He had worked himself into such a frenzy, a purple vein threatened to pop out of his forehead. The reporter, meanwhile, stared at the floor.

"That's Lao Ye, the director of our paper. He looks busy now—let's come back later," the editor suggested smoothly.

We descended to the second level, where *China Daily*—the main newspaper in the building—was located. On the lookout for Party signs, I immediately homed in on a poster of Mao Zedong hanging on a wall and a closed door labeled PROPAGANDA DEPARTMENT. Aside from that, though, the newsroom had the same busy clutter of papers the world over, with reporters hunched over keyboards while their notepads, pens, and dictionaries lay scattered about. As we turned a corner, a connecting room with glass walls came into view where half a dozen *laowai* sat, staring into computer screens. They ranged in age from thirty to mid-sixties and had uniformly white skin. These were the "foreign experts"—the Britons, Americans, Canadians, and Australians flown in on the paper's dime to spell-and-grammar-check the copy. (Considering that most of the reporters knew English only from textbooks, this was no small task. In addition to creative misspellings like "Marilian Menro" and "homos sauce," these experts had to make sense of sentences like "When you count your fingers, you may get surprised that only one is left: There are already nine flower markets in Beijing.")

Aside from a few top editors, Chinese generally did not

enter the foreigners' workspace and the "experts" didn't enter theirs. If a question arose about a story, the experts embedded it into the copy and sent it back to the reporter's computer queue—even if they sat only a few feet away. This is fairly common practice in American newsrooms as well, but there seemed to be more than convenience at stake at *China Daily*. I would later ask the experts if their segregation was by choice or imposed from above, and they said both. Stories abounded of disciplinary action taken against reporters who fraternized too much with *laowai*, so socializing tended to take place outside the office.

By the time we headed back upstairs to our office, Lao Ye's storm seemed to have passed. He greeted me hospitably and showed me to my desk, located in a prime spot by the electric teapot from which my colleagues drank hot boiled water— "white tea"—all day long. (Cold water, they said, was bad for the digestion.) This staff consisted of ten reporters between the ages of twenty-two and twenty-six, most of whom had majored in English but who spoke it at varying rates of fluency. Lao Ye suggested we all get acquainted over lunch.

We walked down a strip of restaurants and chose the upscale one at the far end of the street. A pretty woman in a *qipao*—a slim-fitted silk dress with a thigh-high slit and Mandarin collar—opened the door to a sauna of cigarette smoke and chili vapor. So many fish, crabs, and lobsters had been heaped into the aquariums lining either side of the foyer, they barely had room to wiggle. The eating area was similarly crowded, with dozens of round tables crammed with parties of six and more. It was as noisy and lively as a high school cafeteria, but the mainly male clientele paused midchopstick to take curious note of me as we squeezed past. *"Laowai,"* they mused.

A second woman in a *qipao* escorted us into a banquet room

equipped with a couch, a karaoke machine, plastic plants, and a team of waitresses. An enormous round table stood in the center of the room, set with a dozen saucer-size plates, rice bowls, painted spoons, teacups, and chopsticks propped upon tiny porcelain stands. I was instructed to sit at the farthest end from the door, and my colleagues filed in beside me. Lao Ye called for the menu, which turned out to be the size of my hometown telephone directory. As he flipped through it for the house specialties, my colleagues started shouting out their favorite dishes, which the waitresses frantically recorded onto thick pads of paper. Ordering seemed almost competitive: If someone made a poor selection, the others uttered a guffaw. A good choice, meanwhile, won hushed whispers of approval. Food is the ultimate fashion to the Chinese: No one of status would be caught dead eating last year's dish. Eating has traditionally been considered the culture's "first happiness," and the range of options one can sample is truly staggering. Basically, anything that can fly, swim, crawl, or slither can be slathered in batter, deep-fried, and served on a stick. Grasshoppers. Larvae. Beetles. Scorpions. Duck fetuses. I once watched a pigtailed schoolgirl suck on the tentacle of a shish kebabbed octopus as if it were a lollipop.

This was going to be hard for me to handle. Celery salt was the most exotic spice in our cupboard back in Corpus. Mom told Dad on their wedding night that she'd cook once a year, and we learned to relish the lasagna we got each Christmas. I was raised on the fried bologna sandwiches Dad made for lunch and the dish of the day at whatever diner he drove me to for dinner. I ate roast beef and Tater Tots at Furr's Cafeteria on Mondays, chicken fingers with fries at Andy's Country Kitchen on Tuesdays, fish sticks and hush puppies at Catfish Charlie's on Wednesdays. Waitresses knew not only my name, but my latest grades and the most recent score of my team's Little Miss Kick-ball game as well. I was, in short, my father's meat-and-potatoes protégée.

My U2-induced political awakening refined my diet in high school, however. Joining Greenpeace turned me off veal; I boy-cotted frogs' legs after leading a student protest against dis-section. My consciousness climaxed at Royal Co-op in Austin, where we upheld such a strictly enforced meatless policy, we once denounced someone for sneaking in a box of Kentucky Fried Chicken. Our shelves were lined with herbs and spices I'd never heard of, like turmeric, cardamom, and cumin, and my housemates whipped up weird things like black bean moussaka and ratatouille. After three years of this cuisine, I assumed my taste buds had reached their highest evolved state. But I was mistaken: My Culinary Revolution had just begun.

When Lao Ye asked if there was anything in particular I'd like to try and everyone paused to listen, I knew I had to order something tasty enough to impress my colleagues but also eat in accordance with my vegetarian principles. After an awkward pause, I diplomatically replied in Lonely Planet Mandarin that I liked to *chi doufu*, eat tofu. That response brought gales of gig-gles from around the table; Lao Ye turned a deep shade of red. Uh-oh. Had I just mispronounced *doufu*? For the rest of the day, I worried about what I might have said. (A colleague later informed me that saying you like to *chi doufu* means you enjoy giving oral sex.)

Recovering from the linguistics mishap, Lao Ye asked what I wanted to drink. Again my colleagues turned toward me ex-pectantly. As I was about to discover, the guest of honor at a Chinese banquet chooses a beverage not only for him- or her-self, but for the entire group. I'd heard about the exquisite delicacies of a traditional banquet—shark fin soup, bird nest soup, thousand-year-old eggs—but nothing about the beverages that accompanied them.

"How about some Merlot?" I suggested, hoping to sound sophisticated.

Lao Ye looked crestfallen; the waitress seemed confused. My colleagues spoke in hushed whispers.

"Or would white wine be better?" I asked anxiously.

"No, no, we have red wine. Of course. Chinese have fine red wine," Lao Ye said, then yelled something to the waitresses. They bounded off in a hurry as another waitress walked in, lugging a giant trash bag that appeared to have something alive thrashing about inside. I peered in and found a gargantuan, gasping fish. My heart went out to it.

Freshness is one of the most critical components in Chinese cuisine. In low-end restaurants, waitresses roll up their sleeves and stick their arms right inside the aquarium to fetch the sea life of your choice, then bonk it over the head with a mallet and dispatch it to the kitchen. Fancier establishments prepare sea creatures by wrapping their heads in cold cloths and steaming only their lower bodies, so they'll still be alive when served.

"Hao ma?" the waitress asked.

I gulped and nodded that yes, this soon-to-be-sacrificed fish was quite *hao*, good. The woman bowed, slung the sack over her shoulder, and disappeared as another waitress entered with the first course of cold dishes and plunked them atop the spinning lazy Susan in the center of the table. Then she darted out of the way as the chopsticks started flying. It seemed an almost Darwinian pursuit for the tastiest morsels—and only the aggressive prevailed. Fat and bones were spat upon the table; soups were slurped; burps resounded with gusto. I cautiously dug my chopsticks into the nearest sampling without a face—a translucent something decorated with red and green flecks—and gulped it down.

"You like pig?" the colleague beside me—Ji? Jie? Je?—asked.

"That was pig?"

He smiled and tapped his elbow to signify which part of the pig I had just eaten. I smiled meekly by way of reply. Being a closet vegetarian was going to be tougher than expected. Next, I took a scoop from a bowl of bright yellow jiggly somethings that smelled faintly of chicken noodle soup but appeared meatless. The fatty jiggles left a greasy smear as they slid across my plate, but the long, slim, solid thing in their midst looked vaguely appetizing. I picked it out with my chopsticks, popped it in my mouth, and twirled it around with my tongue. Suddenly it bit me—right on my inner cheek. I spat it onto my plate and stared in astonishment. After a childhood of eating "chicken fingers" at diners across America, I had finally been served a real one. Claw included.

My stomach started growling as I gazed at the other dishes rapidly amassing atop that lazy Susan. There was an entire roasted duck, sweet-and-sour spare ribs, stewed pork belly with veggies, squid with green peppers. The fish that had been flopping only twenty minutes before had been steamed and served head to fin on a bed of what looked like grass. It all smelled heavenly, but there wasn't a thing my vegetarian self could eat.

"Don't you like Chinese food?" Lao Ye suddenly boomed from across the table.

One by one, my colleagues turned to face me. I panicked. "Oh no! I mean, yes! Yes, of course!" For reasons that elude me, something Julia Child once said popped into my mind. "I could happily eat Chinese food every night for the rest of my life!"

My decision became clear. I could either offend my new boss and colleagues by sticking to my college principles or I could sample an ancient cuisine that boasted thousands of dishes.

Can't morals be shoved aside for a little culture now and then? I'd be in China only once. How many times in my life could I try barbecued bear paw?

Seized with inspiration, I kissed off my vegetarian inclinations and added my chopsticks to the frenzy. I gobbled up prawns smothered with garlic, which—admittedly—were rather scrumptious. The chicken served Sichuan style with whole red chilies and peanuts was downright delicious. Taiwanese dried beef tickled my taste buds; the scallops made them sing. Initially I munched for culture, but before long, I crunched for pleasure. Oysters and black bean sauce. Fish ball soup with white radishes. MSG. The succulent tastes converged in a party on my palate; a taste bud had an orgasm. I had never quoted Julia Child before, but she was really on to something here!

An hour into the banquet, a busboy appeared, breathless and sweaty. In his hand, he triumphantly held the bottle of wine I'd requested. He had probably been sent halfway across Beijing to find it—to save the face of both my editor and the restaurant. Guilt and amazement welled over me.

The wine had a cap instead of a cork and was cherry red in color. The waitresses poured equal amounts into tiny shot glasses and placed them along the edge of the lazy Susan. Lao Ye raised his glass, and the rest of us followed suit. *"Gan bei,"* he said. Dry the glass.

"Gan bei!" we repeated as we plunked our glasses against the lazy Susan. In typical Russian fashion, I downed mine in a single gulp and then looked around the table for my colleagues' approval, fully expecting a dozen drained glasses. Instead, there

were deep flushes of red spreading slowly from their chests to their necks to their faces, like mercury rising through thermometers. One grabbed a towel and mopped his face; another chased her wine with tea. The others shook their heads and grimaced.

That's when I realized the fundamental difference between Russians and Chinese: One bonded over drink, the other over food. My upcoming year would be a challenge not of the liver, but of the stomach. After an intestinal transfer of power, I swiped up my chopsticks and dove back in.

14. THE TAO OF BICYCLING

WITHIN A FEW days it became apparent that everybody in Beijing had a bicycle but me. And I wanted one. Bad. Preferably a proletarian model forged from industrial steel that weighed fifty pounds and had a basket for cabbage storage and a tinny silver bell. That way, I would be just like everyone else.

Liu was my first recruit in the purchase. Whereas the other reporters at the paper fawned over my tones, she put me in my place my second day on the job: "I know you are just learning Chinese, but you keep mispronouncing my first name. I am not an 'Evil Fish.' " So I trusted her to tell me if I was getting a good deal or not.

Envisioning Chinese bicycle salesmen to be as wily as American car salesmen, I decided a male should tag along, too. Xiao Yang happily agreed. His name means "Little Sheep," but I liked to call him—in English—"Lambchops," to which he cheerfully replied: "I am a sheep, not a lamb."

The three of us ran down to the canteen to discuss the purchase. My first week at the paper, I was impressed by the way editors and reporters sprinted into line and shoveled down their food at lunchtime, imagining them in a great hurry to get back to their stories. But after a few days of returning to an office that remained desolate for another hour or two, I realized they were rushing back to their dorms for their *xiuxi*, or afternoon siestas. Liu and Lambchops grabbed the tin dishes and chopsticks they stored in the lockers just outside the entrance, bought booklets of the tissue-thin meal tickets, and bounded toward the three different food lines, which the Chinese referred to as *hao, bi jiao hao,* and *zui hao le* (good, better, best) and the foreign experts as "indigestion," "heartburn," and "diarrhea." Either way, the prices could not be beat: 50 cents for a heaping serving of fluffy white rice, a huge ladle of stir-fry, and a steamed bread ball called *mantou*.

Lambchops asked a few questions between bites of chicken and cashews and—after determining that I really did not want a model "more appropriate for foreigners"—said he knew just where to go. After washing our plates and storing them in the lockers, we headed out to the street to hail a taxi. Legions of cabbies inhabit Beijing's streets, but the cheapest were the yellow vans known as *miandi*, or breadboxes. Lambchops flagged one down and, as per Communist protocol, hopped in the front seat to keep the driver company. Liu and I shared the backseat: a tire with a towel draped over it. Off we roared, dodging daredevil *xiali* cabs to the left and jam-packed buses to the right, and eventually pulled up to a department store that advertised its wares on colorful banners that spilled down its facade. Dozens of bicycles were parked in its front rack, guarded by an eighty-year-old attendant with a wispy white beard who nodded as we walked past.

The first floor consisted largely of women's apparel that would strike many a blow to my self-esteem in upcoming months, as I could never pull any of the Asian-size pants past my kneecaps. We rode the escalator to the basement, and there—

between the washers and the dryers—stood a rack of Chinese
bicycles, solid as tanks and twice as heavy. Black Forevers anchored one side, purple Flying Pigeons the other. Lambchops
disentangled a Forever for me and, with considerable effort,
turned it upside down. I rotated the pedals and squeezed its
brakes. "Let's take it out for a spin," I suggested.

Giggling nervously, Lambchops translated my request to
the two salesmen who had just joined us. The one with Coke-
bottle glasses grunted before shouting, first at Lambchops, then
at me.

"Ah, Stephanie. It is not permissible to ride this bike until
you buy it," Lambchops translated.

"But how am I supposed to know if it is a good fit?"

The men folded their arms across their chests and glared.
Apparently, I wasn't.

In Russia, I generally did as I was told, largely because people there intimidated me. Being half a head taller than almost
everyone in China, however, felt oddly empowering. Deeming
that orderly department store in need of some civil disobedi-
ence, I turned to the sales clerks and, in staccato Mandarin, declared: "I ride before I buy."

With that, I uprighted the bike, straddled its seat, rode past
the dryers, and headed toward the refrigerators in the neighboring aisle. The clerks were stunned. Lambchops was morti-
fied. Evil Fish was amused. And I was the proud owner of a
Chinese bicycle. All I needed now was the basket. And the bell.

IN THE MONTH that followed, not one cyclist passed me on
the road. This had less to do with my athletic prowess than the
fact that Chinese rode at the same pace they did tai chi. Yet
everyone I passed always caught up with me at the traffic lights,

which were interminable. I would bolt ahead as soon as the light turned green, but they rejoined me at the next red light a block away. Even though I rode twice as fast, we all arrived at the same place at the same time.

Moreover, my Chinese Forever couldn't be ridden like my mountain Mongoose back home. There was no hunching and pumping on this set of pedals: When I tried to stand, the bike threatened to keel over. For the longest time, this exasperated me: How else was I supposed to burn off those yummy pork buns I devoured for breakfast? But like the Russian pastime of *gulyat'*, or strolling, biking is a far more meditative endeavor in China, even when used for utilitarian purposes. Life is hard enough—why exert more energy than absolutely necessary?

Eventually, I learned to sit in a fully upright position like everyone else and ride slowly, with the flow, taking in the peoplescape as it glided past. Barbers tended to their customers beneath shade trees, their combs and clippers peeking out of their pockets. Bicycle repairmen squatted in the middle of the sidewalk with their tools and pumps, waiting for someone's tires to blow. Black marketeers spread out their pirated CDs (Céline Dion), DVDs (*Titanic*), and software (Windows 98) atop tarps. Blind men read palms and told fortunes. Provincial-looking men dug ditches in tattered suits and ties; construction workers pulverized dilapidated buildings wearing only hard hats for protection.

The most enterprising roadside capitalists were the food vendors. Peasants roasted chestnuts over open fires and baked sweet potatoes atop oil drums. Old men in Mao jackets shish ke-babbed hawberries and dipped them into syrup that dried into a candied crunch. *Baozi* ladies sold dumplings straight off the bamboo steamer. Noodle ladies doused your choice of rice, egg, or glass noodles with vinegar and soy sauce and served it in a Styrofoam box. There were duck egg ladies. Phallus-shaped fried bread ladies. My favorite was the pancake lady, who parked her cart just outside my compound. With a ladle, she spread her batter over a pizza-size griddle and cooked it like a crepe. Once it solidified, she expertly flipped it over with a spatula, added green onions, sauces, and spices, cracked an egg on top, and let it cook a few seconds more. Then she folded the whole thing into quarters, scooped it into a piece of brown paper, and handed it over, hot and delicious.

Alongside these *xiao chi*—small eats—vendors stood the produce peddlers. Each morning, peasants pedaled cartfuls of fresh fruits and vegetables into the city, and you could tell the season by their selection. When I first arrived in August, there were bright orange persimmons, scarlet pomegranates, and clumps of sweet litchis. Farmers hauled in cabbages by the truckload in November, which everyone left in the sun to dry a week or two before storing them for the long winter ahead. During the cold season, carts yielded carrots, potatoes, radishes, and lotus roots shaped like baby arms. Cherry blossoms and wild vegetables announced the arrival of spring; strawberries, pineapples, mangoes, and melons meant summer was near. Bananas were perennial, and foreigners apparently had a reputation for liking them, because every time I rode past a guy selling some, he'd grab one and jiggle it at me. (Female banana vendors, incidentally, never did this.)

Rounding out the food sellers were the meat mongers, whose offerings were equally fresh. Schools of eel quivered in half-filled wading pools; too many fish crammed into murky tanks. Crabs, lobsters, and crawfish attempted escape by forming decapodan pyramids and boosting one another out of their bins. Hens, ducks, geese, and pigeons scrunched into chicken-wire cages; carving blocks were strewn with bloody chunks of pork and beef.

Equally vivid was the scene inside the bicycle packs. Like eating, working, showering, and shitting, cycling was a communal activity in China. Couples held hands as they rode side by side. Girlfriends chatted about their day. Street chefs toted their kitchens; guys, their dates; husbands, their wives; mothers, their children. Bicycles were an indispensable mode of transportation for millions of residents, and their numbers didn't waver with the weather. When it started raining, cyclists simply pulled over and broke out the brilliantly colored ponchos designed especially for them, with extra long fronts that stretched over their handlebars and covered the contents of their baskets. Then they continued with their journeys, a kaleidoscope of yellow, orange, red, green, and purple polka dot. These were the times I felt most part of this world: cruising down the street with a basket full of eggplants, dodging a downpour in a peacock blue poncho, on my way to where I needed to be, with no better way of getting there.

**THIN ICE IS ONLY A PROBLEM FOR
THOSE WHO CHOOSE TO GO SKATING.**
—*Chinese saying*

You never really had to go out looking for a copy of
China Daily. It found you, showing up on your hotel doorstep or landing—unsubscribed—in your apartment's mailbox. I
met one traveler who swore a copy "just appeared" in her backpack after she went strolling through a crowded market. As the
official English mouthpiece of the Chinese Communist Party
(CCP), *China Daily* took its job seriously.

But the *China Daily* complex was actually part of a dying
breed in Beijing. It ran as a *danwei,* one of the old-school administrative institutions that practically everyone belonged to
before foreign ventures trickled in during the late 1980s. As
such, it operated like my personal point of reference—the old
King Ranch where my mother's family hailed from—but with
an additional purpose of social control. Among other things,
this *danwei* provided employee housing, set salaries, paid a hefty
percentage of medical and dental care, approved the paperwork
for marriages and divorces, oversaw the birth of everyone's al-

lotted child, and—by holding passports—monitored all travel. It also guided workers through their daily lives, blasting exercise music through the loudspeakers of the housing compound early each morning to wake them from their slumber and call them into the courtyard for calisthenics. Its canteen served hot, cheap meals three times a day, its showers ran from 12:00 to 1:30 P.M. and 5:00 to 6:30 P.M., and it allotted *xiuxi*—siesta—between lunch and 2:00.

Not surprisingly, this paternalistic system couldn't bear to see its workers go. *China Daily* recruited its employees straight out of college and made them sign five-year contracts off the bat. No one was required to live in its dormitories, but many did, as it cost very little and alternatives were scarce. Rookie reporters generally shared rooms with two or three colleagues—a vast improvement from their college days, when they had as many as eight roommates. Plus, the *danwei* rewarded loyalty, offering journalists private rooms after four years of service, by which point many would have already married. Private quarters were often enticing enough to sign another five-year contract. Around the time most were thinking of their allotted child four years later, they were often eligible for apartments off-site. Another five years down the line, they could apply for scholarships to study overseas.

So people tended to stay at *China Daily* for the long haul, and a Logistics Department tried to make it an enjoyable one. In addition to organizing weekend outings and karaoke contests, the department issued quarterly rations of toilet paper, shampoo, toothpaste, soap, and—for the married couples—boxes of condoms. Even *laowai* like me received a big box of "moon cakes" stuffed with coconut or red bean paste for Mid-Autumn Festival, cooking oil and noodles for National Day, and crates of thousand-year-old eggs for Spring Festival.

My colleagues weren't as impressed by these perks as I, though.

"We each have our own favorite shampoo—who would use the kind they give us?" Liu muttered when I pawed through her ration box one day. "They only have a Logistics Department so that more people can have jobs."

With a population of 1.2 billion and rising, the Chinese were indeed masterful job creators. I once saw a vending machine with two employees: one to take your money, the second to push the button and hand you your drink. But despite the enormous applicant pool, it was nearly impossible to get fired from the *China Daily danwei*—and quitting was equally tough. According to Liu, contracts could not be broken for the first two and a half years—and then, reporters had to pay the *danwei* 5,000 renminbi (RMB) for each year they reneged (roughly $625, or the equivalent of two and a half months of salary). This particularly posed a problem for those who aspired to study abroad (which, among my staff, was everybody). Since papers sent only a few of their top reporters each year, many sought other ways—covertly, though, as such ambitions could make them appear "uncommitted" to the *danwei*. Staffers passed around ragged copies of GRE prep books as though they were samizdat and could recite long lists of English vocabulary words I'd never heard of. If accepted to an overseas graduate program, they then had to prove their "loyalty" (that is, not emigrate) by leaving behind a 12,000 RMB ($1,500) deposit, which the *danwei* refunded in exchange for their passport upon their return.

The intrepid found ways to bend the rules, however. One *China Daily* legend told of a reporter who relinquished the deposit, got her passport, went abroad, and dutifully returned. Because she earned its trust, the *danwei* accepted her claim that she left her papers at a friend's and refunded her money. She was instructed to give back the passport first thing the following morning.

That left her just enough time to pack her bags and leave in the middle of the night.

Some of these rules applied to "foreign experts" as well. Soon after my arrival, one received a lucrative job offer in Singapore. Not wanting to fork over a substantial chunk of his income for breaking his contract, he and his wife grabbed their stuff and went into hiding on the expatriate "underground railroad" until his new employer sent him an airline ticket. Then there were the more dramatic departures, like the unhappy housewife who flung herself out of the *danwei*'s fourteenth-story window on her husband's birthday in the mid-1990s. They say her body lay there seven hours before a police unit that specialized in foreign affairs arrived to scoop it up.

SOMETHING I TRIED to keep in mind at the paper was that, with relatively few exceptions, Chinese media have been tightly regulated since the presses started running some 1,200 years ago. According to a *History of the Media* book in the *danwei* library, the earliest official paper—*DiBao,* or *Court Gazette*—consisted entirely of the emperor's edicts. So when Mao Zedong founded *People's Daily* as the official mouthpiece of the CCP in 1948, he basically just followed in his predecessor's imperial footsteps, writing the most important editorials himself while his cronies altered facts and figures to please him. The results were often catastrophic, as when Mao vowed to surpass the steel production of England and the United States in fifteen years. Rather than tend to their crops, peasants were forced to scramble about, tearing down their shingles and doors to use for charcoal as they melted their woks and nails into iron. Their neglected grain, meanwhile, either rotted in the fields or got seized by Party officials. By 1958, a famine had struck that ultimately claimed between twenty and thirty million lives, but you wouldn't have known it from reading *People's Daily*. Headlines claimed that wheat fields were so thick, a baby could not bend the stalks if he rolled through them, while cabbages reportedly weighed a quarter of a ton.

When his power started waning in the mid-1960s, Mao used the media to implement a "Great Proletarian Cultural Revolution" that sent teenage Red Guards to the countryside by the millions to be "reeducated" by the peasants. This too proved disastrous, as overzealous students carried out Mao's orders to eliminate the "Four Olds" of old ideas, old culture, old customs, and old habits by publicly humiliating, assaulting, and even murdering "enemies of the people"; desecrating temples and evicting the monks; destroying ancient works of art; and burning priceless scrolls and books. *People's Daily* replaced classroom textbooks altogether, and copies were considered so sacred, wrapping a fish in one could be deemed "counter-revolutionary activity." Anyone caught listening to "corruptive imperialist" media (the BBC or Voice of America) was subject to imprisonment.

So when put in historical context, the newspapers at the *danwei* were downright purveyors of journalistic excellence. The Party loosened its media reins when Deng Xiaoping, Mao's successor, introduced market-oriented economic reforms in the late 1970s, and the press have endured brief periods of guarded openness followed by hard-line restrictions ever since. Some fairly hard-nosed investigative journals have even emerged, like Guangzhou's *Southern Weekend*. English-language media are more conservative than their Chinese counterparts, though—perhaps because, as a colleague put it, "you can tell your own people about certain problems in your country, but not foreigners. We have to save face."

That may have explained why *China Daily* was stodgy, but the weekly newsmagazine where I worked supposedly catered to Chinese college students and young professionals who studied English. And our list of "untouchable" topics was staggering. We were flat-out forbidden to write about religion, orphans, capital punishment, gays and lesbians, or human rights violations committed in China or by any "friends" of China, like Vietnam or North Korea. The coverage of other "sensitive" topics depended largely on context, however. Tibet received more coverage in the *danwei*'s papers than any other province, but articles invariably crowed about the achievements of the Chinese Ministry of Health's cataract centers there (and were given headlines like BLIND CURED IN TIBET). Another stock article, headlined LIFE IS GOOD INSIDE, heaped praise on prison conditions in Lhasa. The exiled Dalai Lama could be cast only in a negative light, though. We ran numerous editorials claiming that Tibetans were serfs and slaves under his reign, but when he made a cameo appearance at one of Michael Jackson's benefit concerts for the children of North Korea, his name got nixed. Then came the day the Nobel Prizes were announced. During our weekly news conference, a reporter asked Lao Ye if we could include past Peace Prize winners in our graphic of recipients from the previous ten years.

"Of course. Why wouldn't you?"

"Well, the Dalai Lama won a few years ago. . . ."

"Oh." Lao Ye's face fell. "Then you can't."

"So what are we going to do?" I asked. "Leave a blank space by the year he won?"

"Yes, that's it. We'll leave a space," he resolved. "We can't write positive things about the Dalai Lama. This is a very sensitive topic for the Chinese. The Censor Board may not look favorably upon it."

"What about the Associated Press article on the protests in Washington and Boston over President Jiang Zemin's visit to America?" I pressed.

"No, no, no," Lao Ye said.

"I also saw an interesting article on Kim Jong Il somewhere—"

"No!" he snapped. "North Korea is one of our friendly countries. We don't write about our friendly countries negatively. It's too sensitive. You should know this by now."

I did, but I persisted. Those first months at the paper, this sort of antagonism felt like my journalistic duty. I would scan the Associated Press, Reuters, and Agence France-Presse wires for hours, select every article related to free expression and human rights, and download them into my colleagues' queues, wishing that someone would someday acknowledge them.

Overtly political stories weren't the only targets of the Censor Board's wrath. We once tried to run a picture of a Hong Kong musician in tandem with an article about an upcoming jazz festival in Beijing. The caption mentioned that jazz was currently unpopular in Hong Kong and this musician was "fighting to prove his music." Later that evening, I noticed the photo had been replaced by one of Demi Moore and Bruce Willis. I asked why and was informed: "Hong Kong and China are now unified, so it is sensitive to show that they are not unified in music selection as well."

Sex also got covered up from time to time. Ann, the foreign expert I grew closest to, often helped out our paper by editing, among other things, the lyrics to the American pop songs we reprinted each week. If the lyrics got too salacious, she had some explaining to do. Lao Ye once called her to his desk to discuss Bruce Springsteen's "I'm on Fire." He read aloud the first few lines of lyrics and paused at "I got a bad desire."

"I think this 'bad desire' is too strong," he said, rearranging the hairs on his chrome head. "Make it 'bad feeling.' "

Ann nodded; Lao Ye continued reading.

" 'At night I wake up with the sheets soaking wet . . .' Now what does he mean by that?"

"Uh, he's sweating?" she tried.

"No, I don't think that's it."

"He's crying?"

"No, I don't think that's it, either."

Out it went.

Strangely, the same issue that had Bruce "burning with a bad feeling" on page twelve featured a man covered head to toe in a condom on page four for AIDS Awareness Day. I once counted the word *sex* forty-one times—three times in headlines—in an issue that supposedly focused on Beijing's housing crisis. The world *violence* was mentioned sixteen times, *genitals* four times, and *pornography* and *libido* twice apiece. The Censor Board may have balked at our cover story about Singaporeans having the most voracious sexual appetites in Asia, but they okayed our special issue on the wonders of Viagra.

Articles insinuating that the Party's policies strayed from the Western world's were pulled as well. At another news conference, a reporter shared her idea to lead the front page with an Associated Press story about Karla Faye Tucker, the former child prostitute who went on to kill an ex-boyfriend and his partner with a pickax, found Jesus in prison, and became the first woman to be executed in Texas in 135 years.

"The article doesn't mention China at all—except for one sentence about how we have the most executions worldwide, but I deleted it," she said. "I also want to include a story about how Chinese think differently about this case. We feel she deserves to die and is just pretending to be Christian so she can escape the death sentence."

Lao Ye eyed her suspiciously. "I haven't seen any articles about this in any of the other newspapers. How come?"

"Editorial policy?" she offered in a low voice.

"No. I don't think so," he boomed. "It is too sensitive! Some people might relate this back to China. Our readers might start to question the situation in China."

Then he turned to me. "Capital punishment is a very sensitive topic in China. We don't like people talking about human rights or religion here. Even if we discuss the situation of capital punishment around the world, it still begs the question of our own human rights policy, and we don't want to do that."

I nodded. Another story was selected. End of discussion.

Most alarming were the articles that got pulled to prevent a "panic," like those on global warming or AIDS. In 1997, the virus wasn't yet considered a threat by most Chinese, largely because the media dismissed it as a "bourgeois" illness infecting only those who cavorted with drug users, homosexuals, or foreigners. (Even its name—*aizibing*—was a homophone for the Chinese characters meaning "the sickness of loving capitalism.") But the virus soon exploded in rural areas where impoverished villagers routinely sold their blood to government-sanctioned clinics that were unconscionably unsanitary and irresponsible. A reporter from *China Daily* once approached me in confidence to express her concern about a study she'd read that predicted this outbreak of AIDS. She wanted to write an exposé, but every time she turned in a draft, her editors demanded a "less sensitive" version.

"I've rewritten it five times now, but they still won't accept it," she said, her eyes wide and anxious. "They would rather save face than lives."

WHEN IT CAME to covering "official" business—meetings between heads of state or other Party matters—our newspaper turned to Xinhua for guidance. A wire agency similar to the Associated Press in format, Xinhua held the rank of semiofficial state organ and wielded as much influence over China's English-language media as *People's Daily* did over Chinese-language media. That included everything from official "interpretation" of events to the selection of stock phrases, right down to the adjectives. For instance, Zhou Enlai—Mao's highly respected premier—was always described as a man "with a lofty spirit."

Mark, a foreign expert who'd been polishing propaganda for years, best explained the power of Xinhua. He went to work one morning to discover his colleagues sitting quietly at their desks, their hands folded in their laps. When he asked what happened, they informed him that Deng Xiaoping had died the night before. Excited to finally see some action, he asked how they would cover it.

"We're waiting for Xinhua," they replied.

I caught this dynamic during the conference when our entertainment editor suggested running a story on China's withdrawal of two films from the Tokyo Film Festival in protest of an American film that depicted Tibet "unfavorably" (that is, sympathetically).

"We can't print that article! It's not entertainment; it's politics," someone hissed.

That piqued Lao Ye's interest. He asked the editor if it was a Xinhua story and, upon learning it had been swiped off the

AP wire, thundered: "We can't run stories about our government from the foreign press! They don't see things from our perspective. We have to wait for the official response from Xinhua."

"But this article has nothing to do with perspectives," I reasoned. "It does not offer an opinion; it states a fact. It can be verified with one phone call that China withdrew the films from the festival."

Ignoring me, Lao Ye pressed the entertainment editor. "Did Xinhua write about it?"

He admitted it had not.

"Well, if Xinhua didn't say it happened, it didn't happen," Lao Ye resolved. And that ended *that* discussion.

But for the most part, my colleagues instinctively knew what would and wouldn't fly with the Censor Board. It was practically a motto with them, and they grinned when they said it: "There is no censorship in China. We self-censor."

WHEN EXPATS LEARNED where I worked, one question immediately followed: "Do they actually believe the crap they write?"

This had been a major curiosity of mine as well, and the short answer came when the monumental Fifteenth National Congress rolled around and our paper got pocked with leads like this:

The 15th National Congress of the Communist Party of China will lead Chinese people of all ethnic groups in an all-round advancement of the great cause of building socialism with Chinese characteristics into the 21st century, a spokesman for the congress said.

But even the authors themselves dismissed such stories as "propaganda." At *China Daily,* one foreign expert found a pair of rhetoric-heavy stories in her editing queue slugged "Shit I" and "Shit II" by the reporter. Another received a story with an apology attached: "Dear editor: Sorry, but this story has Chinese characteristics." I interpreted this as meaning my colleagues were at least aware that their stories fell short of standards set by, say, the *International Herald Tribune.* Yet "propaganda" doesn't carry quite the negative connotation in China that it does in the United States. There, it is merely a synonym for "advertising." And the idea of a government advertising in a newspaper didn't appear too terribly heinous to my colleagues. Businesses could do it—why not the Party?

"Our government owns the media, so of course we have to say nice things about it. It's the same in your country. ABC can't say anything bad about Disney, can it?" my colleagues liked to point out.

Moreover, while even the registered Party members stifled groans over Communist cant, staffers generally seemed to agree with its sentiment (that is, the Dalai Lama "oppressed" the Tibetans, Taiwan should be "reunited" with the mainland, and so on). What I couldn't figure out was whether they had drawn these conclusions independently or if they had been conditioned, over time, to think this way. When I asked a colleague, she deferred it back to me: "Don't Americans usually believe what their government says?"

Good question. I certainly did—until I discovered Howard Zinn and indy media like *The Nation, Utne,* and *Mother Jones.* But what about my three hundred million fellow citizens? The "average American" seemed to swallow our own government's cover-ups for the Iran-contra affair and CIA operations in Nicaragua, Guatemala, El Salvador, Panama, Chile, and Cambodia. Why? Did they sincerely believe that our country had no blood on its hands—or had it never occurred to them to question? Did they just not know—or did they simply not care?

After watching me struggle for an answer, my colleague opined: "Chinese do."

IT GOES WITHOUT saying that Chinese journalists are more businessmen than probers of truth and justice. In *China Pop*, Jianying Zha quotes a popular ditty: "The first-rate reporter plays with the stocks; the second-rate reporter gets advertisements; the third-rate reporter takes bribes; the fourth-rate reporter writes for other papers; the fifth-rate reporter writes for his own paper."

But which came first, the shady businessman or the shifty journalist?

It is supposedly illegal to pay reporters to attend press conferences in China, but my colleagues rarely returned empty-handed. One told me that the first time she received a bribe, she promptly gave it to Lao Ye out of fear she'd get in trouble. But he returned it with the prophecy "You'll be getting a lot more in the future."

Within a few months, she was accepting bribes without a second thought. "If you refuse, the company won't give you *guanxi*, and *guanxi* is what gets you interviews," she explained, using the slang for connections. "We can't appear stupid, as though we don't know how to do business. Plus, we may want to leave journalism someday, so we'll need good relations with these people."

An acquaintance who worked for *People's Daily* justified it on purely practical terms. "We don't have expense accounts like you do in America. I use those bribes to reimburse my taxi fare to and from the conference," he said.

When I pointed out that he received at least 100 RMB per conference and taxi fares never exceeded 30 RMB, he shrugged. "That's just the way things are done here."

He had a point. Like Russia, China functions on a system of back-scratching and palm-greasing. That very same month my acquaintance accepted money for covering a press event, he also bribed a driver's ed instructor with ten cartons of cigarettes to secure his license, filled a policeman's pocket with RMB to get out of a ticket, and gave a doctor a watch to ensure a thorough examination.

"Businesses keep us happy with gifts; we keep them happy with articles," he reasoned. "It's a mutually beneficial relationship."

"Chinese think that flexibility is a good quality," another colleague philosophized. "Sometimes you have to sacrifice your principles to be flexible—and we think that's okay."

I didn't know what to make of this. Having just graduated from journalism school and interned at *The Washington Post* and *The New York Times*, I held this profession—and its practitioners—in the highest regard. Hearing my Chinese colleagues so matter-of-factly justify their actions disturbed me profoundly. But after I started attending their press conferences, I found it hard to condemn them.

My first Chinese press conference was held in the swanky Hilton Hotel by Austrian Airlines on the eighteenth of the month. (Since eighteen sounds like "get rich" in Chinese, many businesses give press events that day.) Reporters filled every seat in the conference room, but not one took notes during the event, which lasted less than fifteen minutes and revealed no news. The doors then opened up to a reception hall, where waiters with white towels draped over their wrists served us juices, ales, and wine from silver platters. I had just joined the pack of journalists from *China Daily* to ask about the point of the conference when a few dozen Austrians in matching hats, vests, and knickers strode past. They turned out to be the hired entertainment, flown to Beijing especially for us. Then we got ushered into a dining room featuring a buffet of roasted rabbit; half a dozen fish, pork, lamb, and beef dishes; soups and salads; breads and cheeses; and an incredible array of custards, pastries, and pies. An airline official took to the podium, thanked us for coming, and urged us to visit him when planning our next vacation. "For journalists, anything is possible. *Anything,*" he purred.

Sensing my discomfort, a colleague asked if I wanted to leave. I did—until I spotted a magnificent cheesecake on the buffet table. With cherry swirls that called out my name. And suddenly I understood why my colleagues attended senseless press events like these. It was a chance for them to eat roasted rabbit, drink wine, and listen to live Austrian music, to sample worlds that would probably never be obtainable to them otherwise. But what about me? Was I supposed to be a Western journalist in a Chinese newsroom? Or should I be "going native" in an attempt to better understand my colleagues and the system in which they worked?

These questions would irk me throughout the year. But that afternoon, I let pragmatism—and hunger pains—win out. There has got to be some correlation between a journalist's corruptibility and their standard of living. At least, that's what occurred to me as I wolfed down a fat piece of my favorite dessert.

—

IN THE END, the most challenging aspect of working in a Chinese newsroom was neither the censorship nor the corruption. It was the way Lao Ye treated my colleagues. Anything from tardiness to typos could send him on a rampage, and when it did, his bellows could be heard two floors away (as I discovered my first day there). He would march up to the offending reporter's desk, demand they stand, and proceed to abase them, starting with their most recent mistake, relating it to all the mistakes they'd made in the past, and concluding with a critique of their character. Lao Ye would work himself into such a frenzy, veins would bulge across his massive bald forehead and his face would turn bright purple. The longest "criticism" I personally witnessed lasted nearly ninety minutes, but his record was supposedly just under four hours. All the while, the reporter would simply stare at the ground—never objecting, never flinching, barely even blinking—until Lao Ye got called to the phone or a meeting (he never just quit). Once their anguish ended, they would sit back down, flick on their computer, and resume their work.

This behavior astounded me. During a stint at the Associated Press in Austin, I once transposed a number in a story that appeared in dozens of papers across the state the following day. When the bureau chief realized we needed to print an admission of error, he called me into his office, shut the door, and bellowed: "Fucking up in the AP is a *huge* fuck-up, Stephanie!" I barely made it to the bathroom before I started blubbering. How could my colleagues get chewed out on such a personal level and never bat an eyelash?

For the longest time, Lao Ye served as my metaphor for the Chinese government; my colleagues, the Masses. My empathy aligned with the Masses, of course, but after witnessing them getting struck down time and again, something in me—the

American, I suppose—wanted them to at least try defending themselves. I wanted to see someone stand up to Lao Ye: to fight back, yell back, or at least look back.

But my colleagues were, by their own admission, pragmatists who keenly sensed the limits of their system. If fighting it wouldn't get them anywhere—and it often wouldn't—they simply worked around it. For all his tyranny, Lao Ye had astute business sense, vision, and powerful *guanxi*. Putting up with his temper tantrums for a couple of years got his staff where they wanted in life. Since I've left Beijing, nearly all have gone abroad, free of charge, to study or attend conferences. Several have saved enough money to move out of the *danwei*'s dorms and into apartments of their own (the Beijing Dream). Others used the newspaper as a springboard to bigger and better-paying lines of work. That was their way of "fighting back"—and it was remarkably effective.

Had I applied these tactics to my own affairs, I probably would have enjoyed a more successful year in China. Alas, self-righteousness too often interfered. Take the time I asked Lao Ye for permission to teach a series of writing workshops for the *danwei*. I didn't know then that foreign experts far more qualified than I had been asking to do the same for years and been repeatedly denied. I also did not appreciate the number of strings that needed pulling before I could do so. I just asked and two weeks later was standing before a room full of reporters. The experience exhilarated me. In News Writing we discussed the five Ws and H of journalism; in Interviewing Techniques I invited over a fellow *laowai* so they could practice the art of tactful interrogation on her. The classes went so well, I started thinking I was preparing them for that day in the unforeseeable future their media opened up. And in my subsequent excitement, I forgot the rules. When a flack from the Waiban (Foreigners Office) asked for the title of my next workshop so she could draw up a flyer, I said, "Investigative Reporting," without considering the weight of those words.

That afternoon, Lao Ye stormed over to my desk. "What is the meaning of this 'Investigative Reporting' workshop?" he roared. "You know that Chinese journalists aren't allowed to be critical of the government. We can't be political!"

"But investigative reporting doesn't have to be political."

"Everything in China is political!" he boomed. "Anything we write that is negative reflects back on our government. That is because we are a totalitarian state—your country gave us that name!"

I was about to interrupt again when I realized what was happening. After months of watching my colleagues endure humiliating public "criticisms," my turn had come. So I rose from my chair, bowed my head, and let his anger lash over me.

"I don't know why you Americans always want to control the world. Yes, you are more advanced in technology and computers than we are, and you have freedom of the press. But we're more advanced in other ways. We have no crime. We have one of the most advanced social welfare systems in the world. I don't know of another country where crippled people are taken such good care of as in China. And our orphanages are among the best in the world! But what happens? We have two bad ones and you journalists go and make a documentary about them!

"Western press is too critical of China. It is not always the journalists' fault—they may know the truth, but their editors back in the USA, who have never even been to China, want negative stories about China. They are still scared of socialism, they still fear our Communist system. The only thing they know about China is Tiananmen Square. But we're neither socialist nor Communist—we're our own system with Chinese characteristics. We cared about politics twenty years ago, when the government first opened up, but now we just care about money. We just want good jobs, a nice home, and then we're happy. All of our officials think we should have more freedom in government and in the press and in human rights, but we just don't want to give it to the people all at once and have chaos. We want to make our change gradually, not like Russia.

"You Western journalists think our Chinese journalists are lazy and uninformed. But that's not true. Chinese journalists are more informed than Western journalists. We are good friends with politicians; we can call the police anytime and get statistics. We have complete access by cooperating with our government—not like in the West, where you are adversaries. We just can't print what we know.

"We also have a very responsible press. What happened to Princess Diana could never happen here. We're not allowed to follow movie stars around. Western journalists have too much sensationalism, too much freedom—and we don't have enough. These are the two ends of the scale, and the best is to be in the middle.

"We're taking a big risk having you here. You're not like the other foreign experts. We let you work among us, so that you can see what it is like to be a journalist in China. We want you to learn from us, and let go what you heard about us in the West. Other editors don't think you should be here, but we are not afraid."

At that point, Lao Ye got called to the phone and left me with my head spinning. His inaccuracies were so absurd (a 1996 Human Rights Watch report showed that more than one thousand orphans succumbed to unnatural deaths over a four-year period in Shanghai alone), I hardly knew what to make of his analysis. Did he really believe everything he said? Or did he just want me to?

I inquired about that third workshop on a nearly daily basis for an entire month. The Waiban kept stonewalling me with "We're looking into it." I never did hold it. Rather than learn from that experience, however, I kept repeating the mistake. When I was later invited to lecture for a journalism class at a university, I stupidly asked if a friend visiting from *The New York Times* could tag along. Not only was he denied entry, my own invitation was rescinded. Then, hoping to broaden my perspective of Chinese media, I tried to arrange meetings with professors of the All-China Journalism Institute and editors at *People's Daily*. They naturally called the Waiban to see if I had permission to contact them—which, of course, I didn't. That slipup became the subject of my second criticism, about "being too sneaky."

But my problem was that I wasn't sneaky enough. During the turmoil of the Cultural Revolution, people learned to lie and cheat as a survival skill. Rules could be bent in China, I was often told. They just could never be outright broken.

16. *LAOWAI:* THE FOREIGNER

**THROUGHOUT THE AGES, THE CHINESE HAVE HAD
ONLY TWO WAYS OF LOOKING AT FOREIGNERS:
UP TO THEM AS SUPERIOR BEINGS OR DOWN
UPON THEM AS WILD ANIMALS. THEY HAVE NEVER
BEEN ABLE TO TREAT THEM AS FRIENDS, TO
CONSIDER THEM AS PEOPLE LIKE THEMSELVES.**
—*Lu Xun*

I'M A SUCKER for museums. Never miss a one. Even if the subject matter doesn't interest me in the slightest. So when I passed by a sign that said NATURAL HISTORY MUSEUM in a new area of town, I plunked down 10 RMB without a second thought. One lady handed me a ticket, which I gave to her companion, who punched a hole in it and passed it to a third lady, who waved me inside.

The first room looked and smelled like a high school biology class, its shelves lined with reptiles, birds, and aquatic life pickling in jars of formaldehyde. The specimens were split down the middle to expose their entrails, which flowed from their stomachs like mermaid hair. Feeling queasy, I hurried on to the adjacent room, which showcased the entire mammal kingdom—anteater to zebra—neatly labeled behind panes of glass, the monkeys holding their name tags in their hands as though offering business cards. After pondering the exotic dishes each had become before joining the taxidermy zoo, I headed upstairs to the "Miracle of Life" exhibition. This one featured life-size laminated posters of Caucasian nudes in varying stages of pregnancy. Beneath each mother-to-be's stomach, a proportionally aged fetus floated in a bottle of formaldehyde. For the ninth month, however, the women and fetuses had been replaced with a wall-size poster of a gurgling Chinese newborn. Caucasian blondes begetting an almond-eyed Asian?

Mystified, I continued to the room entitled "Human Hall" and nearly bumped into a human torso floating in yellow liquid inside a glass case. I gazed at its intestinal tracts tucked neatly between its bladder and stomach with a sinking feeling in my own. After a horrifying moment, I tore my eyes away and they fell upon a case with an entire arm inside, sliced like the rest of the animal kingdom downstairs. I whirled around and saw rows upon rows of legs, heads, and brains in neatly labeled containers. There was a penis in one jar and testicles in another. Eyeballs. Tongues. Fingers. I turned to run away and smacked right into the ghoulish clincher: three entire corpses preserved in clear caskets. The first male had been completely skinned, save for his lips and fingernails, to exhibit the muscular system. The second was cut to show his digestive system. I was drawn, however, to the female corpse, who lay flat on what remained of her back. Her front had been cut wide open, from the neck to the belly button. In what appeared to be an attempt to preserve her modesty, a black veil was draped across her face, and black socks and purple gloves covered her feet and hands.

As I gaped, two Chinese schoolgirls—neither a day over eight—joined me. If I had seen such a thing at such an age, I would have had nightmares well into puberty, but while these girls looked pensive as they examined the splayed female before them, they didn't seem frightened. After a few contemplative moments, they started talking quietly.

"*Ni kan jian neige laowai le ma?*" the first one said. Do you see that foreigner beside you?

"*Ta de jiao hen da!*" the other replied. Yeah, her feet are huge!

XENOPHOBIA RUNS DEEP in the mainland, and with good reason. By most accounts, the first foreigners the Chinese encountered were the pirates who raped and ravaged their coasts. In the fifth century B.C., an emperor ordered the construction of a Great Wall to keep out these outsiders, but two thousand years and 4,500 miles later, it had succeeded only in keeping insiders in. When the army finally drove out the last of the invaders—the infamous Mongol warriors—outsiders were declared "barbarians" and China became isolationist for several centuries. Only in the Qing dynasty did China kick up her sales of precious silks, tea, and porcelain to the West—but on her own terms. When Britain's infamous East India Company tried to forge an exclusive trade deal, they got rebuffed for refusing to kowtow to the emperor. Incensed, the East India Company started paying for silks with opium instead of silver, which not only addicted China's populace, but devastated her economy. In 1839, a Chinese commissioner responded by destroying 2.6 million pounds of opium, and the British retaliated by launching the First Opium War, which ultimately forced the emperor to hand Hong Kong over to the Crown. A mystical group of Chinese rebels called the Society of Righteous and Harmonious Fists tried to even the score by murdering missionaries, Christian converts, and diplomats under the banner of "Destroy the Foreigner" in 1899, but an international relief force quickly crushed them.

Though no one could tell me the origin of the term *yang guizi*, or foreign devil, it wasn't hard to see how it came about.

Sino-American relations soured when the U.S. Congress refused to recognize the People's Republic of China (PRC) as a nation in 1949. For the next twenty years, the U.S. government harassed and, in a few instances, imprisoned Chinese Americans suspected of being "Communist sympathizers" while the Chinese government terrorized, tortured, and often murdered anyone unfortunate enough to be deemed a "capitalist roader." But once the United States recognized the enormous economic potential of a country of one billion, they extended an olive branch. Nixon flew to China to visit Mao Zedong; Deng Xiaoping donned a cowboy hat at a Texas rodeo. "Foreign devils" became known as "foreign friends," and until the United States bombed the Chinese embassy in Belgrade in 1999, these "friends" could do no wrong. Every light-skinned expat I met in Beijing had been featured in films, cast in TV commercials, invited to lecture at universities, and/or honored at banquets. I was accorded a respect at the paper that, considering my experience, would have been unfathomable in a Western newsroom.

But did this star treatment come from genuine reverence or fear?

One night, a Chinese American friend named Ming and I decided to explore Beijing's disco scene. We chose a club out of a guidebook, carefully printed its address in characters (so the cabbie could read it) and Pinyin (so we could), and hailed a red *xiali*. About twenty minutes into the journey, our driver—a crusty man in his early forties—began waving down other taxis and stopping on the side of the road to talk to them. We soon accrued a considerable tab and appeared to be leaving the city limits. When we asked where we were going, however, he grunted something unintelligible and swerved into another lane. Ming and I exchanged anxious looks as the traffic started thinning and apartments blocks became spaced farther apart. Where was this crazy man taking us?

He pulled over one last time and abandoned us for a clump of cabbies waiting for a fare. Five minutes and 10 more RMB crept past.

"Where the hell are we?" I asked Ming, craning my neck for something familiar.

"I don't know," she replied, her voice thick with concern.

Having lived in Beijing only a couple of weeks by that point—and having read way too many books by foreign correspondents who'd been kicked out of the country—I decided our cabbie was conspiring to kidnap us, to hold me for ransom, and to pawn Ming off to some lonely peasant in a faraway province.

"Let's get out of here!" I hissed.

On the count of three, we opened the doors and bolted for the empty vacant lot, beyond which gleamed a Kenny Rogers restaurant. The cabbie noticed and, naturally, began to chase us. When he demanded, panting, that we return to his cab, we shouted over our shoulders: "Never!"

He soon caught up with Ming, grabbed her by the arm, and started dragging her toward the car. Incensed, I snatched Ming's other arm and pulled her toward me. A tug-of-war ensued, during which I reached out and shoved the driver. Pursing his lips, he narrowed his eyes and held up his index finger menacingly, as if in warning. When I shoved him again and he repeated the gesture, I surmised that while he had no qualms about harassing my Chinese American friend, he would not physically harm me. So I proceeded to push and kick him, demanding that he let her go. Visibly shaken, he asked Ming why she allowed a "foreign devil" to treat a "fellow Chinese" like this.

"I am not a Chinese!" Ming shouted. "I am an American!"

Those were the magic words. The driver released his grip, stunned. And there we stood in the middle of the vacant lot, catching our breath, the cabbie and I looking at Ming—whom we both considered our own—while she stared, bewildered, into the night. After a long moment, she fumbled through her purse and pulled out some RMB.

"We're only paying part of the fare. You should have told us you didn't know where you were going."

The cabbie snatched the money and stormed off, furious. We hurried on to the restaurant, where the glitzy tributes to Kenny and Dolly proved strangely comforting. Then we headed back into the street for another cab. The disco, as it turned out, was just a few blocks away.

LATE THAT SEPTEMBER, I heard word that Lao Chen wanted to meet with me. Widely rumored to have been a People's Liberation Army officer in his youth, Lao Chen had the unenviable job of keeping tabs on the *danwei*'s foreign experts. After politely inquiring about my well-being, he announced that nearly all of his experts had requested the following weekend, Chinese National Day, off.

"So we'd like to offer you the opportunity to work in *China Daily* for us that Saturday and Sunday," he said grandly.

"Oh, I'm sorry. I can't. I've already made plans to go to Shanghai then."

"Why don't you think about it for a few days and let me know what you decide?" he countered.

Assuming he misunderstood, I repeated myself. "I'm sorry, but I really can't. I'm going to Shanghai for the holiday."

"So think about it and let me know."

I stared at him. What was he trying to do, play some Jedi Knight mind game on me? "But . . . I know right now that I can't. My friend and I bought plane tickets and booked a hostel in Shanghai weeks ago."

"Think about it, and let me know if you can help us," he repeated, his face stony.

This continued for five excruciating minutes, neither of us giving an inch, until someone else entered the room. Then I stalked off, furious at both of us: him for being so difficult to deal with and me for not knowing how. Times like that, I almost envied "ugly Americans" for being so blissfully unaware of their cultural faux pas. Far worse is being cognizant that you're blowing it but are unable to figure out how to stop.

In a nation where money and power have traditionally been unobtainable for all but a privileged few, "face," or *mianzi*, has become the de facto measure of dignity. It can be saved, given, or lost in every social situation and in varying degrees. One example is when a guest is ready to retire for the night. You'll make them lose *mianzi* if you simply wave good-bye from your spot on the couch. A little *mianzi* can be given, though, by walking them to the door, more still to the elevator, and the optimal when you escort them to their taxi, bus, or bicycle. They'll fight you every step of the way, insisting you turn back, but that's just part of the ritual.

The best way to have saved Lao Chen's *mianzi* would have been to cheerfully accept his proposition. However, gushing, "Oh dear, I already bought tickets to go to Shanghai that weekend, but I want to help out in any way that I can. Let me see what I can do," would have been equally effective. I would have seemed respectful, cooperative, and eager to please: treasured traits in Chinese culture. Instead, in my attempt to be understood, I came off as individualistic, confrontational, and argumentative. I also garnered an enemy: Lao Chen harbored his anger at me for months until the opportunity arose for revenge. Not only did he veto my requests to hold the third writing workshop, he advised the All-China Journalism Institute and *People's Daily* not to host my visit as well. That's what you must keep in mind about *mianzi:* If you make someone lose it, they'll get you back someday.

But there are occasions when *mianzi* can—if you so choose—be sacrificed for a higher purpose. I learned this the Saturday afternoon my paper held a free screening of *Guess Who's Coming to Dinner* for our readers. To give the event some authenticity, Lao Ye asked me (token American) to introduce the program's hostess, a Chinese professor of American culture. Some 250 college students showed up that day, and— never having seen the movie—I lingered beyond my duty. The screening took nearly three hours, as the professor kept pushing the pause button to expound cultural insight. Her commentary made my blood run cold, though: Not only did she refer to African Americans as "Negroes," she pronounced it like "Nig-gar-o"—and the students followed suit. Unease churned in my belly. Should I correct her, at the risk of her losing *mianzi?* Or let it slide?

After the film ended, the students asked more questions about the present-day status of "Nig-gar-oes," and the professor responded with stats she probably researched in the 1960s. At last, one girl stumped her: "What is the difference between a drive-in and a drive-through?" The professor thought a moment or two before her eyes lit up: "I know—let's ask our American friend!"

I had every intention of promptly sitting back down after my response, but once those 250 pairs of eyes focused on mine, my years of training as a race and diversity facilitator for the dean of students at UT surged forth as an extemporaneous speech about people of color in my country. When I mentioned that the terms *Negro* and *Colored* had been obsolete for at least three decades, the professor—who had been beaming beside me—sank into her seat. I quickly tried to return the floor to her, but a dozen hands shot up, each with a question for me. I spoke for nearly fifteen minutes, during which time the professor left the premises.

My colleagues then brought the program to a close, but a clump of students followed me outside for more discussion. Once their numbers dwindled to a manageable half dozen, I invited them over to drink tea. They stared back aghast, as if I'd suggested smoking crack instead. When one boldly agreed, however, the others trotted behind. As soon as we were locked inside my apartment, the real questions spilled forth. Did I have any black friends? Could I trust them? Why were they so violent? Did they really dress the way they did on TV? What made their hair stand so high?

Never actually having met a black person, they had formed their perceptions largely through Hollywood and news coverage of the race riots that erupted on several Chinese college campuses in the 1980s against African students accused of "stealing" their women. I tried to explain racial profiling and stereotyping by drawing a parallel between blacks and a people a little closer to home: the highly oppressed Muslim Uighurs of northwest China. They didn't buy that analogy ("But Uighurs really *are* violent!"), but the message seemed to stick when I revealed a few stereotypes that many Americans had of Chinese. ("But I'm terrible in math!" one protested.)

By the time the students left, I was on a high, as if that one conversation validated my existence in Beijing. The following Monday, though, I asked a colleague for her opinion about the film screening. After complimenting me glowingly for the "helpful" and "educational" talk, she concluded pointedly: "But that was a professor of China's most prestigious university. Even if she makes a mistake, she must be held in the highest honor."

In other words, she admonished me, while carefully preserving my *mianzi*.

ANOTHER CONCEPT EVERY *laowai* must grasp in the PRC is *guanxi*, or connections. For a Chinese, *guanxi* can determine where you live, what you do, how much you make, and whom you marry. Good *guanxi* can turn the average Zhou into a millionaire; no *guanxi* will relegate the brilliant to mediocrity. People often assumed that—as a foreigner in general and an American in particular—I must have great *guanxi*. How else could I have traveled all the way to China at twenty-three? I had to know *somebody*.

Before I departed for Beijing, my summer Mandarin instructor made me promise to check in on her little brother, Jin. So I asked him to dinner one evening—and silently thanked his sister when he walked through the door. Tall and tan, with enormous eyes and a tastefully shaven head, he was the best-looking guy I'd seen in the PRC. The attraction seemed mutual, and we flirted shamelessly over plates of shredded chicken stomach and tofu smothered in orange sauce. As we toasted our new friendship over numerous rounds of *pijiu*, or beer, he extended open invitations to the theater, the opera, and the park and promised to introduce me to his family and friends.

Then the bill arrived. When I reached for it, he shook his head and handed me another slip of paper instead. It was an application for a visa to the United States, neatly filled out. "Will you help me?" he asked, suddenly serious.

Thinking he wanted me to proofread the application, I agreed and took out a pencil. After making a few corrections, I handed it over. "Looks great!"

He laughed and slid the paper back to me. "Why don't you give it to one of your friends?" he suggested.

"What friends?"

He smiled knowingly. "You know . . . your friends at *The New York Times.*"

I nearly spat out my *pijiu*. "The *Times*? I was just an intern there. But even if I was its publisher, I couldn't get you a visa. The media and the government are separate entities in the United States."

Jin's beautiful smile faded. "Why don't you want to help me?"

"I do want to help you, Jin, but I don't know anyone, I swear."

"Chinese always help each other out," he said glumly. Then he got up from the table to settle the bill.

As Jin escorted me home that night, neither of us said a word. Though empathetic to his situation, I couldn't help feeling used. Had he been flirting with me only to try to get something from me? Jin, on the other hand, was probably confused. Journalists for China's larger media outlets are practically state cadres. He must have assumed that, as a former employee of a major American paper, I had similar clout—or at least *guanxi* with someone who did. My perceived unwillingness to share these connections must have indicated that I didn't place much value in his friendship. And if that was the case, why go any further?

When we reached my compound, I made one more attempt to be understood. "Jin, I'm so sorry, but really, there is nothing—"

"Okay, no problem," he said quickly. "I'll give you a call. See you soon. Okay?"

He shook my hand and walked away. I never heard from him again.

AFTER THAT NIGHT with Jin, I started feeling kind of lonely. My limited Mandarin didn't allow for very meaningful conversation, making it difficult to befriend non-English speakers. Those who spoke my native tongue—like the students at the university next door to my compound—tended to be more interested in free language lessons than companionship. I also wanted to avoid the thriving expat scene, as it could quickly constitute my entire social circle. And while roaming *sola* had brought a whole cast of interesting characters into my life in Moscow, it made me feel like a pariah in Beijing. Dining out was particularly gloomy, as family-style restaurants either sat loners at empty tables for twelve or turned them away altogether.

The older foreign experts at *China Daily* advised me against befriending our Chinese colleagues as well—deeming it "too risky"—yet I felt drawn to two reporters there. The first was Yuer, the only staffer who laughed with abandon. (Whereas the others covered their mouths and giggled politely if something struck them, Yuer had been known to fall to the ground in hysterics, face be damned.) Like her colleagues, she aspired to go abroad, but to slip on a backpack and explore—not to earn an

MBA and make money. During Spring Festival that year, she passed up family time to take a train out to Hunan province and go snowshoeing in the mountains. And when she heard about the temping industry in the United States, her eyes widened dreamily. "If I were American," she said, "I'd travel across the whole country and temp in every city."

Then there was Liu (aka Evil Fish), the woman who helped me buy the bicycle that day. She stuck out of every crowd with her daring wardrobe (sweaters that zipped down the front and form-fitting blue jeans) and the highlights in her long hair. Though she called herself a "soulless" creature who cared only about money, power, and success, her reporting revealed otherwise. She pushed the Censor Board to its limits, publishing stories about the plights of village teachers, women who bypassed marriage to focus on their careers, and a single mom who ran a controversial day care center for children with autism, plus she lobbied effectively for articles on other "sensitive" topics. Frank and sassy, she was the lone reporter brazen enough to challenge Lao Ye's edicts and seemed in turn the sole one he respected.

So when the three of us happened to be the last ones left in the office one Friday afternoon, I invited them to the tiny café on the university campus, one of the few places you could lounge with a cup of coffee back then besides an overpriced hotel or restaurant. (Starbucks had yet to spread across the city like a virus.)

"This is what you do in America, drink and sit in cafés?" Yuer asked as she happily stirred packets of sugar into her first cappuccino.

"Pretty much. You?"

"Chinese just sit at home and watch TV and read magazines," Liu quipped. "And eat salted nuts."

We chatted about the usual—salaries, food, digestive tracts—until I realized the significance of that upcoming weekend and why I'd been feeling so down lately. That Sunday was the one-year anniversary of the death of my housemate back in the co-ops in Austin. My heart hollowed out with the memory. Sensing the change in my demeanor, Yuer asked what was wrong, and before I knew it, a character sketch of Jason was tumbling forth, of how he used to brew beer in the kitchen and play the pink piano in the laundry room and the accordion in the attic and watch *The Simpsons* in the living room and eat peanut-butter *taquitos* in the dining room and act as everyone's psychotherapist in each of the bedrooms, until the morning he died of a freak medical condition none of us knew about, leaving behind a house so full of his presence, we could see and hear and feel and smell him in all of the rooms. By that point, my emotions were surging, and when I looked up to apologize, Yuer and Liu were sobbing right along. I reached out to touch their hands and then we were talking, really talking, the first authentic conversation I'd had since I'd been in that country. I told them how fundamentally Jason's death changed me, how I learned never to sacrifice the present, that the moment was what counted, and they began to wonder aloud how to change their own here-and-nows, as they felt so trapped at the *danwei*. Liu was even considering leaving journalism altogether for public relations or advertising.

"But your media will open one day and they're going to need people like you to lead it," I said, aghast at the thought of Liu wasting her raw talent on detergent or toothpaste.

"If I waited that long, I'd be an old maid!"

"Why don't you go be a journalist in America?"

"Who would hire me? I would have to work at some small paper in a boring town for years and years before I had a chance with the bigger ones. I'm twenty-six and considered very successful for a Chinese: I don't want to start over again."

Yuer, on the other hand, wasn't bothered by the Censor Board, calling herself "apolitical" since she didn't belong to the Party (and seeming confused when I asked if not joining wasn't a political act in and of itself). She wanted to leave the paper for practical reasons: to live with her husband, who resided in the cramped dorm of another *danwei* more than an hour's bus ride away. Because of Beijing's housing shortage, they couldn't rent a flat halfway between their respective workplaces; because of their binding contracts, neither could quit work and join the other. They simply had to live apart, as did many couples they knew, with conjugal visits on weekends.

Over the year that followed, Liu and Yuer became my confidantes and—when I inadvertently broke rules and violated social norms—my protectors. I turned to Liu for commentary on everything about China that puzzled me and Yuer for sheer companionship. At times I felt so close to them, I forgot how different our worlds were—until they'd mention how their parents spent years in the countryside, trying to bring about a "Cultural Revolution" when they barely had enough rice to eat, or how their college boyfriends went into hiding after the Tiananmen demonstrations, or how they couldn't climb further up the *danwei* ladder unless they joined the Communist Party, or how they'd never tasted peanut butter before, and could I please serve them some more?

17. CLOSE ENCOUNTERS WITH EMBALMED COMMUNIST NO. 2

WO AI BEIJING TIANANMEN!
TIANANMEN SHANG TAI YANG SHENG
WEI DA LING XIU MAO ZHU XI
LING DAO WOMEN XIANG QIAN JIN!

I LOVE BEIJING'S TIANANMEN!
WHERE THE SUN RISES OVER THE
GREAT LEADER CHAIRMAN MAO
WHO LEADS US INTO THE FUTURE!
—*Cultural Revolution song*

THE FIRST TIME I hailed a taxi alone in Beijing, the driver and I had trouble communicating. Mandarin failing me, I tried to signify my destination by drawing a big square in the air with my index fingers and pointing at its center—Tiananmen Square—but that only perplexed him more. I was about to give up and flag down another when I noticed a little shrine of Mao memorabilia on his dashboard.

"I want to see him!" I pointed.

"Ni qu kan Mao Zhu Xi?" he asked excitedly, grinding his

cigarette into the overflowing ashtray. You are going to see Chairman Mao?

"Mao! Mao!" I exclaimed, bouncing up and down in the front seat.

"Mao Zhu Xi!" he whispered reverently as he clasped his hands together, raised them to the Mao mobile that hung from the rearview mirror as a rosary would in Mexico, and bowed his head. I repeated the gesture and we set off to see the Chairman.

Chinese have been hanging up Mao memorabilia for the past half century but not always with the same intention. The tradition started out of genuine reverence—as homage to the revolutionary who was creating such dramatic social change. During the latter years of the Cultural Revolution, however, prominently displayed paraphernalia sometimes served as more of an amulet to ward off rabid teenage Red Guards on the prowl for "counterrevolutionaries." After his death in 1976, Chinese disposed of their trinkets en masse, chucking them into lakes or burying them in parks when no one was looking. But Mao came back in vogue after the Tiananmen demonstrations, when the Party attempted to resurrect his cult of personality as a way of restoring social order. Their efforts succeeded—albeit not in the dignified manner they envisioned. Artists and students took to emblazoning his mug Andy Warhol style on T-shirts along with his great one-liners like "Serve the People," while musicians rerecorded Cultural Revolution songs to pop and rock beats. Liu guessed that my taxi driver believed, like many Chinese, that Mao was bestowed with magical powers during his lifetime and so built him an altar in hopes of siphoning his good luck.

Dashboards weren't the only place Mao could be found in 1998. He also graced the covers of the *danwei*'s publications from time to time. (One *China Daily* centerfold told of a man who'd dedicated his life to sculpting statues of the Helmsman—some 1,600 in all. "I felt strongly that I needed to find some way to express my feelings for this great man of our country," he attested.) Nearly every reporter in the *danwei* had at least one of Mao's tomes on their desks, and several times I caught Lambchops dozing on the lounge chair with a copy in his lap during *xiuxi*. Even non-Party colleagues like Liu and Yuer quoted Mao Zedong on occasion, and after I caught on to some of his expressions—like "Shit or get off the pot"—I did, too.

Then there was Mao Jia Tsai, an immensely popular restaurant that served cuisine from Mao's home province about a mile from the *danwei*. Hostesses greeted patrons at the door by fastening tiny gold pins of his portly silhouette to their shirts. His ceramic bust perched on the front table, wrapped in Christmas lights and surrounded by candles, incense, and his favorite dish (pork fat doused with soy sauce and sautéed with garlic and chilies). Each room chronicled a different era of his life via photographs, newspaper clippings, and Velvet Elvis–style paintings. And this was no tourist trap; the clientele was almost exclusively Chinese.

"Mao was famous for having very good taste, so people trust his judgment," Liu explained. "If you say this was Mao's favorite dish, we'll eat it."

MAO CURRENTLY RESIDES in a marble mausoleum that breaks up the expanse of Tiananmen Square. After his death in 1976, some seven hundred thousand "volunteers" built his resting place in ten months flat and flanked both sides with robust statues of peasants and proletariats. (Only the statues' Asiatic eyes differed from the warriorlike figurines of the Soviet Union; I often wondered if the Chinese hadn't simply borrowed the molds and narrowed the lids.)

The day I visited the Helmsman, the line stretched across the full expanse of the mausoleum. Almost everyone was Chinese, but judging from their accents, few were Beijingers. Many wore the blue jackets that constituted the national dress code during the Cultural Revolution; and nearly all clutched bouquets of the plastic chrysanthemums rented from the vendors by the grand stairwell at the front entrance. A red carpet led to an enormous statue of a stately-looking Chairman. The wide-eyed men in front of me approached the statue as if it were Buddha, prostrated three times, and reverently placed their flowers in the thigh-high heap. Mao awaited in the crystal sarcophagus next door.

Like Lenin, Mao never asked to be embalmed and put on exhibition. He wanted to be cremated. But Hua Guofeng, his would-be successor, had studied Stalin's use of Lenin's cult of personality as a political weapon and tried to re-create this fervor to gain power for himself. Mao died at a low in Sino-Soviet relations, however, so his comrades had to preserve him without the expertise of Lenin's embalmers. After his wake, Mao was carted off to a secret bomb shelter beneath a state hospital and submerged into an herbal soup. According to one report, scientists injected him with twenty-two liters of formaldehyde— six times more than the recipe called for. Mao's face was said to have inflated like a balloon afterward, his neck swelling to the width of his head. One of his ears purportedly fell off in the process and had to be sewn back on; formaldehyde leaked from his pores. There is much speculation that the corpse didn't actually survive the ordeal and that the body in the mausoleum is a wax replica. But as in Lenin's tomb, the guards didn't allow for more than a fast glance from a squintable distance. I noted only that Mao's face appeared soggy and squished, as though still thawing from the night before. (He is mechanically raised from a freezer every morning.)

From there, we were ushered into a high-end souvenir shop. The other visitors, solemn only seconds before, formed a spontaneous mosh pit before the glass cases, snatching up the gold and silver revolutionary badges as fast as the salesladies could take them from the shelves. I elbowed through the body layers to the back door and found another crowd surrounding a lady making commemorative cards that bore a gold embossing of the day's date, sealing one's proof of pilgrimage. The stairwell descended into a maze of souvenir stands hawking everything from kites and pocketknives to sun visors and T-shirts—each branded somehow with Mao. Red Guards' fists formed the hands of alarm clocks; Mao-shaped music boxes played "The East Is Red." Photographs depicted the Helmsman at every stage of his life, including his current one. *Little Red Books* were printed in a dozen languages. And the Chinese snatched them like rations.

Should Mao Zedong be remembered as the visionary who believed social reform lay in the hands of the peasants? The leader who organized one hundred thousand men, women, and children in a six-thousand-mile Long March across eighteen mountain ranges, twenty-four rivers, and twelve provinces toward safety from the Nationalists?* The liberator who ordered women to remove the wraps that had bound their feet and

---

*In 2003, two of my *China Daily* "foreign expert" pals, Andy McEwen and Ed Jocelyn, raised a ruckus when they completed a 384-day recreation of Mao's historic march. Their conclusion: The route was more like thirty-seven hundred miles long.

broken their toes for centuries? The messiah who ended thousands of years of feudalism? The forefather who declared, "The Chinese people have now stood up," on October 1, 1949?

Or should he be remembered as the dictator whose ill-fated "Great Leap Forward" destroyed the lives of tens of millions of his own people? The despot who sacrificed legions of soldiers in the Korean War? The sadist who either shipped his dissenters to the *laogai*—Chinese Gulag—or had them shot on the spot? The autocrat who tried to strip his ancient nation of its sacred culture, traditions, customs, and ideas?

Or was this buying frenzy just another case of "Founding Father syndrome"—the one that inspired my own nation to honor Christopher Columbus with a holiday and to feature Andrew Jackson on the $20 bill, despite their abhorrent treatment of indigenous people? Did we rationalize that our leaders' ends justified their brutal means? Or did we just not know about their transgressions—or care?

It was one of those dilemmas travelers have experienced since the days of Marco Polo. Join in? Take notes? Or head back to the hotel? I thought about it a few moments, weighing each side carefully, then tossed aside the anvil of history. Those Mao Zedong chopsticks were going to look *fabulous* alongside my Elvis Presley salt and pepper shakers.

18. THE JUNE 4
REBELLION/INCIDENT/MASSACRE

**LIES WRITTEN IN INK CAN NEVER
CONCEAL FACTS WRITTEN IN BLOOD.**
—Lu Xun

THERE WAS A time when I connected Tiananmen Square to bloodshed to such an extent, I could hardly say its name without tacking "massacre" at the end. I'd been a highly impressionable fifteen-year-old when troops gunned down those student protesters, so the night of June 4, 1989, was my foremost association with the People's Republic of China. I obsessed about the square during my predeparture days. Would it still be filled with tanks? People's Liberation Army soldiers? Mourning mothers and grieving fathers? A documentary filmmaker once told me the pavement bled during the first heavy rain after the shootings: Would blood be mixed in with the mortar? Or would the square be silent and still, like the haunted banks of Wounded Knee Creek, where more than three hundred Lakota men, women, and children got slaughtered under a white flag of surrender for resisting the U.S. government's assimilation policy?

I tried to mentally prepare for my first visit there, as though on my way to a hallowed ground. But the sun shone over Tiananmen that afternoon, and the one-hundred-acre public square bustled with children flying kites and teenagers playing soccer. Families eating ice cream. Couples strolling hand in hand. Tourists snapping pictures. Provincial Chinese shyly asking me to pose in their photographs. Schoolchildren shouting, "Hullo!" and then laughing delightedly. McDonald's serving Happy Meals and the biggest Kentucky Fried Chicken in the world ladling gravy over biscuits across the street. Nothing seemed solemn or reverent in the least.

I felt relieved, of course, but also the slightest bit disappointed—as a foreigner who knew Compton only from the Rodney King riots might feel if he traveled all the way to Los Angeles just to find families barbecuing in their backyards and kids dribbling basketballs.

TO TRULY APPRECIATE the valor of the 1989 student demonstrators, one must first observe Chinese college life. At the university next door to my compound, reveille sounded each morning at 6:00. Students had fifteen minutes to run downstairs for roll call and their daily exercise regimen. Several classes followed, which the students generally did not select themselves. Then they got shuffled into the canteen with their lunch tins and chopsticks for stir-fry and steamed rolls. *Xiuxi* lasted an hour and was followed by afternoon classes, dinner, and study time. Students had to be in their dorm rooms (which they shared with as many as eight others) by 10:30, and lights went out at 11:00, no exceptions. On Fridays, they tidied their rooms for weekly inspection. Administrators awarded the cleanest room with 200 RMB (about $25), while the messiest residents had to pay a fine. Students also paid for the showers, which were often so crowded, they shared the spigots. Calls went through the operators who guarded the phones at the ends of every hallway, and conversations could be overheard by passersby.

Yong, the twenty-two-year-old wife of a *China Daily* foreign expert, strongly condemned her nation's education system, comparing its graduates to Beijing ducks: "There is a special machine used to feed the ducks that makes them equally fat. They just open their bills and get stuffed with food. It's the same with students—they stand in line, open their mouths, and wait to be filled with knowledge. They never ask questions; they just inhale. And they all walk away with the same information, the same degree, the same education."

So it took considerable courage for these students to even skip class—much less occupy their nation's most prized piece of real estate. Yet after the April 15, 1989, death of Hu Yaobang, the reform-minded Party general secretary who'd been booted out of office, they did just that. "The one who should not die, died. Those who should die, live," they cried as they congregated on Tiananmen Square wearing black armbands and brandishing funeral wreaths. And they returned every day after, in greater numbers than before. In the initial days, they were calling for Hu's rehabilitation (and improvements of their canteen food), but by late April their demands had evolved to political reform, an end to official corruption, a general rise in the standard of living, and more personal freedoms, such as an open media. The Western press summarized these mandates as "a call for democracy," but that's not quite accurate. The bulk of the protesters interviewed then didn't want to replace communism with an American-style democracy of open elections and a representational government. On the contrary, many contended China wasn't ready for such a system—the peasants were "too uneducated." Rather, they sought to reform their own system.

The students won support from all walks of life: vendors, merchants, monks, businessmen, and even Party hacks. Grandmas flocked to the square bearing blankets; schoolkids proffered Popsicles. Even pickpockets announced publicly that they'd gone on strike in the name of solidarity. The students responded with rallies and marches held throughout the nation. They also wrote proclamations. Read impassioned speeches. Sang. Demanded meetings with government officials and—when denied—held press conferences and faxed releases to student groups at Oxford and Berkeley. Beijingers vowed to stay on the square until their demands were met. "We, the children, are ready to use our lives to pursue the truth. We, the children, are willing to sacrifice ourselves," Chai Ling, a prominent student leader, screamed from a megaphone.

But while it attracted the most attention, the student movement wasn't the only one fomenting at that time. Denouncing their deplorable working conditions, a group called the Beijing Workers Autonomous Federation (BWAF) also entered the fray, demanding the divide between the ruling elite and the working class be addressed. They didn't elicit much sympathy, though, not even from the students. Rather, they were perceived as troublemakers capable of bringing down the entire republic (the way the Solidarity Workers Union was doing in Poland). It is widely thought that they were the targets the tanks got sent in to crush.

Around this time, journalists from every corner of the globe descended upon the capital to cover the historic Sino-Soviet Summit. The young protesters made far sexier footage than Mikhail Gorbachev and Deng Xiaoping, though, so the reporters quickly turned their cameras away from the meetings at the Great Hall of the People (which anchors one side of Tiananmen) toward the rallies held strategically beneath the one-hundred-foot obelisk memorializing the People's heroes of the Chinese Revolution (which sits in the square's center). The world marveled over these students flashing peace signs and espousing slogans like "Give me liberty or give me death," and shipped them sleeping bags, tents, food, and money. The top student leaders became such celebrities, reporters had to pass through heavily guarded checkpoints to interview them (causing some, in retrospect, to muse on the "authoritarian" nature the young protesters quickly acquired).

When the momentum slowed in mid-May, the student leaders announced another act almost without national precedence: a hunger strike. Within days, students were collapsing by the hundreds and getting shuttled off to hospitals, where they pumped in intravenous fluids and then rushed back to the square. When the head leaders finally won a meeting with Party chiefs, one showed up in hospital pajamas and upbraided the premier on national TV while clutching an oxygen bag.

And that was as much as the Party could take. Between the failed Sino-Soviet Summit and the hunger strikes, the students had made them "lose face big time," as journalist Jan Wong put it. After an intense power struggle between the reformers and the hard-liners of the Party's upper brass, the latter triumphed and declared martial law in late May. The loudspeakers on Tiananmen warned protesters to evacuate immediately.

By that point, the demonstrators were physically and emotionally exhausted and divided on what to do. Some wheeled in a thirty-seven-foot *Goddess of Democracy* statue, positioned her before the giant portrait of Mao overlooking the square, and then returned to their campuses. Those who remained wrote out their wills. The citizens of Beijing, meanwhile, erected barricades around the city and begged PLA soldiers to leave. Incredibly, few troops knew why the demonstrations even took place, as they had been sequestered from all media save military propaganda. But when Deng Xiaoping ordered them to "recover the square at any cost" just before midnight on June 3, they carried out their orders.

What happened next depends on whom you ask. The Chinese Red Cross released figures of 2,600 casualties, based on hospital surveys. American intelligence gave initial estimates of 3,000 deaths but later scaled it back to between 1,000 and 1,500. *The New York Times* put the death toll at 400 to 800. The Chinese government said that 200 civilians were killed (including 36 college students) and that martial law officers and soldiers sustained some 6,000 injuries and scores of deaths. It is doubtful the real number will ever be known (or, rather, released), but the government is probably correct in its contention that no one died on the square. Thanks in part to the persuasive powers of pop star Hou Dejian, the troops there held their fire until the students retreated. The bulk of the slayings occurred on the streets surrounding the square, like the Avenue of Eternal Peace.

In the months that followed, as many as forty thousand Chinese—mostly workers, but also students and intellectuals—were arrested. Unknown scores of workers were publicly executed with a gun to the neck in sports stadiums, and—as is customary—their families got billed for the bullets. The students who avoided arrest endured rigorous "reeducation" courses before being allowed back on campus, and the entire freshman class of several universities underwent extensive military training before they could enroll. Many of the students who actually led the movement escaped, however, and have since become successful entrepreneurs overseas.

The Party tried to peg the demonstrations a "counter-revolutionary rebellion," but it didn't stick. They have since settled for the more innocuous "June 4 Incident." Foreign investors quickly pulled out of China as a symbolic slapping of the hand, but once the nation stabilized, their money poured back in. It hasn't ceased since.

EITHER BECAUSE THE demonstrations impacted me so deeply as a teenager or because I knew of very little else that had happened in China in my lifetime, I hungered for personal stories about that June night. But it wasn't exactly a topic for the banquet table. As my friend Ann from *China Daily* put it, there were three forbidden topics in China: Taiwan, Tibet, and Tiananmen. During her two-year stint as a lecturer at a Beijing university, she was instructed never to mention those three Ts in class. "But you'd always see British and American teachers sauntering out of their classes, saying, 'Guess what *we* talked about today,' as though they were proud to have gotten around the system," she said. "They thought they were justified in putting their own value system—freedom of expression—over the Chinese's and tried to turn their classrooms into Democracy 101. Didn't they know every class had a student monitor who reported what was said and done each day to the Party?"

Indeed, too many black marks on a Chinese's dossier could ruin his or her chances of ever finding decent housing or employment back then. More than one American journalist told me horror stories about colleagues who'd helplessly watched their sources go to jail for being too outspoken. Though deeply curious about Tiananmen, I was afraid of broaching the subject. As a colleague interjected the one time I foolishly tried in our newsroom: "Every day of my life, I have been told not to talk to foreigners about politics."

So instead of conducting interviews, I read. Every expat had at least one banned book about China tucked away: I inhaled them all and grew ridiculously paranoid in the process. If the telephone made clicking noises, I wondered if it was tapped; if my notebooks seemed out of place, I suspected the cleaning attendants of spying. I started locking my notes in a suitcase, self-censoring my e-mails, and devising such an elaborate code for my journals, I could barely understand them myself when I got back home.

At some point in this process, I decided to seek out the "official" version of events and began spending my *xiuxi* at the *danwei* library, combing the shelves. My initial searches yielded nothing but mind-numbing reports about the state's agricultural, industrial, and economic advancements, but I eventually located the *China Daily* archive bound into monthly volumes. Naturally, there was a three-month gap between April and June 1989. I couldn't very well ask the librarian about it, so I kept returning every week or so, searching without appearing to be searching, until I unearthed a box hidden behind some old copies of the *International Herald Tribune*. Holding my breath, I opened the lid, lifted a black piece of felt, and there they were. The lead story on June 6 read:

> As a result of the "shocking counterrevolutionary riot" instigated by a handful of people with ulterior motives, according to *People's Daily*, the riot, which began early on Saturday, was aimed at "negating the leadership of the Communist Party, denouncing the socialist system, and

overthrowing the People's Republic." The statement said it was under such circumstances that the PLA was compelled to take action to quell the riot. In the course of action, the PLA martial law units "tried their best to avoid bloodshed, but some casualties nevertheless occurred, most involving military personnel," according to the statement.

This is where the subtleties of state media come to play. It is a given that *People's Daily* toes the Party line; by noting three times in a single paragraph that they were the source of the information, it was clear that the government had regained control over the media and that no original *China Daily* reporting had been used. In other words, this was not what happened, but what the state wanted you to *think* (or at least *say*) had happened.

Yet Chinese media had actually known—or, rather, created—a brief period of openness prior to the June 4 crackdown. On May 4, some two hundred journalists took the grave risk of marching through the streets wearing headbands that said "Our pens cannot write what we want to write" and "We tell lies. Don't believe us." Less than a week later, more than one thousand journalists from thirty papers signed a petition requesting a dialogue on the freedom of the press and delivered it to the All-China Journalists Association. Consequently, reporters suffered in the crackdown. Scores of publications got shut down, including the highly influential *World Economic Herald*, and many lost their jobs. The government expelled a British journalist as well, causing the foreign press corps to either steer clear of "sensitive" stories or risk jeopardizing their bureaus.

But the fact remained that for several weeks in May 1989, some Chinese journalists disregarded the "official" interpretation of the demonstrations and reported on what they themselves witnessed on the square—and their editors allowed them to print it. This proves they have the gumption—and the skill—to be part of a democratic media, whenever that day might come.

WHEN I FINALLY started talking to Chinese about the events of June 4, 1989, patterns emerged. The first thing they'd usually say was, "That was one black page in our history," "We are no longer a political people," and, "We've moved on." I initially assumed they were lying, likely out of fear, and that once I "broke through" to them, their real opinions would come forth. But no matter how close I got to people, the same sentiments surfaced.

"I was in high school during the 'June 4 Incident,' and those protesters made me so mad!" Liu remarked as we lazily sunned on a rock after climbing Fragrant Hill one afternoon. "My mother predicted it would be just like the Cultural Revolution, when all the colleges closed down for years. My classmates and I thought the protesters were being very selfish."

"Selfish?!" I sputtered, shocked. "They were trying to make a revolution, to bring about social change!"

"But what would be the point of revolution if there was no one to benefit from it? Democracy is not within our tradition, and our education is very undeveloped here. We would have to go through a very turbulent period to have such a transition, and we just can't afford that right now," she reasoned calmly, accustomed to my outbursts. "Given the choice between democracy and a thriving economy, Chinese will always take the economy because that is what affects us most."

According to Jasper Becker's *The Chinese*, China actually experimented with democracy as recently as 1930, when citizens could join political parties, participate in elections, read a free press, and stand before an independent jury. But either the nation suffered from collective amnesia or the censors had purged it from their history books, because no one ever mentioned it. Rather, people I spoke with said that their national focus had shifted from politics to the economy. I even heard this sentiment a few years later from a guy who participated in the demonstrations himself. During the spring of 1989, Zhang was a student at Beijing University, the most politically charged campus. He first learned about the rallies by reading the giant *dazibao*—political posters—that plastered the university. Although he had recently submitted an application to become a full-fledged member of the Party, the *dazibao* intrigued him. When he heard about a group of classmates planning to march out to Tiananmen Square, he joined them.

"I had no idea about democracy, I was just moved by the situation," he said.

His initial impression of the demonstration was of "anarchy" and "confusion," but he found it exhilarating. For four and a half days, he went on a hunger strike—although he admitted to drinking orange juice and beer. (American reporters saw—but rarely reported—a number of students cheat on their strike. I met one who even bought one leader dinner.) As the protests entered its second month, however, Zhang's enthusiasm started to fade. Party leaders still refused to compromise, and the student leaders bickered among themselves. Many of the original demonstrators dropped out, although the students and workers who were arriving from distant provinces daily by train quickly replaced them.

Zhang and most of his classmates returned to their campus two weeks before the PLA seized the square. He didn't lose anyone close, but the bloodshed so outraged him, he withdrew his application to the Party, as did everyone else he knew. In the years that followed, he—like many others—suffered from "survivor's syndrome," oscillating between bouts of depression and fits of rage. But once the economy picked up, he realized China was going places. Not one to be left behind, Zhang resubmitted his application to the Party seven years after the shootings.

"Everybody should believe in something, but I had nothing to believe in. So that's why I joined the Party," he explained. "It is the only way to a utopian society. It's not the best way, but it's the only way we have now in China. My country is ruled by Communists, and it will remain this way for a long time. So if you want to succeed, you have to hold this special pass."

At twenty-nine, Zhang's plans for the future consisted of obtaining his MBA in America and returning to Beijing to *xia hai,* or jump in the capitalist sea. "People my age go one of two ways. Either they are disenfranchised and hate the government, or they are opportunists pleased with the growing economy. I understand the other side, but I think they are going about life in the wrong way. You can do anything you want in China—just don't cause any trouble," he said with a sideways grin.

WALL-SIZE PORTRAITS of Marx, Engels, Lenin, Stalin, and a nuclear explosion greeted me in the rotunda of Beijing's Military Museum; a statue of Mao Zedong and an enormous rocket waved me through its many mazes of aircraft, armored tanks, missiles, grenades, and machine guns. My research on the official take on the demonstrations led me here to an exhibit on the PLA, the three-million-strong militia that for years was the pride of the nation, memorialized in campfire songs and glorified in propaganda. Never in its history had the PLA turned its guns on the citizens of the People's Republic. When they opened fire that June night, many demonstrators did not rush for cover because they couldn't believe their soldiers would actually shoot real bullets.

The underlying theme of this exhibit, however, was "Soldiers as Victim." The photographs displayed mutilated bodies in uniform with captions condemning the "counterrevolutionaries" responsible. Several foreign journalists witnessed soldiers getting ripped to pieces by angry mobs on June 4, and in the months that followed, bands of youth launched some 170 assaults against them that resulted in at least 21 deaths. In *Mandate of Heaven*, Orville Schell observes that the soldiers were almost as traumatized as the civilians by the end.

But when Chinese schoolchildren get herded into this museum by the busload, they learn only this latter half of their history. The Party has subverted nearly every image of the demonstrations, including the June 5 footage of that citizen of unfathomable courage who stood down a column of tanks, blocking their path, before climbing aboard one and screaming at the soldiers inside: "Turn around! Stop killing my people!" According to the Party: "This scene . . . flies in the face of Western propaganda. It proves our soldiers exercised the highest degree of restraint."

I tried to see this exhibit as a schoolgirl might and decided the rows of nearby souvenir stands would distract me from asking too many questions. Tucked between the Mao Zedong Zippos and Zhou Enlai badges, rolls of Tweety Bird stickers declared: I WUV YOU. Amid the toy tanks and model airplanes, miniature plastic violins lit up and played "Jingle Bells."

A few have tried publicly to memorialize the killings over the years. On several anniversaries, citizens have set out to lay commemorative wreaths on the obelisk that served as the students' headquarters. (Security agents generally drag them away before they succeed, however.) Computer "hacktivists" have programmed viruses that cause "Remember June 4!" to pop up on terminals. But the government has yet to acknowledge any wrongdoing in the slayings or express any regret. When Barbara Walters asked President Jiang Zemin to reflect on the events of 1989, he replied: "It's like much ado about nothing."

This attitude seemed to have spread among foreigners as well. The longer the expats I met had lived in China, the more nonchalant they had grown about Tiananmen.

"I am so sick of everyone running around, trying to land an interview with the parents of Wang Dan [the student leader who, at that time, was serving his second term in prison]," a Chinese American reporter who'd spent most of her adult life in Asia complained over dinner. "He's wasting his life in prison. People here could care less about him. The real story in China is about the economy, not the dissidents."

"The same damn journalists keep bringing up Tiananmen Square at every single news conference we go to. They need to get over it," another American reporter, who had lived in Beijing for years and married a Chinese, said over lunch.

Could we? Should we? Was there really an alternative? The government had, after all, clearly shown the consequences of dissent. The consequences of forgetting, however, seemed equally dire in my Western eyes. I wanted to see a memorial plaque on Tiananmen, even if it just collected dust, even if—in one hundred years—nobody ever stopped to read it. I wanted a Chinese Howard Zinn to step forth and set their history straight.

But my friends thought that day was still far away. As Liu put it: "We're powerless to change our situation, so we just focus on the things that affect us directly. Like housing and health care, and having a good life."

19. UIGHUR DREAMS

**IF I CANNOT DANCE, I WANT NO
PART IN YOUR REVOLUTION.**
—*Emma Goldman*

SO WHO SUFFERED most in Stalin's and Mao's "Grand Socialist Experiments"? Landowners? Intellectuals? Religious leaders? Artists? Nearly everyone fell victim to these repressive regimes, including some of the Revolution's most loyal supporters, but I found myself most taken with the "fringe" communities that got sucked into the madness: the racial, ethnic, and religious minorities stripped of their indigenous cultures and mashed into the socialist molds. I encountered quite a few of these brave individuals during a quick trip to the Baltics before returning home from Russia. One was a Latvian woman whose sister got sent to the Gulag for laying flowers at the feet of Milda, the lovely statue symbolizing Latvian independence that for years faced down one of Lenin in the center of that nation's capital. Another was an elderly Lithuanian who spent three years in prison for refusing to denounce his Jewish faith. Throughout the Soviet Socialist Republics, people risked their lives to continue speaking and publishing in their native languages and worshiping in their temples, mosques, and churches.

This steely defiance exists among China's fifty-five ethnic minority groups as well. During the Long March, Mao promised the minorities he encountered that they would be granted the right to self-determination if they helped out his army. But soon after taking power, he implemented a rigid assimilation program that tossed dissidents into prison. The Tibetans are best known for their rejection of the ways of the Han (who account for 91 percent of China's population), but the Uighur people of Xinjiang have fought just as hard. Their land—a desert basin in northwest China that once served as a caravan route on the ancient Silk Road—was first policed by the Chinese some two thousand years ago. The two have been at war practically ever since, with tensions escalating after the People's Republic declared Xinjiang an "autonomous" province in 1955. By 1997, the Uighurs had dropped from 93 percent to 47 percent of Xinjiang's total population, according to Chinese statistics (Western estimates were even lower). More racially akin to Turks than Han, the Uighurs felt far more allegiance to Muslim Central Asia than Beijing and resented the presence of Han on their ancestral land—especially the cultural intrusions. Among other things, the government converted the Uighurs' Arabic script to the Latin alphabet in the 1960s and then switched it back twenty years later, making those who learned only the "new" language illiterate. I met families whose parents relied on their children to translate documents written by their grandparents.

Over the years, Uighurs have protested Chinese rule through riots, bombings, and political assassinations, but Beijing retaliates quickly. Government troops shot at scores of protesters in 1990, and as many as ninety people were killed when one thousand independence-minded demonstrators took to the streets in 1997. According to Amnesty International, throughout the 1990s Beijing shut down mosques and Koranic schools, tightened control on the Islamic clergy, and executed political prisoners for crimes as slight as hanging a banned flag on a statue of Mao. (This suppression intensified tenfold after September 11, 2001, but that's another story.)

Why is this desert wasteland so valuable to Beijing? For starters, it shares a border with the former Soviet Union, Afghanistan, and Pakistan. Xinjiang is in such a geographically strategic position, China has made it home to army divisions, air bases, and a good portion of its nuclear ballistic arsenal. Xinjiang is rich in oil and mineral reserves as well. Throw in Beijing's vow to keep its Motherland "united" and it's apparent that the only way Xinjiang will ever secede from the mainland is over the Party's dead body.

So why has there never been a *Seven Years in Urumqi* movie or a "Free the Uighurs" benefit concert? Perhaps Mark, the *China Daily* foreign expert, said it best: "If Tibetans are the panda bears on the list of China's endangered minorities, Uighurs are the alligators."

THE CULTURAL DIVIDE between Han and Uighurs was immediately palpable in my backyard. On the restaurant strip a few blocks from my compound, Uighur eateries lined one side of the street, Han cafés flanked the other, and apparently only *laowai* like me ate at both. Han colleagues often lectured me about frequenting the "dirty" Muslim restaurants, while Uighurs wondered why I pumped money into their nemesis's coffers. Perplexed, I zigzagged between the bustling streets and ultimately gave in to the whims of my palate.

The Han restaurants had a feminine touch, invariably cheery and bright with tasseled red lanterns, plastic plants, overstocked fish aquariums, and laminated cutouts of Chinese children in traditional costumes hanging on the walls. Giggly girls with high-pitched voices stood in the doorways and called out the daily specials to passersby. If a potential customer opted for a competitor's eatery, the girls shrieked in unison, *"Ni cuo le!"*— You made a mistake! But if he looked even mildly interested, the girls hooked their arms in his and led him inside, chattering all the way. Then they rushed to the kitchen for a fresh pot of tea and a menu.

Testosterone ran the Uighur show across the street. Much of the cooking was done barbecue style right on the sidewalk. Teenage boys tended to well-seasoned mutton strips that cooked on skewers over smoky coal fires. Old men with flour-powdered hands stretched and pulled fat lumps of dough into rows of noodles and tossed them into vats of boiling water. Puffy disks of steaming *nan* cooled in the sun. Uighurs greeted passersby with hearty shouts of *"Peng-you!"*—Friend!—and rigorous back patting before dragging them into the grotty confines of their restaurants, where Arabic music blared from the speakers. Because I was a regular, they treated me to a chorus of "Alo! Ah luv yooooouuuuu" as I wove through their barbecue pits and noodle stands toward the café at the far end, where Arik worked.

A stringbean of a man with a straggly goatee and bloodshot eyes, Arik could usually be found nursing an enormous green bottle of *pijiu* and gazing through his restaurant's front window. When I joined him, he would point to the chaotic street life outside and we would shake our heads and laugh. There was something immediately bonding about being strangers in a strange land. Arik missed his hometown in Xinjiang as sorely as I did Austin, but he stayed because his family needed the money. He slept on a mattress behind his café, washed his clothes in the nearby canal, and left that strip of Uighur restaurants only when necessary. Though Chinese by nationality, he was Uighur racially, culturally, and ethnically, and that almost made him as much of a *laowai* as I was (minus, of course, the perks). Yet Arik had lived in Beijing for so many years, he was finding it difficult to reconnect with his people back home. The Uighurs' plight is known to first-generation immigrants the world over, but I would argue that the children had it worse. Parents at least had the privilege of knowing the rich culture that made them so different: The kids were simply outcasts. Some of the Uighurs would attend school and assimilate to the dominant Han culture, losing their native one in the process; the rest would help their parents with the restaurant until they someday ran it themselves.

While I usually arrived at Arik's unaccompanied, he ensured that I never ate alone. If he happened to be busy, he'd send over a pack of kids or—even better—one of the women from the kitchen to sit with me. With their colorful head scarves and long, flowing skirts, Uighur women reminded me of the Romanies back in Russia: saucy and free. Rather than run for the menus like the Han girls, they sat at my table and filled me in on the latest gossip. They spoke only Uighur, a Turkish dialect, but were so expressive with their hands and faces, they managed to give me the latest installment of their *telenovella* lives regardless. We wouldn't get to my food order for twenty minutes, and if they didn't have what I wanted, they simply borrowed the ingredients from their neighbors next door. In that mini Uighur village, everyone was like family.

THE PINNACLE OF Uighur existence in Beijing was Afanti's, a raucous restaurant tucked in an alleyway. Oriental scarves and

American beer promos hung from its high ceilings, long wooden benches covered its floors, and scores of drunken Westerners, Arabs, and even the occasional affluent Han caroused in between. Waiters decked out in crisp black-and-white uniforms and Santa Claus caps acted as disco balls by dimming the lights and twirling their flashlights in the air. Depending on the music, Greeks in the audience would clamber on stage to perform impromptu circle dances, Brazilians would samba, or Americans would dance like go-go girls. And when the restaurant was jammed to its hilt, the deejay would blast the song that united us all: "The Macarena." Dishes would break and beer would spill as tables were frantically cleared to be danced upon. With the possible exception of the pee-pee dance, the Macarena was at that time the world's most international jig.

One night, just as the crowd was getting rowdy, the deejay relinquished the stage to three wispy-bearded men in skullcaps and embroidered robes. Each carried a traditional Uighur instrument, including a two-stringed guitar called a *dutar,* a zitherlike *rewab,* and a snakeskin drum with iron rings inside its frame. They squatted on their haunches and strummed an old caravan song that seemed to whisper of a sandstorm on the ancient Silk Road, its chords deep and searing. When they kicked up the pace to tell of a happier time, perhaps of bountiful harvests or newborn sons, a striking young woman in a crownlike headdress appeared. She wore a pale rose dress as gossamer as a butterfly wing with a tight black vest and slippers. Nodding at the musicians, she raised her arms to the sides and began to snap her fingers and stamp her slippers to the beat. Having caught the tempo, she transferred the focus of the dance to her neck, which either lacked or possessed something the rest of ours do not. Her head swiveled from side to side in spine-defying movements in perfect time with the music—refined and precise, but playful and fun. After a time, the musicians rose, they all bowed, and the deejay reclaimed the stage.

We had just called for our bill when the houselights dimmed a second time and a song of an entirely different sort blasted forth—one that sent electric currents surging through my body. The syncopated beat of the *durbuka* drum, the haunting call of the *nay*, the blare of the *mizmar*, and the intricate melody of the *oud* lifted everyone to their feet as the Uighur dancer seized the stage, this time in a fringed-and-beaded bra and coin belt with a sparkly skirt. She stared down the audience defiantly. And then she began to belly dance.

I had discovered this art form at a nightclub in Cairo a few years before. Its music struck an immediate chord in me, in a way no other has before or since. I shimmied to it almost instinctively, as though my father's gift of percussion—honed from decades of drumming—had been passed on to my hips. But the dancers were what truly enthralled me: voluptuous women who played the intricate textures of the music right on their flesh. They revolutionized my perception of the female figure. In this dance, the bigger the belly, the better the dancer. I enrolled in a class upon my return to the States and had been shimmying ever since—so much so, I had brought a stash of Arabic cassettes and a coin belt with me to Beijing. After her riveting performance, I followed her off stage and asked if she'd show me how to dance like a Uighur.

Ayih arrived at my apartment the following afternoon in tight white jeans, high heels, and big hoop earrings. Her hair, dyed chestnut brown with blond highlights, tumbled in tightly permed rivulets down her back. Rather flamboyant for the average Uighur, but then she studied at Beijing's prestigious Drama

Academy, which graduated China's most prominent actors, including Gong Li of *Raise the Red Lantern* and *Red Sorghum* fame. Ayih aspired to be its next star.

Uncertain how to begin our lesson, I put a Lebanese cassette in my deck and simply started dancing, showing Ayih what I already knew—sways, *mayas*, the *ghawazee*. Within a song, she had removed her shoes and loosened her clothing to expose her midriff and was dancing beside me. Together we moved across my living room floor, communicating through hip drops and snake arms, expressing mood through melody and exchanging energy through rhythm, Ayih following my moves and I imitating hers. Within a few songs, we could anticipate each other's movements and danced in synchronicity, as though we were bilingual children teaching each other words from our respective mother tongues and then incorporating them into the one we shared, so that by the time the tape ended, we had each expanded our vocabulary.

This is said to be the oldest dance form in the world, as its most basic step—the pulsation of the hip—keeps perfect accordance with the body's heartbeat. In prebiblical times, the dance's stomach rolls were performed as an imitation of the contraction of the uterus in childbirth. In some indigenous tribes, midsisters danced around the woman in labor so she could imitate their moves during her contractions. It is still passed down from mother to daughter in many Middle Eastern cultures today.

"My mom had me shimmying as soon as I could walk," Ayih explained. "Singing and dancing are like eating and breathing to us Uighurs."

Indeed, dance plays a role in every Uighur rite and ritual, from weddings and family get-togethers to visits with heads of state. As the legend goes, when a young Chinese prince failed to perform for the Uighur court back in the eighth century, they whipped him to the brink of death.

Once we'd exhausted my collection of Arabic music, we headed down to the restaurant strip to borrow more from Arik. Bedazzled by Ayih, every Uighur we passed followed us into the café bearing gifts of fresh *nan* and bags of hand-pulled noodles. We sat down and a lively conversation ensued. At one point, Ayih said something that caused everyone to clasp their hands to their hearts and gasp. Arik looked at me, his bloodshot eyes awed with wonder. "She said she's going to Hollywood next," he translated.

This happened from time to time in the world I came from: small-town kids buying one-way tickets to the city and making it big. It even had a name: the American Dream. But for those Uighurs, meeting one of their own pursuing Hollywood fortune and fame wasn't just a dream, it was a flat-out miracle. When we returned to my flat with handfuls of cassettes, I pumped Ayih for details. Her luminous aura darkened.

"I don't know," she admitted. "I don't even have a Beijing *hukou* yet."

Like Russia, China had an oppressive paper bureaucracy that kept "undesirables" out of the major cities. In 1998, Chinese could more or less live where they pleased but could work (officially) only in the city where their *hukou* had been issued. At birth, they got assigned the same *hukou* as their mother, and only the most powerful institutions and businesses could change those vital documents. Since this was Ayih's last year of college, only a few months remained to find an employer with enough clout to issue her a Beijing *hukou* so that she could earn enough money to go overseas. Such would be almost impossible in Xinjiang, where unemployment was rife and wages rock-bottom.

"I've looked and looked and Afanti's is the only place that will hire me—and they can't issue *hukou*," she said quietly. "No Han theater company wants a Uighur on stage."

I'd heard this dilemma before, of course: from Kari, the Tajik student in Moscow. By virtue of studying in their nations' capitals, these young women had become too "modern" to find contentment with their old lives in their native provinces. Yet because they were minorities, that's exactly where they were headed.

It's hard to describe what Ayih stirred in me that afternoon, revealing what it was like to be an ethnic minority in China. Not the "this could be you but for the grace of some higher power" kind of guilt, but the penetrating, paralyzing, quasi-Catholic, "you should be suffering, too" guilt. The kind I felt when my dark-skinned Latina friends back home complained about getting the "taco beat" at newspapers, or when my cousins got harassed by the cops. Not that you have to be victimized to be a "real minority," but when you're already insecure about your authenticity—like many light-skinned biracials—you often feel as though you've got something to prove. You want to tell stories about how your *abuelita* suffered, and how your great-*abuelita* suffered, and how her great-great-*abuelita* suffered, too, and that's why you deserve those affirmative action scholarships and job opportunities you've been given. But deep down, you wish your skin were darker and accent stronger so that you could *understand*—not empathize—when another person of color told you nobody wanted them on stage.

"You're lucky," Ayih said curtly, reading my mind. "Nothing prevents you from pursuing your dreams, but everything keeps me from mine. I'll probably end up back in Xinjiang with all the other Uighurs."

With that, she took a cassette of traditional Uighur folk music out of her purse and put it in my recorder. Holding her arms out to the sides, she snapped her fingers, closed her eyes, and danced as her ancestors had for millennia on my living room floor. The *dutar* sounded sad but sweet.

20. CHINA'S WELL-FED ARTISTS

BEIJING'S POLLUTION MAY turn your shirt, snot, and tongue black and force you to plug your nose when passing canals, but the city is noticeably lacking in that other universal sign of urban sprawl: graffiti. The only kind around was of crudely drawn profiles of human faces. Scrawled in black spray paint, these profiles outlined a crescent-shaped forehead, a flat nose, open lips, and a jutting chin and often bore an obscure insignia, like "18K" or "AK-47." One by one, the faces sprang up throughout my neighborhood, along freeway bridges and upon the crumbling walls of buildings marked for demolition. The Chinese press pondered the identity of the "hooligan" responsible and how they should be punished, but their significance remained a mystery. They seemed to be making a statement of sorts, but what? My admiration for the artist grew as more and more faces cropped up across the city.

EARLY ONE SATURDAY morning, Liu called to invite me on a tour of some art studios she wanted to write about. Though I loved accompanying her on stories, I hesitated. All the Chinese art I'd seen thus far consisted of calligraphy scrolls and land-scapes, both of which had grown monotonous to my untrained eyes. Liu, however, knew just how to convince me. "Their work has been banned by the government," she said in a singsong way.

There's just something about that b-word that perks a young journalist's ears and curls her fingers into a note-taking position. "Banned? Really? Sure, I'll go!"

We met an hour later in front of our office, hired a *miandi* (breadbox) driver for the day, and set off for the first studio, which was tucked inside an apartment block. Housing was yet another institution the Chinese modeled off the Soviets, mean-ing the buildings were uniformly high-rise, concrete, and ugly. But the door on the eighth floor opened to a surprisingly spa-cious apartment filled with bookcases and stacks upon racks of canvases. The artist in residence was a beautiful woman in her late twenties named Feng who greeted us in a silk Mandarin jacket and velveteen slippers. As she and Liu chatted, I gravi-tated toward her work, which consisted of scantily clad Chi-nese women with hot pink rouge smeared all over their faces. According to her English statement: "China does not accept di-rect nakedness. In my work, cosmetics act as a protective mask against the women's inner world. Chinese women can dress se-ductively in Western negligees because they know they can hide behind the makeup. They can relax with their masks."

But these ladies looked anything but relaxed. In one piece, a chorus line in evening gowns wore ghastly grins on their pasty faces. This was Feng's view of high society: "Their expressions reveal their misery."

Her "banned" work included a teenage girl lying seduc-tively in bed near a rag doll with a funny-looking flower plopped atop its face. The flower had originally been a Chinese flag, but in order to display the painting publicly, she was instructed to blot it out. Another prohibited piece showed a mother and child posing in front of the Forbidden City, the five-hundred-year-old imperial palace that sprawls out behind Tiananmen Square. The mother was positioned directly against the giant hanging portrait of Mao Zedong, so that her face fit inside its frame. "This represents women's future in China," Feng explained, a smile playing on her lips. "We'll be taking over someday."

I instantly liked this feisty art, finding it clever and daring. Liu, however, whispered, "I don't quite like it," when I sought her opinion. Before she could elaborate, Feng emerged from her bedroom in street shoes and offered to be our guide for the day. We headed down to the taxi together and ventured off to the next studio, tucked inside a *hutong*, one of the labyrinths of neighborhood alleyways that date back as far as the Ming dynasty (1368–1644). *Hutong* were one of the few places Beijing felt like "Old China," but in the city's effort to expand its congested roadways, hundreds were in the process of being pulverized by men with mallets and hard hats, while their residents got shipped out to the suburbs.

A lanky guy with tobacco-stained teeth and a ponytail answered the door of the second studio and, squinting like a bat in the sun, ushered us into his cold, dark space without a word. His banned series was called *Square*, as in Tiananmen. One depicted naked Chinese toddlers with tanks pointed at their crotches and police batons aimed at their heads; another featured a Western woman's portrait where Mao's should be. A Red Guard girl and the Mona Lisa beamed from either side of a red cross while tiny stars emblazoned with Mao twinkled in the background; a Chinese peasant and child stood beside a Madonna and child while tiny Santa Clauses showered upon them; and a Western woman's bikini-clad ass squatted in front of the Forbidden City with Coke and Sprite cans by her side. The final piece depicted psychedelic goldfish swimming over the Forbidden City, symbolizing the artist's idea that intellectuals would soon be taking over.

After Liu conducted her interview, we headed back to the breadbox with Feng. When I remarked how refreshing it was to see something besides calligraphy scrolls, Feng agreed. "I used to like art that was just beautiful and simple, but not anymore. That is just technical art, with no feeling behind it. Now I need art with meaning."

Liu raised an eyebrow but said nothing. We sat quietly until an apartment building festooned with one of those phantom graffiti faces whizzed by. Feng laughed when I inquired about it. "Those are Zhang Dali's," she said. "We're heading to his house right now—you can ask him yourself."

Zhang lived and worked in a *siheyuan*, or a richly restored courtyard apartment, in a *hutong* behind a high gate. A profile constructed out of pink neon lights dangled in his studio's entryway; black-and-white photographs of some of the two thousand faces he'd drawn in different *hutong* slated for destruction decked his walls. "I call my work *One Man's Dialogue with the City*," he explained grandly.

"Who is the man?" I asked.

"Me." He grinned. "These profiles are a depiction of myself speaking out. I hope that amid the rapid changes in our society, people will see this symbol waving to them as a reminder to speak out as well."

"Don't you worry about getting caught?"

He grinned again. "I work at night."

I immediately fell for Zhang, too, admiring his courageous, creative way of reminding his city of the consequences of rapid modernization. But Liu—as usual—differed. What struck her was not the man's art but his life. Right after the Tiananmen crackdown, he fled to Europe with his Italian wife, became a citizen, had two little girls, and then returned to Beijing six years later a wealthy man, installing a Western-style toilet in his tiled bathroom and a Japanese entertainment system in his living room. While I viewed that as opportunism, Liu thought it almost traitorous. Chinese often perceive those who leave—even to escape political persecution—as outsiders hopelessly out of touch with their people. But what seemed to bother Liu most was how Zhang "rubbed" his fortune in other's faces.

"He makes art about speaking out, knowing full well he can just go back to Italy if there is any trouble, while anyone else would go to jail," she sniffed.

From there, we continued on to a suburb of Beijing known as the Cultural Development Zone, where painters, sculptors, writers, and poets lived in a thriving artistic community of California ranch–style houses. The artist we visited there—who had the requisite ponytail and sun-starved skin—led us into a warehouse filled with banned works that he sold to Hong Kong businessmen, overseas Chinese, and Westerners for $2,500 to $10,000 a canvas. Nearly all depicted a peasant's nightmare. Gigantic grasshoppers fed off the blood that ran down farmers' battered arms, legs, and faces. A man screamed in agony over the cornstalk growing out of his head while millions of faceless Masses fled in the background. Another portrayed the open legs of a woman and the Masses that ran—terrified—in, around, and through her. Naturally I was impressed, but when Liu walked by she hissed, "This guy is a psycho," in my ear.

After showing off his daunting collection, the artist invited us into his dining room, where his maid had laid out a full side of lamb, *mantou* rolls, and jugs of red wine. An assortment of artists and intellectuals joined us at the polished wooden table. This was like a fantasy for me, yet I felt uneasy watching them rip off pieces of meat and dunk them into delicate porcelain bowls. How were these "starving artists" leading such lavish lifestyles?

The poet seated across from me spoke halting English, so I asked him about the Party's repression of art.

"It goes in spurts," he said. "Of course, 1989 was the biggest crackdown. Nowadays, the government just closes or cancels exhibitions. They don't put artists in jail as much as they used to, although a good friend of mine is still there. He got in trouble for holding a 'sensitive' exhibit while the Fifteenth Party Congress was in session."

"What is the situation like for writers?"

"We sit around and wait for someone to make the first move. Then we'll have lots of readings, then disperse, then regroup, then start over again."

The artists invited us to spend the night in the Cultural Zone, but Liu declined. We soon said our good-byes and headed back into the city. Liu had a lot to unload, particularly about the last artist. "He's so insincere, painting about the lives of peasants as though he understands their hardship. And then he sells them to foreigners and keeps the money for himself!"

She turned to stare out the window and, after a long while, added: "Sometimes artists create work not because they have an idea they want to express, but because they want money. They want their work to be shown in the West, and they want to win some prestigious international awards, so they do what they think Westerners will like. They paint with the intention of being banned."

To be sure, every piece we had seen that day seemed primed for a gallery in SoHo or New Bond Street. But why? It wasn't skill: The scrolls displayed in China's state-run galleries showed superior craftsmanship. Was it because their work was so refreshingly original? Maybe. We Westerners love creativity and ingenuity, after all.

But I had to admit the art's main attraction was that it illustrated dissent. Why was I so fascinated by Chinese who spoke out against their government? Was I intrigued by subversion in general, by solitary voices that rose above the Masses? Or did something in my American psyche want to be reassured that the Chinese, in particular, protested their Communist system?

Whatever it was, the Chinese seemed to have it figured out. And the talented ones were churning a profit.

21. TABOO TO WHO?

I LEARNED ALL about sex in the fourth grade. Mom told me about it one evening as she did the laundry. I must have followed her back and forth to the garage—where we store our washer and dryer—half a dozen times before the facts registered. And a good thing, too: I was under the impression babies popped out of their mothers' belly buttons.

Such mother-daughter talks are practically a rite of passage in many American homes, but my Chinese friends found the very notion scandalous. Not one learned about sex from Mom or Dad, and their teachers didn't raise the subject, either. One friend was kept in the dark until her wedding night. With 1.2 billion people running around, they obviously partook in carnal pleasures, but they sure didn't like to talk about it—or, rather, not while I was around. Take the time a pack of editors and reporters locked into a spontaneous debate in the middle of our newsroom. Though they were arguing in Mandarin, they kept shouting out "sex" in English every few moments. When they finally split up, I cornered a colleague. "Doesn't your language have a word for sex?"

His face broke out in bright red splotches. "W-we . . . have, but Chinese don't talk about s-s-sex. When we do, we use English," he explained, then hurried off.

How did sex become such a taboo topic in China? Both Taoism and Buddhism view it as a fundamental part of the cosmic paradigm—the very yin and yang of life. One of literature's most debaucherous books, *The Golden Lotus,* was written by a Chinese scholar nearly three hundred years ago. He scrawled the tale of concubines and little boys on fine rice paper with a camel-hair brush dabbled in ink mixed with poison, then sent it to his nemesis. The poison caused the pages to stick together, so the reader had to lick his fingers in order to turn them. They say he dropped dead before he got to the end. The emperors were famous for their salaciousness, tucking away hundreds of concubines into their private chambers and castrating males for miles.

As in Russia, here it was the puritanical Communists who halted the licentiousness. Soon after taking power, Mao closed down the brothels and opium dens, banned "bourgeois decadence" (pornography), and gave prostitutes a good, sound political education. Yet he was as big a hypocrite as Stalin, filling up his swimming pool with underage Red Guards and having virgins brought to his bed so he could penetrate them, as per the Taoist belief that it would tack years onto his life. But while he encouraged his countrymen to procreate ("Every mouth is born with two hands attached!"), Mao limited the frequency with which they could copulate: once every three to seven days for newlyweds and once a week or two for everyone else. The Masses weren't supposed to enjoy it, either: Commie slang for the entire courtship, dating, and marriage process back then was *jiejue geren wenti,* or solving your personal problems. Under Deng Xiaoping's "Campaign Against Spiritual Pollution," Chinese could be fined for so much as holding hands with someone who wasn't their spouse. Being caught with "girlie" pinups could be grounds for imprisonment.

But as happened in Russia, when China began to open up economically, puritanism gave way to prurience. The porn trade emerged in the mid-1980s, and sex scenes popped back up in fiction. By the early 1990s, even propaganda had loosened up: The official mouthpiece of the Ministry of Culture, *China Culture Gazette*, kicked off 1993 with a New Year's issue chock-full of photographs of nude women (mainly Westerners). Concubine villages have also made a comeback along the southern coast, where young mistresses wait for their Taiwanese and Hong Kong sugar daddies to stop by on their business trips.

Yet my colleague's almost juvenile squeamishness about sex that day in the newsroom—as well as interactions I'd had with others—gave me the impression that, when it came down to it, they were prudes, at least compared to my American or Russian friends. That notion lasted until the Saturday morning a tampon-seeking expedition brought me to a neighborhood drugstore. There in a glass case, tucked between some ginseng and a jar of dried sea horses, was a stack of soft-porn photos. Porn hardly warranted a second glance in Moscow, but those contorted bodies seemed bizarrely out of place in Beijing, especially in a family pharmacy. So I examined them more closely and saw they were condom covers. Though they appeared to have been packaged in China, they depicted voluptuous blondes and busty redheads—Westerners, naturally, instead of Chinese. After gaping at them a minute or two, I realized they were surrounded by dildos and vibrators in every imaginable color and an impressive assortment of sizes. And alongside those were a dozen boxes of strange hairy things. I bent down for a closer look: rubber vaginas!

"*Ni yao shenme?*" a voice interrupted my voyeur trip. I

glanced up to see an elderly Chinese woman in a lab coat waving a silver key. Did I want anything in her little sex shop?

I shook my head furiously. *"Wo zhi . . . wo zhi . . . wo zhi shi kan-kan!"* I stuttered. Just looking. Then I hurried off as my face turned beet red.

I PASSED MANY a night in Texas fantasizing about the men I might meet in China. They had known suffering, and suffering meant angst, and angst meant passion, and passion meant hunger. And that, by my calculations, meant not only damn good stories, but damn good loving. I dreamed of dashing young dissidents who had denied themselves food and water in the name of democracy. Of troublemakers on the run from the Public Security Bureau.

But I arrived to find that Chinese men thought of me as an overly tall, frizzy-headed freak. Not that I enjoy catcalling, mind you, but going a whole year without so much as a second glance is a little hard on the ego. Your breasts start to droop like lonely lumps of flesh; your legs grow hairy from neglect. Only two men expressed the slightest bit of interest in me that year, the first of whom was a taxi driver. In his mid-thirties with a workman's tan and smoker's teeth, he appeared to be the silent type, failing to ask the usual "Where you from/Why you here/How much money you make?" But when we got stuck in traffic on the Second Ring Road, he rolled up a sleeve, rubbed his baby-butt-smooth arm, and grinned: *"Wo mei you maoer!"* I have no hair!

I rolled up my sleeve and twisted a patch of Chicana black arm hairs. *"Wo you!"* I have some!

He leaned over and—as I held my breath—caressed my

arm. Then he lifted his pant leg to expose a second hairless limb. *"Hai mei you!"* he said. None here, either!

Not having shaved in months, I had an impressive collection in store. *"Wo you!"* I cried as I pulled up a jean cuff. I do!

"Aiya!" He cringed, then looked away.

We sat in silence for the rest of the trip. I assumed my gorilla-girl legs had been a major turnoff, but he slipped me a piece of paper as I climbed out of his cab. A phone number was scribbled across it. As I looked up in surprise, he blew me a kiss before roaring away.

Okay, so that wasn't much. But at least I started shaving again.

Then that spring, a neighbor turned me on to Johnny's, a bona fide coffeehouse just a fifteen-minute bike ride away. I dropped in one afternoon to catch up on my journal and there he was, whacking an espresso scoop against the countertop. My heart beat double time as he took off his baseball cap, rubbed the glistening beads of sweat from his brow, and hacked. Then he ran his slim white fingers through his sleek black hair and glanced up at me. Our eyes locked through the coffee bean steam of the espresso machine. With a cappuccino in one hand and a banana nut muffin in the other, I slid into an empty seat in his full view. As my fingers slowly unwrapped my muffin in a suggestive manner, my eyes wandered up and over my coffee toward the counter, up the espresso machine to the shoulders, up the neck toward the dimpled chin, past the button nose to the ebony eyes staring right back at me. We exchanged flirtatious glances as I polished off my coffee and sifted through my journal.

Talk to me talk to me talk to me.

He didn't.

An hour later I rose to leave and, making as much noise as possible, slid in the chair and headed toward the door. He beat me to it. His name was Chen/he came from Hubei province/he studied at Jing Mao Daxue. Then he took a breath, paused, and shyly asked me on a date.

Who could be more angst-ridden than a college student with eight roommates, a part-time job, and so many rules and regulations?

Chen arrived at the front gate of my compound the very next evening on a polished Flying Pigeon and grandly offered the space between the handlebars and the seat, known to Chinese as the "love seat." But I wasn't ready for that—I mean, we hardly knew each other. So I wedged myself between the seat and the back wheel, where locals usually strap their cabbages. I had about thirty pounds on the average Chinese woman, but if I was a heavy load, my date hid it well. He stifled a gasp, swerved, and teetered forth.

Call me a romantic, but I had been fantasizing about riding on the back of one of those proletarian bicycles—of slipping my arms around some manly waist and scissors-kicking my feet, of unbraiding my hair and letting it whip in the wind. What I did not anticipate was the balance required—especially in a city where crossing the street is akin to playing the video game *Frogger*. We wobbled in, around, and through the taxi, bicycle, and foot traffic, defying gravity at every turn. He let me ring his tinny silver bell.

We eventually pulled up to a Korean dive packed with locals gathered around barbecue pits that belched out cherry sparks and clouds of spicy smoke. Soon after we slid onto a vacant bench, a waitress appeared with a tray piled high with bite-size chunks of raw mutton and two giant green bottles of *pijiu*. Chen grabbed a handful of skewers and dangled them over the fire to cook as he chugged his beer. After downing five skewers in a row, he looked up and asked why I wasn't eating.

"I'm not that crazy about meat."

He looked surprised. "Are you Buddhist?"

"Catholic. You?"

"I'm Chinese," he said as he took a swig of *pijiu*. "I'm Marxist."

"That means you eat a lot of meat?"

He beamed and inhaled another skewer.

This guy had potential. "What do you want to do after you graduate?"

"Go to America and get an MBA."

"To make the State-Owned Enterprises here more efficient?" I asked hopefully.

"To play the stocks."

"That's Marxist?"

"No," he said, signaling for more mutton. "That's Chinese."

I stared at him, amazed. "And you're how old?"

He blinked. "How old do you think I am?"

"Twenty-one?"

"Right," he said—a little too quickly.

That probably meant he was nineteen. I was nearly twenty-four. What sort of law did China have about that sort of thing? Before I could ask, he changed the subject.

"Chinese girls. You have to be with them one year, two years, three years, four. Then they'll be your girlfriend," he speculated as he chewed more mutton off a skewer and spat out the fat. "Japanese girls. Korean girls. They'll be your girlfriend right away. What about American girls?"

Was this going where I thought it was? "Are you asking me about sex?"

There was *that word* again. Chen choked on his beer,

coughed, sputtered, and turned red. Then he smiled sheepishly. Before we could continue, the restaurant owner—a five-foot Korean—barged in. She surveyed her patrons, zeroed in on us, and marched up to our table. "What are you doing with this *laowai*?" she demanded in Mandarin. "She's got to be twenty-five, and you're only eighteen. . . ."

"Nineteen!" he interjected, and stole a glance at me.

I couldn't help myself, really: I laughed, hard and loud. As the restaurant grew still and the color ebbed out of Chen's face, I realized the severity of this mistake. My laughter had been interpreted as mockery, which not only lowered his status in the eyes of the restaurant owner and the patrons, but injured his pride as well.

Our ride home was a solemn one. Chen didn't offer me the love seat. I could not ring the bell. He said not a word as he carted me across the city, past the late evening strollers and the candlelit cafés, beneath the cypress trees. When he pulled into the driveway of my compound, he shook my hand without making eye contact. And then one of the last generations of self-declared Marxists turned his bike around and pedaled into the night.

WITH OUR WEEKLY deadline looming overhead, Yuer rushed over to me one evening with a broadsheet in bad need of an edit. "Should this be 'it's' or 'its'?" " 'Your' or 'you're'?" " 'I am a sweater' or 'I sweat a lot'?"

She scribbled down the corrections and was about to dash back to her cubicle when another question occurred to her. "Oh, and Stephanie? What's the difference between homosexual and faggot?"

I sat Yuer down for a quick lesson about gays and lesbians, dykes and fags, queens and queers, and transvestites, transgenders, and transsexuals, writing out the definitions as we went along. She thanked me and returned to her desk clutching the paper. I thought she'd throw it away or—at the very least—hide it in a drawer, but she taped it to the wall of her cubicle.

About a week later, Liu asked Yuer and me to accompany her to a party she'd been invited to by someone at a press conference. When we stepped out of the cab in front of an upscale apartment complex just outside Sanlitun, Beijing's Bourbon Street, campy music drifted down the stairwell. "You can get yourself cleaned, you can have a good meal / You can do whatever you feel." The Village People! "YMCA" grew louder and louder as we ascended to the fifth floor, where we cautiously knocked on the door. A Chinese with gel-spiked hair, a black muscle shirt made of netting, and silver hoop earrings flung open the door and threw his arms around me. I peeked over his shoulder and marveled. The apartment walls were painted hot pink and decorated with black-and-white photos of girls kissing girls and boys kissing boys. Pink triangles fashioned out of pipe cleaners hung from the light fixtures; a rainbow flag covered the back wall. Several dozen Chinese in hip-hop gear danced a *lambada* around the hostess, a Western diva draped in turquoise velvet who wore horned-rimmed glasses.

I turned to Liu. "Are you sure this is the right place?"

"Yes, I think so," she said, pulling out her invitation to check.

"Cool! Let's dance!"

Holding hands like schoolgirls, Yuer and Liu joined me on the living room floor, put their arms on each other's shoulders, and stepped side to side in time to the music, while I sandwiched myself between two guys wearing rainbow-colored rings around their necks. We flung our hands in the air and shouted every time Madonna cried out "Cherish." A few songs later, Liu, Yuer, and I took a break on a couch. "Great party!" I exclaimed.

They nodded pleasantly, still holding hands as Chinese friends often do.

"Y'all ever been to a party like this?"

"Like what?" Liu asked innocently.

Oh, boy. They didn't know. "Yuer, Liu. Every single person in this room is gay."

Yuer's face lit up with recognition. "You mean *homosexual*?"

I nodded. Liu's jaw dropped. Yuer's eyes grew huge. "How do you know?" they asked.

I looked around the room. Where to begin? The music? The pipe cleaners? The two women fondling each other in the love seat across from us?

"Trust me," I assured them.

AS IN RUSSIA, homosexuality has only recently been considered taboo in China. For two centuries at the height of the Han dynasty (206 B.C.–A.D. 220), ten openly bisexual emperors ruled the country. Of particular note was Emperor Ai, who once cut off his own sleeve so as not to awaken the male lover stretched out across his robe. The famous poet Ruan Ji wrote extensively of homosexual relations, calling boys "young peach and plum blossoms . . . joyful as nine springtimes." Lesbianism is largely absent from historical texts—perhaps because men did the bulk of the recording—but there are references to women's "jade gates" pressed together "grinding bean curd."

But when the West started exporting missionaries to China,

sexual liberalism got pitched into the proverbial closet. Mao sicced the Red Guards on gays and lesbians during the Cultural Revolution, and unknown scores were either imprisoned or killed. Diagnosing homosexuality as a mental illness, doctors often prescribed electric shocks as "treatment," which sometimes left their patients permanently incapacitated.

Gay culture noticeably reemerged when lesbians from around the world traveled to Beijing for the UN's Fourth World Women's Conference in 1995. Their information tables drew surprising numbers of locals, many of whom swapped business cards with one another. In 1997, some two hundred gays and lesbians—including one from Beijing—flocked to Hong Kong for a conference on being a gay Chinese. By the time I arrived, the capital boasted half a dozen gay-friendly bars and discotheques, salons, and underground libraries.

But despite their contribution to population control, gays and lesbians are still persecuted heavily by the Party to this day. When police are instructed to round up the "bad elements," they are among the usual targets, along with dissidents, prostitutes, and drug addicts. Jail sentences aren't always what their captors have in mind, though.

"They once detained a friend of mine and made him do spring cleaning at the station," Jayne, the British diva who hosted the party that night, told me. "The whole time he was cleaning, the guards laughed about how they used to round up immigrants to do this job, but gay people were so much better because they didn't smell bad and were much more meticulous."

"Gays are so afraid of getting caught, they just fuck and then run and hide," added Wang, a Chinese Australian I later met at a popular gay bar called Half and Half. "I bet there are men here who have never spent the entire night with their boyfriends before. It would be impossible to have a meaningful relationship in this country."

That was probably an exaggeration, but there certainly were risks involved with being openly gay in China—even in cosmopolitan cities like Beijing and Shanghai. Police brutality was not unheard of, and homosexuals risked losing their job or apartment if too many people learned their secret. Yet the average homosexual likely worried more about disappointing their parents than they did a crackdown by the Public Security Bureau. Chinese have traditionally felt morally obligated by filial piety to bear their parents a grandchild, and the One-Child Policy has magnified this responsibility, since no one can depend on a sibling to uphold their family's gene line. Even gay activists contend that it is "wrong" to come out to one's parents, as their grief would be too great. According to Wang, most gay men married for this very reason and had relationships on the side.

Things seemed different for lesbians, though.

"It's easy being gay if you're a girl," Gong, a twenty-two-year-old with bleached blond hair and a nose ring, declared that night at Jayne's party as she cuddled with her girlfriend.

That might be because it is culturally acceptable for Chinese women to be outwardly affectionate with their girlfriends, be it snuggling, hand-holding, or slapping their bodies together on a dance floor. In fact, if anything differentiated the lesbians I met in Beijing from my straight friends and colleagues, it was their auras: They positively radiated freedom, from their elfin haircuts to their flamboyant platform shoes. They were also politically aware. During a salon I later attended at Jayne's house, a dozen lesbians sat in a circle and took turns sharing information and resources about everything from AIDS prevention to feminism. Several volunteered at a hot line for gays and lesbians in need of counsel. In many ways, these women were the closest I came to real "activists" or "dissidents" in China. They had even co-opted the Cultural Revolution term of *tongzhi,* or comrade, as their moniker.

After observing a bit of the gay community, I took an informal poll of my straight colleagues' views on homosexuality. I suspected their range of acceptance would parallel my own country's, with Party members being aligned with the American religious Right and progressives being uniformly open. Yet again I was mistaken.

"If a society offers so many options to its people, as America does, then I can see how some will choose to be homosexual. But in a country like China, the tendency to be gay would be killed before the person even discovered it," Liu reasoned. "Why else would there be so many gay people in America and not in China, where there are so many more people?"

"Proportionally, there are probably just as many gay people in China as in America," I replied. "They might just be too afraid to act on it. Or maybe they do act on it, but only in secret."

"No, I don't think so. It's not that people are trying to hide the fact they are gay: They just don't even think that it is an option. We Chinese are so set in our ways, there just isn't any room for gay culture here."

THERE IS NOTHING more humiliating than having your lousy Spanish corrected by a bald-headed, red-bearded gringo whose polka-dot boxers gleam through his tight white trousers. Although nearly everyone in my seventh-grade Spanish class was at least half Mexican, we couldn't do much more than curse ("Stupid *pendejo!*"), and even then, we didn't know what we were saying. So Mr. Sprinkle had to devise some fairly innovative ways of teaching our language to us. Once, he drew a great big tree on the chalkboard and wrote *yo* (me) on the trunk and hung words like *madre, tía, sobrino,* and *primo* from the branches. Then he asked who could identify a term.

I glanced up and recognized one right away: "*Tía* means grandmother."

Mr. Sprinkle looked at me in bemusement. "Good try, Stephanie, but that's incorrect."

Huh? But that's what I'd been calling my grandmother for years.

Melissa, my gringa friend who sat behind me, raised her hand. "*Abuela* means grandmother."

Abuela? As in *abuelita?* That couldn't be right. That's what

I called that sweet, crinkly old woman who lived on the King Ranch—the one who hand-rolled tortillas even though she could no longer see the *masa* or the stove owing to the glaucoma that had left her eyes dark and cold. I turned to Melissa. "No, it doesn't. *Abuela* means great-grandmother."

Mr. Sprinkle watched me curiously. "Actually, Melissa is right. *Abuela* means grandmother and *tía* means aunt."

Aunt? I had loads of aunts—Alicia, Amanda, Consuelo, Diane, Elida, Emma, Francis, Herlinda, Margie, Maria, Mary, Mary Lou, Toni, Ventura—but all of them were my mother's age, give or take a few decades. But *Tía* must have been pushing seventy, not to mention the fact that she and *Tío*—Grandfather? Uncle?—raised my mother. How could *Tía* be my aunt?

Just then, my thoughts drifted to the sepia-toned photograph on my mother's nightstand. That somber young woman in the gingham dress had a long, oval-shaped face like Uncle Meme's and thick curly hair like Mom's (and mine). Who was she?

I waited until another one of my mother's laundry days to ask.

"She's my mother," she said brusquely, shaking out a pair of hot jeans.

"So she's my grandma? But I thought *Tía* was my grandma."

"She is."

"But how can *Tía* be my grandma if that lady is your mom?"

"Can't you see I'm busy?!" she snapped.

Patience—like cooking—wasn't among my mother's virtues. So I resorted to that which little sisters and aspiring reporters do best: snooping. While Dad mowed the yard after school one day, I started poking around the deeds and insurance papers filed in the fireproof lockbox beneath my parents' bed and the mementos stuffed inside Mom's musty jewelry boxes. I didn't know what to look for, exactly—an old diary? a faded letter?—until I found a death certificate for someone named Barbara Silva Elizondo tucked inside a yellowing envelope at the bottom of a drawer. The name struck a chord in me, as Barbara was my sister's name and Elizondo was my mother's maiden name. I remembered hearing somewhere that my sister had been named after my grandmother. Was this her death certificate?

I examined the first few lines of the document and calculated that this woman died in 1949, at age twenty-five. My mother had five full-blooded siblings—could her mother have died so young? If so, how? I read until the end, where something sent a chill down my spine. Under cause of death, it said gunshot wound to the head.

GROWING UP, I didn't know much about my mother. She marched off to work in the morning in a power suit with shoulder pads while my father fixed my Cap'n Crunch and walked me to school. Yet even at an early age I noticed the strange dichotomy between her Louis Vuitton handbag and the *barrio* she came from. Born in a one-bedroom bungalow with no air-conditioning and six people to share it with, she was raised on beans, rice, and Catholicism. As the youngest daughter in a first-generation Mexican family, she was expected to stay home and take care of her parents in their aging years. So she caused quite an *escándalo* when at twenty-one she fell in love with a thirty-year-old white musician she met at a jazz club and married him three months later. Then Dad whisked her away to the Northeast, where he joined the Naval Academy Band.

Dad showed Mom a great deal of America those first few years, but since he'd vowed never to ride another plane after retiring from the navy—and hasn't—her travels were confined to the continental United States. That seemed terribly unjust to me, especially since my mother devoured the world archaeology tomes and classical literature she checked out of the library with such delight. When I started bugging her about visiting me in Asia after I received the Luce scholarship, however, she rolled her eyes and said, "Puuh-lease." Mom didn't relate to my fascination with the developing world: She lived it growing up.

"Why can't you go to London or Rome?" she asked as I tried on down coats for Russia.

"Why do you always go to depressing places?" she implored when I got my shots for China.

Knowing this would be a hard-won battle, I waited until the morning of my departure for the coup de grâce. When the flight attendant announced the final boarding call, I gripped Mom's arms and, as tears streamed down my face, cried: "Promise me you'll come to China! I'm not getting on this plane until you do!"

What could she do?

At age fifty-two, Mom applied for her first passport and sent off for her first visa. And that May, she made her first flight across the Pacific. Solo.

THE MORNING OF my mother's arrival felt like the eve of a blind date. I scrubbed the walls, polished the floors, and filled big bowls with fresh fruit, scripting where we'd go and what we'd do those two weeks. It had never been just the two of us. When I was growing up, my family either did things as a foursome or in couples, with Mom pairing off with my sister and me wandering off with Dad. When Barbara left for college, we became a happy threesome. But now it would be only Mom and me. What if we ran out of things to talk about? (I jotted down a list.) What if she had nothing to eat? (A woman of habit, she subsisted on Rice Krispies for breakfast, Granny Smith apples and rice cakes for lunch, and tomato-and-cheese sandwiches for supper. How would she handle turtle juice and thousand-year-old duck eggs?)

What if we didn't get along?

I ran down the street to my favorite florist, a gruff man with slicked-back hair who puffed on smokes while sprucing his roses and pruning his tulips. I explained the occasion and he gathered an armload of Easter lilies, tied them with a long pale ribbon, and hosed them down with a fruity fragrance. Then I darted into the street for a taxi and headed to the airport, my stomach quivering with nerves. An eight-layer mosh pit thrashed alongside the arrival gate. Chin up and elbows out, I waded through and thrust myself against the barricade. Then time began to stretch like Arik's hand-pulled noodles, the faces of the incoming passengers melting and merging as they shuffled past—until a familiar one magically appeared. Gripping her suitcase with clenched white knuckles, my mother peered cautiously around the gate.

"Mom!" I called out, waving the lilies like a flag. *"Mom!"*

She couldn't hear me above the Mandarin din, though, so I jutted backward and squirmed through the crowds toward the end of the gate, hollering her name. By the time I made it, she was already there, her back toward me. "Mom," I said, placing a hand on her shoulder. She whirled around to face me, her eyes swollen with anxiety. We fell into each other's arms and suddenly I was crying, overwhelmed by the connection I shared with only this person. She stroked my hair with soft, smooth hands and rocked me back and forth. When at last we parted, calmness had replaced our fears. Slipping her hand in mine, she smiled and said: "Where to?"

MY MOTHER ARRIVED my ninth month in China. By that point, shish kebabbed scorpions, sidewalk beauty parlors, and people sounding as though they were hacking up thirty-pound hairballs had become my daily landscape. The only sight that got me gawking anymore was goofy-looking *laowai* getting off a tour bus. Ironically, the person who reopened my senses to Beijing's marvelous chaos was the same woman who watched me discover mudpies and roly-polies.

"Look at that little boy!" she exclaimed, pointing. "His pants are split wide open."

"That's so he can go to the bathroom."

She stared at me in bewilderment. "Isn't that what diapers are for?"

"Diapers are wasteful. Besides, he's more comfortable that way," I replied, Chinese logic having become my own.

"His little butt cheeks look so cute hanging out there like that!"

I looked. They did. I'd forgotten that.

Moreover, I extracted a certain pride showing my mother the 250-ton marble carved with dragons undulating through clouds in the Forbidden City or the fifty-five-foot Maitreya Buddha carved from a single piece of sandalwood at the Yonghe Gong Lamasery. I may never have brought home a suitable boy or studied anything that would pay my rent, but I sure could haggle with a Beijing street vendor and nab a good cab fare! I failed algorithms in Precalculus, but listen to me rattle off Maoist theory!

I also prodded my mother in basic etiquette like tapping two fingers on the table when the waitress poured our tea or holding objects with both hands and bowing slightly when passing them on to someone else. I grabbed *her* hand before crossing busy streets and reminded *her* to say *xie xie* when someone was kind. At times, it seemed she had temporarily transferred her maternal powers on to me during our embrace at the airport. But more often—like when we picked up the sex talk we started on that laundry night years ago—she felt like a friend.

THE FIRST THING Liu and Yuer said when they learned my mother was coming for a visit was: "Oh, good! Now we get to have a real Mexican meal!" They'd heard me pine for chicken enchiladas so long, the manna of my ancestors had taken on an almost mythical quality. Not having the heart to tell them Mom had never made a *mole* in her life, I called the week before she left to warn her that my friends expected a home-cooked meal.

"A what?!" She cringed audibly.

"They want to try authentic Mexican cuisine."

She thought for a moment. "I guess I could bring them a can of refried beans."

"And maybe one of those Old El Paso spice packs."

The only Mexican food I'd ever made was the co-op kind: burritos stuffed with tempeh and spinach and a dollop of low-fat yogurt on the side. Mom, meanwhile, had shoved all the dishes she was once required to make into the far recesses of her memory. You'd think the Mexican in at least one of us would have channeled through once we'd piled stacks of tortillas and cans of jalapeños, beans, and enchilada sauce on the kitchen counter, but we just looked at each other helplessly and squinted for the directions.

Fortunately, my friends didn't know the difference. Using their tortillas as plate covers, they happily picked out the chicken fajita filling with their chopsticks.

BUILT IN THE early eighteenth century by Emperor Kangxi, Yuanmingyuan was once considered the Chinese Versailles, an elegant palace of more than two hundred pavilions and temples built around lakes connected by marble footbridges. The French and British destroyed it in 1860, however, to make the Chinese acquiesce in the Second Opium War. Only the stone-and-marble foundation skeleton remained of its imperial splendor, but the sparse crowds made it a great spot for picnics. Toward the end of Mom's visit, I packed some sandwiches and melons and took her there. We spread out a blanket in a wooded area alongside a pond lined with willow trees. When our conversation reached a natural pause, I asked the question that had gnawed at me for nine years: "How did my grandmother die?"

Mom took the question in stride, capping her orange juice before replying: "She killed herself."

My entire body numbed. "Why?"

"She had five kids before she turned twenty-five. That's reason enough."

Mom was only three at the time, so she retained no memory of the event. The little she knew, she pieced together over time, through snippets of conversations whispered behind closed doors. It happened in the middle of the day. Barbara's husband was still at his barbershop. She tucked the children into the bed they shared—an old mattress on a hardwood floor—and kissed them one by one. Then she walked into the only room with a door and locked it behind her. A shot rang out moments later. The eldest daughter pounded on the door and, when she heard no response, gathered her brothers and sisters and herded them next door, where *Tía* and *Tío* lived (the ones I thought to be my grandparents).

Theories abounded, of course. She did it because she was depressed. Because she was pregnant again. Because the father of her next child was not her husband. Because her husband was unfaithful. Her own mother declared that she didn't kill herself at all, that someone slipped into her bedroom and shot her. Police didn't fully investigate homicides back in the 1950s, though, at least not those of impoverished Mexican women. Even if they left no note and said no good-byes.

Soon after, the kids got doled out to their mother's sisters while their father remarried and had an additional seven children. *Tía* and *Tío*, who had no children of their own, inherited Mom and two of her brothers and later took in the twins a neighbor had abandoned. Though saintly in their actions, they were mercilessly strict. Mom couldn't wait to escape that patriarchal household. Then Dad came along: happy-go-lucky, unpretentious, and eager to support her career—the antithesis of Mexican machismo. His music took them to some of the whitest lands in America—West Virginia, New Hampshire, and Annapolis, Maryland—before they settled back down in Corpus with my sister and me.

It must be tough raising biracial children. Whose language do you use? What music do you play, and which foods do you prepare? Finding a balance, of course, is the best strategy, but whatever my mother's efforts, I took little interest in learning about my Mexican roots growing up—probably because white people seemed so much more interesting. Everyone on TV was white; the characters in my books and magazines were white; the musicians who packed into my father's garage for late night jams were white. I didn't even consider myself Mexican until a high school counselor pointed out that a Hispanic *H* on my transcript would get me a lot further with scholarship committees than a white *W*. When I made it to UT with full funding and started meeting "real Latinos" (that is, those who bore the hardships of their skin color), however, I realized I'd reaped only the benefits of being a minority and none of the drawbacks. Guilt overwhelmed me. Had I snatched away scholarships from a *real* Mexican kid out there? If so, what should I do? Give back the money I received? Take out a loan? Transfer to a cheaper school?

I resolved instead to become the *H* emblazoned on my transcripts. I started calling myself a Chicana and adorning myself with what I perceived to be Latino symbols (decorating my room with images of Frida Kahlo and the Virgen de Guadalupe; reading Sandra Cisneros; getting a Colombian lover; stocking up on Selena tapes; drinking lots of margaritas) and doing what I could for *La Raza* (working at the minority recruitment center at the Office of Admissions; taking classes on Chicano politics; teaching English to Mexican kids). I changed my white-bread middle name of Ann to Elizondo and made everyone use it. Despite my liberal views on abortion and gay rights, I delved back into Catholicism.

Yet even then, I hadn't considered mine a culture worth serious exploration, choosing instead the "exotic" worlds of the East.

As I looked around that imperial garden in which my mother and I were sitting, it occurred to me that perhaps we weren't so terribly far removed from what had transpired in that ancient country. Though I would never compare any event to China's outrageously destructive Cultural Revolution, the United States had found its own way of eliminating Mao's Four Olds of old ideas, old culture, old customs, and old habits. Like whipping slaves for worshiping their African pantheon in the eighteenth century. Like "civilizing" indigenous youth by taking them from their tribes and throwing them into boarding schools, cutting off their hair, denying them sweat lodges, and beating them for holding ceremonies in the nineteenth century. Like punishing my mother for speaking Spanish to her brother in class in the twentieth century.

But those, of course, are the extreme cases. First- and second-generation immigrants are often so eager (or desperate) to "fit in" to mainstream (white) America, many shed their Four Olds willingly and raise their children on English and macaroni and cheese. Those who don't risk losing their children as soon as they hit grade school and get teased for their funny accents, clothes, and lunches. And often it doesn't take even *that* long. Kids realize at a very early age who the "privileged" of society are, and we do everything within our power to fit in, be it Anglicizing our names or begging our mothers to straighten our kinky hair. I certainly never respected my native Spanish-speaking peers' struggles in mastering a second language in elementary school. On the contrary, being an "ESL student" seemed synonymous with being remedial, disabled, or just plain dumb, and I treated them accordingly.

Never knowing that my own mother had once been in their shoes.

Or that she sacrificed so that I wouldn't have to be.

23. SUNSET OVER CHINA

BY JUNE, THE schizophrenia of editing my colleagues' "happy news, please" stories by day and reading ominous books by exiles by night had taken its toll: My thoughts had become thoroughly, hopelessly muddled. This is actually a well-documented phenomenon. Foreign correspondents joke that if you go to China for one month, you'll write a book; six months, a long article; a year, barely a letter. The Chinese even derive a perverse sense of pride from their complexity.

"Of course Westerners don't understand us," Liu sniffed when I griped about it. "You don't, either, and probably never will."

"Never ever?"

"No. You're too strong-minded. Everything you see in Chinese culture runs counter to your nature."

I mulled over that comment a long while, then composed a list of what I might need to change about myself to continue living in China with inner peace.

Stop shuddering when people clear out their chest cavities. Build higher stamina for turtle soup, fish heads, and other *hen hao chi*. Refrain from glaring at peasants who sell freshly killed kittens in plastic bags. Be more practical and pragmatic—why not sell executed prisoners' corneas?—and less spontaneous and passionate. Hide emotions, but dwell in sentimentalism. Save everyone's face. Compile good *guanxi*. Brush off compliments with a self-effacing *nali*. Sing more karaoke. Don't judge those who think there is no persecution in Xinjiang, Inner Mongolia, or Tibet. Look beyond the Tiananmen Square Rebellion/Incident/Massacre. Disregard politics. Quit questioning. Embrace socialism with Chinese characteristics. Focus on family and finances. Accept fate. Find center. Chill.

Liu was right. I couldn't do it—and for the reason she cited. China had caused me to question so much about myself and what it meant to be a journalist, a human rights advocate, a citizen of a democracy, and an American that it was frightening me. By that point, I was losing arguments on what I valued most, including the right to an open media. My foremost antagonist in this realm was not Chinese but, interestingly enough, a former Soviet. Sergei was a handsome man who lived in my compound with his wife, Zhenya, and ten-year-old daughter, Masha. They moved to Beijing from Leningrad in the late 1980s because Zhenya (who was half Chinese) got a job teaching Russian at the university next door. I spent many a Sunday afternoon with them, trading an hour's worth of English tutoring with Masha for conversational practice with Zhenya or heated debates with Sergei. Although he seemed progressive in other ways, he could not fathom the point of a free press.

"To make the People aware of what is happening! To give the People a voice! To expose injustices so that the People can unite and create social change!" I'd cry.

"But what happens when the corrupters are powerful and the people are poor and helpless?" he'd ask.

"The People rally together and make Revolution!"

"Who the hell wants to go through that mess? People would be much happier if they didn't even know what was happening in the first place. If you can't do a thing to change your situation, why know at all?"

Hearing such comments from a man whose nation had won those very freedoms just seven years before completely unnerved me. But while I refused to believe open media was anything less than a fundamental human right, I found it increasingly difficult to rebut his arguments the longer I lived in China.

Equally disturbing was when I caught myself engaging in behaviors I'd condemned only ten months prior. My colleagues' practice of running stories and cartoons from Western publications without permission had once been the catalyst for many a tantrum, but that late night they asked me to take the call of an uppity editor from a British tabloid, I actually defended it.

"Pardon me, but we just discovered that your publication reprinted one of our cartoons!" he exclaimed.

"Yeah, so?"

"Well, I call because, you see, we have laws about this sort of thing. It is not permissible!"

"Uh-huh," I murmured as Yuer handed me a broadsheet that needed to be edited *hen kuai*.

"Do you plan on paying our cartoonist for his work?"

"Probably not. Listen, can you call back? We're on deadline."

"I apologize for my insistence, but really—your publication plagiarized! Who is in charge over there? Let me speak with someone else."

"This is China. Call the Party," I instructed before hanging up with a flourish.

MY TENURE AT the paper culminated as it commenced, with a two-and-a-half-hour banquet. Moments after our waitress bounded off to the kitchen with a notepad of our requests, another returned with our still-breathing main course for the ceremonial nod of approval. The snake, upward of three feet in length, thrashed madly in her clenched fist, but the turtle remained tucked inside its shell. We protested. Smiling broadly, the waitress removed a hairpin and jabbed it up the turtle's rump. Its arms, legs, and head shot out.

"Hao, hao," we murmured, and dismissed her with a wave. I tried to picture how the cooks would prepare the turtle and decided they would shish kebab its little stumps. Mmmm.

As my colleagues began their usual banter of whose home province served which tastier dish, I reflected on the year I had spent with them. Sure, we'd written our fair share of stories about the Fifteenth Party Congress and Beijing University's latest class on Deng Xiaoping theory. Yes, the Censor Board rejected our groundbreaking article about Chinese lesbians. But we did manage to get in interviews with three fairly controversial feminist writers and an exposé on the discrimination faced by teachers at rural village schools. Though it took some serious prodding, we even admitted that the women on China's Olympic swim team had deeper voices and hairier chests than normal.

And because I had seen the raw talent of reporters like Liu, I'd taken to defending them, too. When the Beijing bureau chief of a major U.S. paper scoffed to me, "You can hardly call them journalists. They accept bribes and kickbacks and favors and are totally corrupt," I shot back, "And they also live four to a room and brush their teeth in a trough. They only have access to hot showers for three hours a day, and it's so crowded, they sometimes share the same spigot!"

He countered, "The point is that their stories are not legit," but to me, the real point was that this Ivy League reporter had an apartment complete with ceiling-to-floor bookshelves, a spacious living room, dining room, two bedrooms, a cook, a housekeeper, a nanny, and a company car in a country where millions huddled in shacks. Of course, I wanted my colleagues to rise above corruptive practices, too, but it's probably a lot easier to pontificate ethics when you've got an expense account. Chinese journalists aren't trying to be martyrs; they are workers hustling for a taste of the "good life"—and they are the first ones to admit it. As a colleague once put it: "Our moral system hasn't yet been established in China, so we don't really have a sense of right versus wrong. If there is a loophole in our system, we'll take advantage of it. This is endemic to our society as a whole, but you see it more in journalists because we are public figures."

But where did that leave me? While I never figured out whether to "go native" in the Chinese newsroom or stick by my Western principles, I did learn that there is only one real way to change things there. Lao Ye said it best: "You won't get anywhere by being arrogant and demanding information or trying to change the way we do things. The best way to approach China is through quiet influence."

Halfway through our incredible meal, a waitress carried in a silver platter of shot glasses filled with dark red liquid. Chinese liqueur was usually red, so I didn't think much of it until Lao

Ye gallantly proposed a toast to me and we raised the glasses to our lips. Then it occurred to me that the liquid did not look very smooth. In fact, it was borderline chunky.

"*Zhe shi shenme?*" I whispered to Yuer. What is this?

"Snake blood," she said matter-of-factly, and gulped down her glass.

I closed my eyes and shuddered. Granted, I had digested a lot of crazy things that year, but no way could I go back to calling myself a vegetarian if I drank the freshly squeezed essence of life. Greenpeace would revoke my membership. The People for the Ethical Treatment of Animals would put me on their hit list. This was worse than eating veal.

On the other hand, Chinese had been drinking snake blood for at least one thousand years for its cooling properties, as a way to purify their bodies. Moreover, this was my last banquet with my colleagues. How could I refuse? So I took a deep breath, tilted my head back, and chugged the blood. It burned like vodka and left a trail of residue. Just then, a burp escaped. A primal one, with an aftertaste. My colleagues looked at me in surprise. Smiles crept across their faces as I unsheathed my chopsticks and gave them a good rub, like a butcher sharpening her knives.

"*Hao chi,*" I said nonchalantly. Tasty.

EARLY EACH MORNING, just after sunrise, Beijingers amass upon all available stretches of green—including medians—to perform their daily exercises. In the park surrounding the canals by my compound, septuagenarians gathered beneath the willow trees to practice tai chi as though rehearsing for a yogi's ballet. Opera fans reenacted their favorite scenes inside a pagoda. Bearded men rolled metallic balls in their palms beneath magnolia trees, focusing intensely on unfixed points in space. Old men in Mao jackets aired out their finches by hanging their bamboo cages from tree branches. Fathers and sons played *xiang qi*—Chinese chess—atop tree stumps. Power walkers charged down the dirt trail forward one lap and backward the next. Friends played badminton with no nets. Couples ballroom-danced with no music. Loners threw themselves against the trees the way the *babushki* did with birch branches back in Russia, only in reverse.

Soon after my departure, some of these early morning enthusiasts became the target of intense political persecution. Though they did little more than meditate and exercise in quiet unison, the Falun Gong would be deemed an "evil cult" and be banned on charges of "corrupting minds" and "posing a threat to the public order." Tens of thousands of practitioners would be arrested for holding peaceful demonstrations, hundreds would claim to have been tortured in prison, and dozens would die in captivity.

But in the early summer of 1998, the *yang ge* dancers drew the most attention. These sixty-to-eighty-year-old women dressed in matching pantsuits and waved little red flags as they pranced around a live ensemble of cymbals, drums, and an *erhu*, or Chinese violin. *Yang ge* dancing dates back to the Revolution, when comrades celebrated military victories and called for bountiful harvests through performance. The sassier dancers alternately puffed on smokes and hacked.

These were the people I most wanted to see that last day in Beijing—the ones who would keep on meditating, exercising, singing, and dancing long after I'd returned home and who would be there when I returned someday. I stole to the canals at dawn and stayed until the last *yang ge* lady left. At lunchtime, I headed over to Arik's. As I zigzagged through the mutton grills and the Uighur boys declared, "Ah luv youuuuuuuuuuu," I wondered what it would feel like to regain anonymity, to not be greeted with choruses of *"laowai, laowai, laowai,"* to not be pointed and giggled at by children, to not receive invitations to lecture at universities just for speaking my native language fluently—to not be anything special at all.

Arik had scrounged up a camera from somewhere and snapped photos of me with the Uighur women and their kids inside his new café. Arik's dive used to be the grottiest on the block, but he had recently amassed enough RMB to tear down the old and throw up the new, which he coined "Alibaba's." That afternoon, we shared a *pijiu* and watched Beijing out his window: the bicycle waves, the overstuffed buses, the on-slaughts of taxis, the peasants who transported everything from produce to human waste atop wooden carts, the vendors, the *jiaozi* and *baozi* ladies.

"Will you miss this?" he asked.

So much came over me then—a nostalgia not only for people but for sights, sounds, and smells—words would have cheapened a response. So I nodded. He smiled. "I would, too."

From Arik's, I went to meet Yuer and Liu at our favorite Sichuan restaurant for a final spicy supper. Feeling a panicked need to get out every last question, I started interrogating my friends around our circular table.

"Tell me one more time why you don't care about political prisoners like Wei Jingsheng and Harry Wu."

"They have too many martyr complexes," Yuer offered.

"All countries have rules. If you follow the rules, you will be fine. If you break them, you have to pay the consequences," Liu reasoned. "Dissidents really aren't so important to us any-more. If people believed what they had to say, they would have more followers. But they don't. We just aren't interested."

They were right, of course. Chinese dissidents probably have as much (or, rather, little) mainstream support in their country as prisoners like Leonard Peltier and Mumia Abu-Jamal do in mine. But that didn't make it any more palatable. "Then why do I believe them?" I asked, as much to myself as to them.

"Because you trust those who agree with you. And you think that Chinese who speak positively about their government are Party members or spies or just plain stupid," Liu replied.

Not really knowing how to respond to that, I changed the subject. "And what about the Tibetans? Don't you think they should be free?"

"Chinese like harmony. We don't want to separate," Yuer said. "And you wouldn't, either. How would America like to give up Alaska?"

"Plus, we believe we are doing some good for the Tibetans. We pulled them out of the Dark Ages," Liu said as she ground out her cigarette, then smiled. "Of course, that's just me being arrogant. I should go ask them what they want."

"And democratic elections?"

"What is it really going to change if we have new leaders?" Yuer asked.

"Chinese are more concerned with reality—about our families, our homes, and our jobs," Liu philosophized. "Elections are a symbolic gesture, which is why you're so caught up in them. Americans are idealistic, but we Chinese are very practical people."

It is hard to hear what you perceive to be propaganda from those you perceive to be friends. You wonder: Do they not trust me enough to confide their feelings? Or have they been conditioned over time to say these things (or worse yet, think them)?

As though reading my mind, Yuer suddenly asked: "Why do Americans think they know so much more about our situation than we do? It's our country!"

She was right. How did we?

Chinese often spoke about life in terms of cycles. Kingdoms rose, empires fell, and the process repeated itself again and again. China had crested the world throughout much of its five-thousand-year history, just as it had been dragged through the undercurrent. Many believed they had been spiraling downward in the past century or two but were in the process of making a cyclical comeback. Similarly, they thought the United States—which had been riding the summit for the past half century—would soon be heading toward the valleys.

"China has been so poor for so long, we have to rely on our economy to pull us out," Yuer said. "The issues that concern America—open elections, free media, democracy—will matter to us later, once we have reached economic stability."

It occurred to me then that I didn't want to spend my last evening with these wonderful women talking about politics. So the topic changed to everything but—ambitions, thoughts, plans, dreams. Both Yuer and Liu were applying to graduate programs overseas, both to escape the paper and hopefully to work at a prestigious foreign venture someday. For Liu, this symbolized power and success; for Yuer, a way to meet interesting people and possibly travel. Though both were married and in their mid-twenties, neither saw children in their near futures.

"Since we can only have one, Chinese have to make sure the timing is perfect," Liu said. "It would be best to have them in America so they could be citizens. But either way, we must have savings for their schooling and tutoring. It is so expensive nowadays."

Liu needed to meet her husband soon after dinner, so we

said good-bye in front of the *danwei*, where staffers did their morning exercises. My friend was so strong and proud and confident, I knew her many ambitions would materialize. When I called out her full name as she headed into the street for a cab, she turned around with a cocky grin. "Nice tones. But you can still call me Evil Fish."

Holding hands, Yuer and I walked out into the balmy night, reminiscing over our year together. Shopping for her wedding *qipao*. Playing mah-jongg, singing karaoke, making pork-and-celery *jiaozi*. Hiking, biking, eating, drinking, laughing, being. I introduced Yuer to cappuccinos, belly dancing, and tampons; she showed me acupuncture, shadow puppets, and how to deal with Lao Ye and Lao Chen in a more "Chinese" fashion.

The sun had long since set by the time we reached Tiananmen some three hours later. We joined the families and couples strolling across the square in the moonlight. It was perfectly still but for the laughter of children. So many events had occurred upon that forty-hectare stretch of pavement: the first calls for democracy by students demonstrating against the Treaty of Versailles in 1919; the anti-Japanese protests of 1935; the rallies that kicked off the Cultural Revolution in 1966; the carnage of 1989; the celebration of Hong Kong's return to the mainland in 1997. So much hope, anger, blood, tears, and triumph. But the majority of nights fell upon the pavement without occurrence, much like my last night there with Yuer.

We walked the full expanse of Tiananmen in silence. When we reached the northernmost end, Yuer stopped but I continued toward the portrait of Mao Zedong flanked by red banners that read LONG LIVE THE PEOPLE'S REPUBLIC OF CHINA and LONG LIVE THE GREAT UNION BETWEEN THE PEOPLES OF THE WORLD. I paused for a moment beneath the spot from which Mao once declared: "The Chinese people have finally stood up," then headed toward the Forbidden City, which had closed for the night. Yuer trailed behind.

Through the inchwide crack between the emperor's high red doors, I caught my last glimpse of the palace. The marble bridges adorned with carved torches. The curved roofs with upcurled eaves. Classical texts describe this as a place where "earth and sky meet, where four seasons merge, where wind and rain are gathered in, and where yin and yang are in harmony." Yet during its five centuries as the emperor's primary residency, most Chinese were not even allowed to touch its walls. The emperors must have seemed invincible back then. But their reigns had since passed, as inevitably as history itself.

The night had grown so beautiful, still, and final, it overwhelmed me. I felt myself fall against the bolted doors and slide down to the cold pavement. Within an instant, Yuer was at my side. She held me close as I began to weep.

REVOLUTION IS NOT A BED OF ROSES. . . .

A REVOLUTION IS A STRUGGLE TO THE DEATH

BETWEEN THE FUTURE AND THE PAST.

—*Fidel Alejandro Castro Ruz*

—

AFTER THAT NIGHT with Yuer in Tiananmen, I hit the road with hopes of finding a new life plan. But absolute freedom can be as paralyzing as confinement when you don't know what you want. I spent June and July exploring Mongolia, Uzbekistan, and Kyrgyzstan by jeep, horse, and foot and made it to Moscow in time to catch the Rolling Stones in concert. My old stomping grounds had changed more in my two-year absence than Corpus had in twenty. There were gleaming new shopping malls, richly restored cathedrals, Internet cafés, and trendy bars and restaurants staffed by *devushki* who were downright cordial. People looked better, too, more stylish and sophisticated. But while thrilling to reunite with friends like Elena and Valera, there wasn't terribly much for me to *do* there. I filled the days designing a press kit for a newspaper for the homeless and volunteering at a soup kitchen, wondering, "What next?"

Then, on August 17, Russia's currency collapsed. Bank lines grew longer as the exchange rate of the ruble plummeted further with each passing day. When rumors started spreading about ATM machines closing and Elena cut a hole in their mattress to store their American dollars, it seemed time to go. After a pit stop in East Berlin, I flew out to Istanbul with grand ambitions of selling carpets by day and belly dancing by night. Five days into my stay, however, my passport, credit cards, money, traveler's checks, and driver's license disappeared from the thigh pouch in which they'd been sealed for months. Exactly how remains a mystery—the police said someone probably threw a powder in my eyes that knocked me out while they mugged me—but I took it as a sign that my destiny awaited elsewhere.

Colombia, to be precise.

That's right. Whether out of love, loneliness, or just plain stupidity, I decided to give Mario—the full-blooded, soccer-playing, coffee-picking, sign-of-the-crossing Latino who decimated my heart—another chance. He had visited me in Asia before I departed and left an invitation burning in my ears: "Come to Bogotá and we'll open a coffeehouse together." You can't travel with a man on your mind: Mario so consumed my thoughts, I started passing up world-renowned museums to sit in Internet cafés and have cybersex. Resolving that the only way to ward off life's regrets is to pursue any and all question marks, I flew out to Colombia and discovered a stunning country locked in civil war: roads blocked, military posted, eyes untrusting and fearful. But this very real human drama was overshadowed by the one that promptly erupted between Mario and me. He'd drink, I'd yell, we'd fight, he'd leave, I'd cry, he'd return, we'd make love, and so forth. Looking back, I believe he *wanted* me to hate him, but nothing he did worked— not even abandoning me on a junkie-infested beach in Cartagena at one in the morning. In fact, the worse he treated me, the more determined I became to stay. It was such a beautifully fucked-up story, I wanted to see how he'd hurt me next.

So when Mario suggested we both move back to Austin to

"start over again," I agreed. I got a job at the Associated Press, signed a lease, and happily prepared our love nest, envisioning late night candlelit dinners, lazy Sunday brunches, and sex whenever I wanted. He arrived a few weeks later with plans of enrolling in culinary school (presumably to learn how to bake our future café's pastries). But our first night together in my new apartment, he sat me down, looked deep into my eyes, and said: "Stephanie, this isn't going to work. . . ."

That's right. He dumped me. Again.

And after my contract ended with AP, I wound up back in Corpus Christi. At the washed-up age of twenty-five. Living at home with my parents. Lacking even the wheels to go cruising through the parking lot at Taco Bell.

Then came the fortuitous call from my good friend Machi, who was back in town for the holidays. Machi was the sort of Texan who wore cowboy boots under secondhand Levi's and drove a beat-up truck to yoga class. We first met at a conference for Hispanic journalists back in college, where we bonded over our substandard Spanish. She'd made amends over the years, however, winning a fellowship to study in Mexico and then immersing herself in the Latino community for her documentaries. We talked for hours that night, and before we hung up, she brought up the rapidly approaching end of the millennium. How was I bringing in 2000?

"Probably watching the Dick Clark special." I sighed. "You?"

"I'm thinking about going to Cuba."

"But . . . how would you get there?"

"Through Mexico."

"But . . . where would you stay?"

"In somebody's house."

"But . . . it's illegal!"

"Only if you get caught."

"But . . ." I stopped as it dawned on me that I had been jetting halfway around the world to see red when it was only ninety miles away. "Can I come, too?"

THOUGH I HAD lived within 150 miles of Mexico most of my life and had family in Monterrey, I only vaguely knew of its border towns, which—from my limited vantage point—consisted primarily of sock-and-sandaled tourists haggling over souvenirs, senior citizens hoarding cheap prescription drugs, and college kids slamming tequila shots. So it was a treat to experience the country's interior as Machi and I worked our way south toward Cuba by bus, from the frenetic pace of Mexico City to the tranquillity of Tepoztlán. Yet being around *puros mexicanos*—real Mexicans—made me feel grossly incompetent. Every word I had ever uttered in Russian or Mandarin had seemed like a trophy to me, something I had sought, studied, and conquered. In Spanish, however, my speech felt pocked with failures, as though everything I managed to say were an admission of what more I could not. Though I had invested time in the language that year, studying from workbooks and conversing with my *tías*, I dreaded using it—largely out of fear of the direction a conversation with a *mexicano* might take. "*¿Tu mamá es mexicana? Híjale,* what the hell happened to *you?*"

Machi, on the other hand, was eager to use the Spanish she'd learned over the past few years. She became our spokeswoman in virtually every transaction, from small talk to business negotiations, while I cowered behind, wishing a Kyrgyz shepherd would ramble by so I'd have someone to talk to, feeling more like an *extranjera*—or foreigner—than ever before.

After a few days of wandering around, Machi bargained a great deal on airline tickets at a travel agency in Cuernavaca and we jetted off to Havana. Somewhere over the Gulf of Mexico, paranoia struck. True, upward of fifty thousand Americans sneak into Cuba illegally every year, but it does entail a degree of risk. Under the Trading with the Enemy Act, any American caught spending money in Communist Cuba without Uncle Sam's explicit permission could—in theory—be slapped with fines of up to $250,000 and ten years in prison. We were also a little nervous about losing our passports. We couldn't expect much sympathy from the U.S. Interests Section (America's version of an embassy in Havana) if we weren't supposed to be there in the first place, could we? And what if we ran out of money? American traveler's checks and credit cards don't work in Cuba. We might have to sell our belongings (or our bodies) in a gutter somewhere.

By the time we landed at José Martí International, our nerves had seriously frayed. Machi's personal breaking point came when the airline attendant bade everyone *hasta luego* when they exited the plane—except her. "She took one look at me and said, *'Ten cuidado'*—Be careful!" she hissed. "What did she mean by that?!"

As we got in line at passport control, my entire body began to tremble. Cuban control officers supposedly didn't stamp U.S. passports when asked nicely, but what if mine misunderstood? Or asked for a bribe? Or had a vendetta against Americans? When our turn came, I pushed Machi ahead. She took a deep breath and, with a toss of her silky black hair, marched up to the window and relinquished her blue booklet. *Blam-blam* went the control man. Did he stamp it, did he stamp it? Machi grabbed her papers and disappeared through a little white door without looking back.

Great. My turn. My stomach now churning upon itself, I approached the booth and handed my papers to the officer, who had his back turned to me. *"Por favor, no pone un . . . ,"* I began the carefully rehearsed phrase. Then he turned around. His eyes were amber, his chin was cleft, his skin was a deep shade of copper. I smiled shyly. He gave a sideways grin. Then his hands—hidden beneath the counter—made that horrifying *blam-blam* sound. I hyperventilated. Did he stamp it, did he stamp it?

"No te preocupes, mi amor," he whispered as he returned my unmarked passport. Don't worry about it, honey. Then he winked and buzzed me into one of the few remaining bastions of communism in the world. It smelled of salt and sea and sex.

Before leaving South Texas, I blew $70 in long-distance calls to Cuba tracking down some guy named Jorge who—according to a friend of a friend—rented out a room in his house to foreigners at a fraction of the cost of a hotel. When we showed up on his doorstep in Centro Habana that afternoon, however, he had forgotten our reservation and rented our room out to some Swedes.

"Where are we supposed to stay?" we wailed.

"No problema," he promised, then shifted his eyes into the street as a caramel-skinned, spandex-clad woman in her early forties sauntered by. "Cecilia! Do you have any room for these girls?"

"¿Sí, cómo no?" she replied. Of course.

Machi and I exchanged glances. Could we really just go home with a random passerby? Seeing few alternatives, we followed her to a three-story nineteenth-century house regally designed with high ceilings, carved wooden doors, ornate light fixtures, and grilled ironwork but modestly kept with humble furniture and peeling paint. Vintage Chinese bicycles leaned against the outer wall of the courtyard while two floors' worth of neighbors' laundry dripped dry from above. Cecilia opened a padlock hanging on a door and let us peek inside. For $12 a night, she offered a king-size bed, a dresser, a vase of plastic roses, and a bathroom with a sliver of soap. While we deliberated, she darted off to the kitchen and returned with two steaming glasses of coffee. *"Es negro como la piel y dulce como una muchacha,"* she quipped. It's as black as skin and sweet as a girl.

It tasted so good, it was also the deal maker. "We'll take it."

After stashing our stuff away, we ventured out to explore our new 'hood. With the exception of a 1956 Chevrolet carcass rotting on a curb, there wasn't a car in sight, enabling us to walk directly in the street instead of just along it. The residential area quickly gave way to a commercial strip where a bakery featured bread loaves as long and wide as the pickets of a fence, and a pharmacy sold medicine bottles with handwritten wrappers glued upon them. A dark, musty warehouse served as a melancholic farmer's market, where vendors sat listlessly behind bins of scrawny yuccas, plantains, guavas, and chilies and a butcher sold ham by the slice. Across the street, a long-lashed woman in a window cried out, *"Cerrrr-veeeee-ʒaaaa!"* until a customer stopped by. She whipped out a glass, poured him some beer, and plunked it on the sill; he chugged it down, wiped his lip, slipped her some pesos, and continued down the street as she washed the glass, wiped it dry, and resumed her barter cry: *"Cerrrr-veeeee-ʒaaaa!"* Another vendor—a gorgeous old man in a beret—had scrawled his croquette menu on a piece of cardboard with a

Nike decal stuck on it. When I pointed at the brazen capitalist symbol, he grinned good-naturedly and said: *"Es bonito."* It's pretty.

Up ahead glimmered the Atlantic Ocean, bordered by the famous stretch of limestone boulevard known as the Malecon. Locals strolled upon it in droves, many wearing T-shirts depicting a sullen Elián González crouched behind a chain-link fence. (The child refugee had been plucked from the sea two months before and was still living with his Miami relatives.) Lovers tangled into impassioned embraces while children dangled their legs over the seawall and portly women sold roasted peanuts inside rolled-up newspapers. We passed some fishermen just as one got a nibble and cheered him on as he reeled in a foot-long fish. After ripping the hook from the fish's gaping mouth, he jumped atop the seawall and treated the harbor to a victory dance punctuated with an energetic pelvic thrust.

We hadn't been on the Malecon five minutes when two guys our age asked to join us. Mine, Raul, introduced himself as a saxophonist from Camagüey and politely inquired about me. Uncertain how American journalists would be received here—particularly in light of the Elián fiasco—Machi and I had selected new identities on the plane ride over: Canadian grad students from Toronto and "some town out west you've probably never heard of." This wasn't the first time I'd lied about my nationality: After getting attacked by that *babushka* in the Moscow subway, I'd often claimed a Mexican heritage. That alibi wouldn't have worked in a Spanish-speaking nation, of course, but I thought my country's northern neighbor would make an equally good cover—until the interrogations started. Raul's brother, as it turned out, had recently opened a salsa discotheque in Toronto. Had I heard of it? What type of neighborhood was it in? What other good clubs were in the area? He planned on applying for a Canadian visa himself: What were Canada's immigration laws concerning Cubans? Could he enroll in a university right away? What about health care?

I answered his questions as vaguely as possible and then tossed one back at him: Where could I buy one of those Elián T-shirts?

"Buy one?!" He laughed. "Nobody buys them. They are a gift from, you know . . ." He stroked his chin as though it had just sprouted a beard—Cuba-speak for Fidel Castro.

"Canadians think Elián should return home to Cuba," I volunteered.

"I don't," he said. "There is nothing for him to eat here. There is no freedom. There is no future. He's better off in Miami."

His frankness surprised me, but when I said as much, he shrugged. "Cubans aren't encouraged to talk with foreigners, but we do it anyway."

"Isn't that kind of risky?"

"How else are we supposed to know what's going on in the world? Our papers are censored; our media is controlled." He paused to nod at a police officer standing a few feet away. "You see that cop? If you told him that I was bothering you, he would take me to jail. Foreigners are treated better than Cubans—in our own country."

This was the open sort of conversation I'd dreamed of in Beijing, but having it my first hour in Havana made me nervous. I glanced back at the cop. Could he hear us?

"But these days will soon be over," Raul continued. "There is already a capitalist revolution under way. It won't be much longer before things change for good. I just hope I'm in Canada when it does. So, what do *you* think about Cuba?"

By that point, we had reached the Hotel Deauville, where

friends of Machi's were staying. As she breezed into the lobby to find them, I turned to Raul. What was happening here? Had the Committees for the Defense of the Revolution (Castro's neighborhood watchdog groups) and the state security system caused Cubans to distrust one another as much as the Cultural Revolution had the Chinese and the KGB had the Russians, making foreigners a safe, sympathetic ear? Or did Raul have a more sinister motive? Soviet spies often tried to trick foreigners into bad-mouthing their system so they could get them kicked out of their country—did they do that here?

"It's more complex than I realized," I stated lamely, then bade him good night and walked inside the hotel.

Raul and his buddy watched me for a moment, then headed back to the Malecon. Another group of foreigners awaited.

25. WAITING FOR FIDEL

*PRIMERO DEJAR DE SER, QUE DEJAR
DE SER REVOLUCIONARIO.*

BETTER NOT TO BE, THAN NOT TO
BE A REVOLUTIONARY.
—*René Mederos*

HOWEVER INCESSANT THE Elián González coverage may
have seemed on CNN in early 2000, it couldn't hold a *vela* to
that on Cuba's revolutionary networks. That six-year-old pawn
in the forty-year-old cold war had been the subject of twenty-
four-hour coverage since the "kidnapping" took place, on both
national TV stations and all the radio stations. *Juventud Rebelde*
and *Trabajadores* ran full-spread editorials berating the "Miami
Mafia"; RETURN OUR SON! signs plastered the sides of buildings.
The U.S. Immigration and Naturalization Service had by that
point ruled Elián should be returned to his father, but the ever
vigilant (and affluent) Cuban American lobby seemed poised to
prevent it.

The people we met had a sense of humor about it, though.
When we asked Cecilia about Elián, she scoffed: "You know

what his name stands for? *Estoy Libre! Idiotas, Aprendan a Nadar!*" I'm free! Idiots, you need to learn how to swim!

Then she tossed us a coffee-stained copy of that day's *Granma*, the official organ of the Central Committee of the Communist Party of Cuba (named after the yacht that brought Fidel and his guerrillas to Cuban shores to start the Revolution). The lead story announced that a demonstration would be held the following afternoon in front of the U.S. Interests Section. "It should be a good one," Cecilia mused. "It's for mothers."

Would she care to join us?

"No way." She shook her head. "I'm sick of them."

Early the next morning, Cecilia rapped on our bedroom door before entering with fresh coffee. "They changed the time of the march. It's happening right now."

Machi and I rolled out of our bed and into our shoes. "The Interests Section is so far away—should we take a taxi?" I wondered aloud.

"Naaah, just follow the mothers. They're marching down the Malecon now, all one hundred thousand of them."

I was skeptical of that estimation until we saw the crush of women a dozen deep and a few miles long striding down the Malecon. Many wore the disconsolate Elián shirts; all waved paper Cuban flags as they chanted: *"Queremos a nuestro hijo de vuelta!"* We want our son back.

At last! After four years and eleven bloc nations, I was finally seeing some in-the-streets action! We darted across the four-lane road for a better view. Some women passing by were linked arm in arm and singing something vaguely familiar. *"No hay que llorar / No hay que llorar."* What was it? A revolutionary battle hymn? The Spanish version of "The Internationale"?

Machi looked at me incredulously. "They're singing 'La Vida Es un Carnaval'!"

We would go on to hear Isaac Delgado's rendition of Celia Cruz's hit "Life Is a Carnival" blare from deejay booths, car speakers, and radios on windowsills across Havana, but the first one was belted out by those mothers skipping down the Malecon. And that wasn't the only way this march felt more parade than protest. When the Atlantic crashed a cold wave of rainbow mist over the seawall, the women squealed with delight. When a news helicopter whirled by, they waved their flags and cheered. Only when they passed the periodic clumps of foreign media—easily detectable in their safari vests and camera bags—did they shout out slogans and grimace.

Standing shoulder-length apart along the city side of the Malecon were the protesters' protectors: thousands of uniformed military personnel. Their purpose, however, evaded us. Did they think those mothers would misbehave somehow? Or that the "Miami Mafia" would roar up on speedboats and pick them off, one by one? Perhaps they worried the women would sneak away. They had not, after all, come of their own volition. Every day, the government held a mass rally somewhere on the island for members of a certain profession or grade level and shuttled them there from their work units or schools. Attendance supposedly wasn't mandatory, but it is hard to imagine many would have refused.

Machi and I trotted alongside the mothers, recording sound and snapping photos, until the boulevard suddenly narrowed and the military merged in. Considering they were marching in opposition to our country, we tried backing up, but a mile and a half of women and soldiers trailed behind us. With no place to go but forward, we became demonstrators by default.

The protest came to a climax of sorts when we marched past the U.S. Interests Section. The mothers shook their flags a little harder and yelled a little louder at the stone-and-blue-glass building speckled with mirrored windows. Then, a few blocks later, they suddenly disbanded. Theirs was a march in the purest sense: no speeches, no proclamations, no petitions, no dicta. Just movement. The unity of the crowd dissolved as the moms scrambled about, trying to single out the bus that would drive them back to their work unit.

Another day, another demonstration.

WHEN CECILIA BROUGHT our morning coffee the next day, she informed us that another rally would be held that afternoon. She nodded understandingly when we declined. "I only mentioned it because *Granma* says Fidel will speak," she said.

Fidel?! Could this be my chance to see a Communist leader who wasn't bloated behind a pane of glass?

Machi and I bolted for the paper. It was front-page news: FIDEL TO SPEAK AT OPEN TRIBUNAL. We arrived at the rallying point—a busy intersection in Vedado—an hour ahead of schedule to score a good spot. National flags draped the surrounding buildings; hundreds of people milled about in SAVE ELIÁN T-shirts. Except for the schoolchildren, who got shuttled in on buses, most appeared to have been drawn by the star-studded cast of performers, which included actors and musicians as well as the longest-lasting head of state in the world. The diversity of the crowd was phenomenal: factory workers, doctors, farmers, teachers, bus drivers, and little kids who represented every possible shade of human pigmentation.

At 4:00 P.M., the tribunal presenters mounted the stage and greeted the crowd, which by then numbered in the tens of thousands. After a few speeches, a thick set of scripts was distributed and everyone took turns reading, as though rehearsing for a play. The Miami relatives harboring Elián were deemed the "torturers of his innocence"; the U.S., his "kidnappers." The crowd responded with flag waving and cries of *"Viva la Revolucion!," "Viva Fidel!,"* and *"Viva Cuba Libre!"* It felt like the cross between a political convention and a rock concert.

About an hour into the festivities, I started getting antsy. Where was Fidel? I periodically peeked backstage for a bearded man in olive green fatigues while Machi scanned the neighboring streets for police brigades and black Mercedes-Benzes. Our hopes rose when a cop pulled up on an expensive-looking motorcycle, but he only listened a moment and then sped away.

Another hour passed.

Finally, I cornered a young couple and asked, *"Perdón. ¿Dónde está Fidel Castro?"* They looked at me stonily. *"Yo no sé,"* the husband said in a way that clipped further probing. I don't know.

After getting the same response from two more people, I decided to alter my approach. Cubans often shied away from uttering Fidel Castro's name directly. Supporters preferred nicknames like El Jefe Máximo (the Big Boss), El Líder (the Leader), El Comandante (the Commander), El Compañero Fidel (Comrade Fidel), El Caballo (the Horse), El Barbudo (the Bearded One), El Viejo (the Old Man), or just plain Fidel. Enemies opted for two syllables spat out like a four-letter word: *Cas-tro.* Keeping this in mind, I approached a middle-aged man who looked as though he had a sense of humor.

"Perdón. ¿Dónde está . . . ?" I let my voice trail off as I ran my fingers along my chin, as Raul had two nights before.

He stared at me silently.

"Granma said he would be here," I prompted.

"*Yo no sé*," he said forcefully. Then he turned and vanished in the crowd.

I continued my polling in earnest, but no one wagered a guess, not even a policeman or a news photographer. At the Associated Press, we used to receive detailed digests of then governor George W. Bush's public appearances every week; *China Daily* had tabs on President Jiang Zemin. Didn't *Granma* keep up with her Viejo?

"If *Granma* says Fidel will be there, that's a good sign he won't," a Cuban professor of political science told me later. "I've seen Fidel three times, and each time was a complete shock. I just turned around and there he was. And ten seconds later, he was gone."

According to author Jon Lee Anderson, Fidel is rumored to have other phantom behaviors as well, like entering and exiting his office via a hidden network of hallways and tunnels and having his doors electronically locked and sealed at night with a specially embossed wax. That might sound paranoid, but considering there have been—by his own (inflated) estimation—637 attempts on his life, he probably has reason to be. The CIA, for one, has tried to assassinate him with methods ranging from cyanide milkshakes to cigars impregnated with botulism to chemicals sprinkled in his boots so his beard would fall out. But Fidel has proven indestructible for four decades and counting.

Like Lenin and Mao, Fidel defied all odds on his road to power. When his yacht *Granma* crash-landed off the southeastern shores of Cuba in December 1956, he had a seasick crew of eighty-two that promptly got knocked down to about twenty-two during an ambush by President Fulgencio Batista's U.S.-backed army. But within two years' time, the guerrilla war Fidel orchestrated from a mountaintop not only ended a corrupt military dictatorship, but sent the Yankee *imperialistas* packing as well. Then he won the hearts of liberals, developing nations, and many of his countrymen by pumping money into the health care system, setting up schools for the deaf and blind, slashing rents by half, and lowering gas, electricity, and transportation fees. He even issued one hundred thousand college students olive green uniforms, blanket rolls, and lanterns and dispatched them to the countryside for a year to teach country folk how to read.

But also like Lenin and Mao, Fidel granted these remarkable advances in social welfare at the steep price of civil liberties and human rights. Soon after the Revolution, he oversaw the tribunals that banished accused informers and "counter-revolutionaries" to the firing squads and ordered so many property seizures that the wealthy fled to Florida. Then he started censoring and shutting down critical media and establishing Committees for the Defense of the Revolution that essentially forced neighbors to spy on one another. He also reneged on his promise to hold elections within a year.

It didn't take long for Cubans to realize what Russians and Chinese had years before: Revolutionaries might be genius military strategists, but they are crummy economists. For reasons ranging from incompetence to CIA sabotage, many of the industrial and agricultural plans Castro & Co. cooked up failed miserably. Fidel eventually turned to Moscow to bail him out (at which point he became a self-proclaimed Communist), and for the next two decades, the Soviets bought Cuba's cane and kept its stores stocked with goods, pharmacies with medicines, and libraries with books.

Sugar daddies don't last forever, however, and when his suddenly dissolved in 1991, Fidel lost his primary import and export venues. Cuba quickly slipped into the euphemistic "Special Period in a Time of Peace." Blackouts left entire communities without light, air-conditioning, or refrigeration for up to eight or twelve hours at a time. The sudden dearth of public transportation brought about state-regulated hitchhiking. Factories, nightclubs, restaurants, and hotels closed down. Daily newspapers became weeklies; weeklies went to monthlies; monthlies fizzled out altogether. With no means to distribute them, farmers sadly watched their crops rot in the fields.

Something clearly had to give, and for once, it was Fidel. He legalized the U.S. dollars (USD) already heavily circulating in the black market. He instituted a limited market economy that allowed the formation of joint ventures with foreign companies in addition to some tightly regulated private enterprise. He sanctioned some of the covert living-room restaurants—or *paladares*—that had mushroomed throughout the nation and permitted select families to open their spare bedrooms to travelers. He permitted apolitical émigrés to visit home now and then. Finally, he opened the doors to tourism with an ad campaign of *cubanas* in string bikinis that said COME AND BE SEDUCED. According to *Granma*, 1.8 million tourists responded in 2000 alone.

But how much longer can Fidel continue this manic influx of tourism and still preach against capitalism and imperialism? Will he find a way to open Cuba's doors to political and economic freedom while filtering out the chaos that torments Russia and the corruption that plagues China? And what will happen when Fidel inevitably expires? He may have given up cigars and taken up the exercise bicycle in recent years, but not even a *comandante* can hold out forever. How will Cuba change without him?

I would have loved to ask a Habanero these sorts of questions at the tribunal that day, but I did not. It felt too much like asking a Beijinger about Tiananmen Square: a little risky and way too prying. Instead, I waited to hear what El Jefe Máximo might say for himself in his address. And waited. And waited. It really seemed as though he could have sprung atop that stage and treated the crowd to his long-winded grandiloquence (a recent record being seven hours) at any moment. But when the tribunal's presenters completed their scripts, they shouted a final *"Viva!"* and hopped off the stage. Revolutionary music blasted through the speakers as the crowds dispersed.

My one chance to see a living, breathing Communist leader—and he flaked.

26. THE RUMBA QUEEN

LIVING IN HAVANA WAS LIKE LIVING IN A FACTORY THAT PRODUCED HUMAN BEAUTY ON AN ASSEMBLY LINE.
—Graham Greene

THE WORLD MAY have marveled when Fidel's ragtag band of young men and women overthrew a military dictator backed by the most powerful nation in the world, but it made sense to me. After examining the photographs of Camilo Cienfuegos smoking cigars and Che Guevara flexing his biceps at the Museo de la Revolución, I decided that if I'd seen them and a few dozen other rugged rebels scaling mountaintops, I would have picked up my machete and joined them, too. Somebody ought to put sex appeal in the "Top Ten Most Desirable Revolutionary Traits" in Mao's *Little Red Book*.

And sensuality isn't confined to Cuba's *barbudos*—bearded ones—either. Centuries of mingling Spanish and African blood have created skin colors that range from creamy white to dark chocolate black. Noses are aquiline; cheekbones are well defined. Eyes are framed with extra long lashes. Smiles are vibrant. Gaits are fluid. Movements are rhythmic. But stunning exteriors are only part of what makes Cubans so exquisite.

Theirs is a sensuality that transcends physical appearance. It is an attitude, and it is infectious.

Getting dumped by the same man twice, however, is murder on the ego. It may have been a year since Mario walked out, but I was still feeling pretty undesirable—until I took a late afternoon stroll through our barrio *sola*. Within five steps, I had unwittingly summoned the attention of every male on the block. A father and son tinkering beneath the hood of a faded blue 1954 Chrysler wiped their hands on their jeans and waved. Graying men in white tank tops looked up from their domino matches to grin appreciatively. Two guys sipping Cristal beer on a second-floor balcony clinked their bottles against the railing and called out, *"¡Salud!"*

Then came a noise from the shadows of a doorway that sounded like a cross between a hiss and a slurpy kiss. It grated against my feminist fibers like fingernails on a chalkboard—until the perpetrator stepped into the sunlight. He was six feet two and the color of iced coffee. His features were chiseled. His black eyes glittered. He wasn't wearing a shirt. I wrestled my eyes away from his washboard stomach and continued down the street in a daze. Two steps farther, another catcall resounded, followed by a lasciviously whispered, *"¡Qué guapa!"* Incensed, I whirled around, fists clenched, ready to pounce— and found a tall, dark, and stunning someone grinning at me. The corners of my mouth admittedly lifted before I managed to grit my teeth and glower.

Just then, a teenager pedaled past on a Flying Pigeon, braked, and looked back at me. "Is that a sun you're wearing?" he inquired.

I glanced down at the sterling silver sun tied around my neck. *"Sí."*

"And where is your moon?"

I stared at him blankly.

"You don't have a moon?" he asked, concerned. He hopped off his bike and walked over, grinning. "Well, how about me, then?"

I laughed; he persisted. "Do you have a boyfriend?"

"*Sí*," I lied.

"A Cuban boyfriend?"

"*Sí.*"

"You want to change?"

"No."

"Not even for a little while?"

"No."

"How about just a day?"

"No."

"An hour?"

I peered into the amber eyes of this curly-haired suitor. His biceps bulged in a pleasantly pubescent way; a few stray chest hairs peeked through the buttons of his shirt. There was potential. "How about I look you up in a couple of years?" I proposed.

He beamed and whipped out a pen.

Mom always said to ignore catcallers—or, at the very least, not encourage them—but then, she has never been to Cuba. *Cubanos* may whistle at anything lacking a Y chromosome, but somehow it felt neither predatory nor disrespectful to me. It just seemed like an indiscriminate appreciation of the female body. And it did wonders for my tattered self-esteem. There's just something about an island full of gorgeous men calling you *linda* that makes you start to believe it.

—

ON THE RECOMMENDATION of some backpackers we'd met, Machi and I went to the Cayo Hueso district of Centro Habana that Sunday afternoon to check out the murals an artist had supposedly painted out there. While Cayo Hueso teemed with people, its buildings exuded the lonesome neglect of a long-deserted ghost town. Walls whimpered for paint, scaffolding cried out for support, bricks begged for mortar. Entire buildings had been gutted. The only splotches of continuous color were the hot pinks and lime greens of the Lycra stretch pants hung out to dry.

But when we turned a random corner, an oasis sprang from the architectural desert. A whirl of reds, yellows, greens, and blacks streaked across the high-rises like a comet and exploded into a blur of painted eyes and roots and feathers. A giant black goddess levitated out of a sea of color; a serpent slithered through puffs of smoke. Then we began to hear the pounding of tribal drums and the shaking of dried bones. We turned one last corner into a cul-de-sac to find scores of locals and backpackers dancing so fervently, their hair and limbs had turned yellow from the dust clouds they created. In the crowd's center, impossibly muscular black men pounded fierce sets of rhythms onto tall wooden congas as cigar and pot smoke swirled above their heads toward the instillation art pieces that climbed the neighboring gallery's walls. Bathtubs and cash registers mingled with African masks, Christian crosses, and gods of every sort.

Then the gallery door opened and a bearded, beaded man appeared with a cigar in his mouth and what smoked like sage in his hand. The crowd parted to allow his passage to the drummers, whom he appeared to bless. This was Salvador Gonzalez Escalona—creator of the art, host of the gathering, and master of the Santero ceremony currently transpiring.

Santeria originated with the advent of the Cuban slave trade in the 1500s. Among other atrocities, Spanish settlers stripped the imported Africans of their indigenous religions and forced them to convert to Catholicism—a mandate that particularly devastated the intensely devout Yoruba tribes of southwestern Nigeria. They quickly noticed important similarities between the religions, however: Both worshiped supreme beings who created and maintained the world, and both used intermediaries to talk with them. Over time, the slaves simply fused the religions together, with every Catholic saint corresponding to an African *orisha*, and called it Santeria—the Way of the Saints.

Communist leaders have a history of repressing all forms of worship outside the Revolution and themselves, and Fidel is no exception. But while he canceled Christmas, shut down Catholic schools, exiled foreign priests, and either shipped the Cuban clerics to labor camps or slapped them with restrictions, he allowed *babalaos*—Santero priests—to continue their practice throughout the island. (Theories vary on this difference in treatment. My favorites: As a child, Fidel had to serve as an altar boy, for which he has always been spiteful; as a revolutionary, he was blessed by a *babalao* with longevity, for which he has always been grateful.)

My own Catholic upbringing had revolved around images of a bloodied, tortured man surrounded by grief-stricken women, of golden goblets wiped and shined after each sip, of rosaries wound tightly around my *tías'* fingers as they recited Hail Marys for some poor gone soul. It was a religion of discipline, of confession and redemption, of impending doom pitted against eternal salvation. This tiny taste of Santeria, then, was both shocking and intensely appealing. As Salvador's crew demonstrated, the *orishas* believe their adherents should have a good time here on earth. Burn a little incense, sacrifice a chicken or two, smoke a cigar, then shake your maracas and dance.

I darted into Salvador's art gallery to stash my backpack somewhere and nearly crashed into someone in the process. As I apologized, my eyes traveled up from a pair of black leather shoes to tailored trousers and a button-down shirt to a thick strand of yellow beads and a pair of full lips. Six feet three with sculpted features, he was mocha black and gorgeous.

"I'm sorry," I gasped.

"I'm Harold," he breathed, proffering a manicured hand. "I'm a model. Want to see?"

After grabbing a glossy Euro magazine off a rocking chair, he turned to the advertisements. "That's me." He pointed at a black-and-white photograph of a strapping nude straddled into a complicated yoga pose on a beach.

While I flipped through the magazine, he dug into a closet for more. I sat in the chair as a pile began to form. "Look at me here, and here, and here," he murmured as he hand-fed me pieces of a nearby rum-soaked cake.

The drumming soon came to its untimely conclusion and a hundred sweaty bodies descended upon the gallery. Everyone— including many of the foreigners—seemed to know Harold, who watched over Salvador's gallery when he was away. (When I asked how Salvador acquired so much paint, Harold replied: "Anytime anyone gets some, they bring a little to him. That's how this country works.")

After locking up the gallery, Harold organized a group of us to go clubbing, though it was still the middle of the afternoon. As we headed into the street for taxis, he removed the backpack from my shoulders and slipped it on his own—as Andrei used to do—and took my hand. Figuring that no amount of protest would return that bag until we parted, I swallowed a tirade and accepted the chivalry. (When he reached for Machi's, however, she glared a steely *Try it and you're dead, buddy.*)

An old Chevy showboat slowed just enough for us to climb aboard and then sputtered down the center of the street, swerving in, around, and through potholes and children playing stickball. Our first stop was a bar in Habana Vieja full of local creative types—painters, musicians, writers, a documentary filmmaker—as well as expats and tourists. As Harold made the rounds, Machi and I ordered Cuba libres and slid onto a wooden bench beside a voluptuous woman who introduced herself as Nouris, a former dancer and choreographer at the Tropicana. This was no small claim: The Tropicana opened its doors in 1939 as the world's most flamboyant nightclub, and its showgirls had been dazzling sold-out crowds in extravagant carnival-style costumes ever since, Revolution be damned. She certainly looked the part, though, in her thigh-high black felt boots, fishnets, and miniskirt.

Machi engaged her in a conversation in Spanish, and within minutes I was lost. Jealousy curdled as I watched them huddle together. What was Nouris telling her about? Late night parties and amorous lovers? This woman had performed for diplomats and dignitaries, athletes and movie stars, artists and musicians: I was missing out on the conversation of the trip! Their laughter rang above the mambo band playing in the corner. Why do people laugh harder in Spanish than in any other language?

Desperate for a connection, I waited for them to pause and then informed Nouris that I, too, was something of a dancer. A very foolish thing to tell a former showgirl, because naturally she rose to her feet, grabbed my hands, and demanded a demonstration.

"No, no, no," I protested.

"Baile!" she commanded, twisting her hips and rib cage in opposite directions in a move known as the *moño,* or knot.

Fortunately, there is a belly-dancing move that resembles the *moño* in spirit. Hoping no one would notice the difference, I stood up and did that instead. Some people in the bar—amused an *extranjera* would attempt their prized move with their prized dancer—shouted their approval. My confidence heightened, I stacked on an undulation. Nouris matched it, and we did the movement in synchronicity. Another cheer resounded from the crowd. Then, holding the *moño* and the undulation, Nouris sent her whole body into a trembling vibration—a move similar to the Middle Eastern shimmy. I vibrated, too, and people went wild.

Though it was an intoxicating moment, I wished for a quick conclusion. Professional belly dancers can keep stacking one movement on top of another, but I max out at three. This clearly was not a problem for Nouris, who proceeded to swoop her entire body backward, as though sliding beneath a limbo stick. I couldn't even do that when limbo sticks played a prominent role in my social life in fifth grade, but to show good sportsmanship, I gave it a try. Then I straightened and joined the applause for Nouris, who was defying human anatomy by undulating into a backbend. When the tip of her head hovered two inches above the floor, she held a pretty pose, then gracefully came up, fell down into splits, and—briefly channeling Prince—somehow pulled herself up again. Then she really let loose, twisting, turning, and shimmying almost manically. The bar began to chant her name, but you could see in her eyes that she had left us long ago. Nouris wasn't dancing atop an old bar floor singed with cigarette ash. *Ay,* no—she was nineteen again, wearing a glimmering chandelier headdress and sashaying under the stars to an orchestra, a chorus, and thunderous applause at the Tropicana.

Just then, Harold slid onto the bench beside me. "Want to rumba?"

With that, we jetted off to a club called La Loipa, where a swarm of locals and backpackers had formed around a seven-piece band playing *bata*, *bongo*, and *conga* drums, wooden boxes, wood blocks, and tambourines. Their voices provided the harmony, either leading, following, or arguing with the percussion. This was classic Cuban rumba—not the "rhumba" of Fred Astaire or the "son" of the Buena Vista Social Club, but the rumba born in slavery and raised on the streets of poor black neighborhoods by musicians possessing little more than a cardboard box, a bottle, and a stick. The kind that derives from the verb *rumbear*, which means to party and have a good time. The kind traceable to the religious and ceremonial dances of Africa. The kind that did to the soul what Salvador's murals did to the mind.

As we watched, a beanpole of a man and a big-breasted, big-assed woman in gold stretch pants maneuvered to the circle's center to perform the *guaguanco*, a fiercely flirtatious dance in which a man strives to give his partner a *vacunao*, or mighty pelvic thrust. In this rendition, they appeared to be imitating a rooster and a hen. The rooster strutted about, puffing his feathers as he pleaded, while the big chick stood her ground with complete composure. But as the music escalated, she started swiveling her hips in a tantalizing way, the crowd rooting her on. When the congas suddenly climaxed in a burst of sound, the rooster gave his penetrating *vacunao*. And then the crowd fanned out over the dance floor as the band began another number.

As I scanned the crowd, my eyes fell upon a woman who appeared to be forty years old and weigh approximately 225 pounds. She had swaddled her galactic ass in pink spandex and stuffed her papaya-shaped breasts into a polka-dot halter top. A bouffant of Afro-mermaid hair spilled across her shoulders. The heavily syncopated beat of the *batá* had caught her in a temporary trance: She was slumped in a chair, eyes shut, body still. But as the rhythm sped up a notch or two, it called her feet to action. Her spiked heels began to pound the beat on the floor beneath her chair. The music worked its way through her tree-trunk thighs toward her massive belly, across her breasts, and finally to her head, which started swaying. Suddenly, the music commanded her to stand and, undulating every muscle of her full frame, she gyrated toward the dance floor. Then she began to rumba. Her energy was palpably feminine and undeniably sensual. She was like a Frida Kahlo painting of a fleshy melon bursting with ripeness. She was fertility. She was womanhood.

When I gravitated closer for a better view, she peered upon me with charcoal eyes. I smiled. Winking sassily, she took a fast step to the side, gyrated, and motioned for me to follow. I did, clumsily but obediently. She nodded encouragingly before adding a sensuous hip swivel to the move. When I tried and failed, she seized my hips with her giant hands and swiveled them for me. I beamed my gratitude and she winked once more. Then she closed her eyes and absorbed even more of the rhythms. The deaf could have followed the music's manic beat by watching the rippling of her flesh.

Just then, a hand slipped under the small of my back and whirled me around. It was Harold. He wanted to rumba. With me.

At that moment, all of the inhibitions I had just released on that wooden floor froze back inside me. I can't dance with men. They always want to lead, and I can't follow. I discovered this in junior high, when Arturo Rodriguez asked me to dance to Gloria Estefan with him. "Follow *me*," he hissed as he steered me across the cafeteria floor. I tried to be obedient, but my body refused. After two songs, Arturo gave up and banished me back to the estrogen circle, where my girlfriends awaited. Humiliating, yes—but at least there, I got to do my own thing.

And couple-dancing to Latin music is even worse. Though I love mambo and merengue, my body butchers its rhythms as badly as my lips do its lyrics. Many a *tío* have dragged me onto dance floors at weddings to try to teach me properly, but I have succeeded only in embarrassing us both. (This, naturally, is another biracial complex of mine.)

Yet it was becoming apparent that while Russians bonded over drink and Chinese over dinner, Cubans connected through dance. Reluctantly, I stepped into Harold's arms. My eyes dropped straight to his feet. They always do that when I have to dance with a man. It comes from fear, I think. Fear of stepping on his toes. Fear of losing the rhythm. Fear he's scanning the room for the woman he *really* wants to dance with. But a few turns into the music, Harold cupped my chin and lifted my gaze toward his. Pressing me deep against him, he stepped forward with such will, I had no choice but to fall back slow, quick, quick, slow, quick, quick, then turn out to the crowd and back to his arms.

That's the point where my feet usually reassert their independence with a stumble or two. I mean, why does *he* get to decide when we go forward and when we go backward?

But Harold drew me closer still, so close that his breath warmed my ear. His body softly began to speak, not to command but to engage. And mine, for the first time, responded.

27. AN AFTERNOON AT EL CASTILLO DE FARNES

ONE AFTERNOON, Machi and I visited the restaurant where Fidel and Che dined upon their triumphant arrival in Havana after two years in the Sierra Maestras: El Castillo de Farnes. At the open-air bar, we ordered *mojitos*. With a knowing nod, the bartender plunked down two highballs, tossed in heaps of fluffy white sugar, squeezed in the juice of half a lime, stuffed in fragrant *yerba buena* (mint) sprigs, added ice, poured in Havana Club rum, and topped it off with soda. Cold, refreshing, delicious. Sipping slowly, I ambled over to the old woman rolling cigars with stained, wrinkled fingers in a nearby booth and asked how long she'd been a *tabaquera*.

"Longer than you've been around."

"I'll take two."

She handed them over, and I joined Machi at a table that straddled the bar and the sidewalk. Neither of us had a lighter, but when we raised the cigars to take in their spicy-sweet pungency, the guys at the next table whipped one out. They were about our age and, judging by their Nike sportswear and thick gold chains, appeared to be tourists. They watched us puff with interest and asked about our plans for the afternoon.

"No idea," I said.

"Then you should come with us. We know the best night-clubs in Havana," one said grandly.

"We don't even know you."

"I'm Camilo and this is Randy."

"Where are you from?"

"Somos cubanos."

My sketchy *biznes* detector, programmed in Kirill's flat in Moscow, began to beep. Unless they had some seriously generous relatives in America, those threads probably couldn't have been acquired in an honest way.

Rising from his chair, Camilo extended a hand. "Come on, let's go."

Before I could reply, someone tapped on my shoulder. "How much did you pay for that cigar?" a scraggly man standing outside rasped.

"Two bucks."

"I could get you a whole box for fifty dollars."

"No, gracias. I just wanted to try this one."

"Forty-seven?"

"I'm not trying to bargain. I don't actually smoke."

"Forty-five?"

"Are you coming or aren't you?" Camilo interjected.

Just then, a young woman in 1980s acid-washed jeans sauntered in, surveyed the scene, and zeroed in on me. "I like your pants," she announced. "How about twenty dollars?"

"¿Perdón?"

"Your pants. I'll give you twenty dollars for them."

It really used to piss me off when cold war travelers mused about Soviet citizens stopping them in the street and wistfully asking for their jeans and sneakers. I always thought I would have happily handed mine over and continued on barefoot in my underwear. But now that someone actually wanted my H&M hip-huggers, I felt strangely attached to them. "I'm sorry . . . I don't think that's possible."

"Why not?" she huffed.

"She'd be naked," Machi observed.

"So I'll trade her my jeans. That's a good deal. Come on, there's a bathroom over there."

"Listen, you really don't want my pants. I've worn them five days straight."

"Trust me, she has." Machi wrinkled her nose.

"And you are so much slimmer than me," I said, trying another tactic. "My pants would be way too big for you. Really, your jeans are so nice, this wouldn't be a fair trade."

She glared at me. "I want them."

"Are you girls coming or aren't you?" Camilo insisted.

"Forty-three?" the cigar man pleaded.

A Cuban would have called these three *jineteros*, or jockeys, for the way they were trying to "ride" us. In touristy areas like Habana Vieja, *jineteros* were ubiquitous. Some initiated contact under the pretense of friendship, like those Nike guys (who probably wanted to escort us to a club where they could earn a commission). Others were more up front about their desired transaction, like the cigar man and the jeans maven, and could become aggressive if you turned them down. Of course, no one could be blamed for wanting hard currency. At an exchange rate of 1 U.S. dollar (USD) to 20 pesos, theirs wasn't worth so much in 2000. But while the 1993 legalization of USD had saved Cuba's economy, it had also re-created the social inequities the Revolution strove to end—largely because the government continued to pay its employees in *pesos* while the black market and tourist industries paid theirs in USD. This meant bellhops, hotel clerks, and waitresses earned significantly higher salaries than the nation's top lawyers, doctors, and engineers. It also birthed a whole host of social ills, including *jineteros* and their female counterpart—*jineteras* (who mainly sold their bodies).

This was especially tragic considering that the Cuban Revolution was *supposed* to teach people to sacrifice so that someday, everyone would stand on equal footing. Yet Fidel's ruthless policies had turned his people into second-class citizens, forcing many to depend on the tourists who not only showed them what they lacked (Nikes and Nikons), but took away what little their country actually did produce. The choicest fruits and cuts of meat went to hotel restaurants instead of lunch counters; the finer beaches and resorts and hotels banned locals from the premises (unless, of course, you were a *jinetera* with a high-tipping patron). Cuba exported so much of its coffee and sugar, exiles actually brought it back to the island with them as gifts for their local relatives.

Inner dilemmas abounded that afternoon at El Castillo del Farnes. Could I justify my trip to Cuba because I was funneling badly needed dollars into its fallen economy? Or was I taking away food and resources that might otherwise have gone to a local who needed them? And what should I do about the *jineteros* surrounding me, knowing that my nation had contributed to their miserable predicament and that I would probably be turning the same damn tricks had I been raised in Camagüey instead of Corpus?

As I racked my brains for a way out, I noticed two *cubanas* with long, beaded braids staring at me from the street. I waved at them as if they were old friends and grabbed my backpack, thinking I'd run out and join them. Before I could communicate this plan of action to Machi, however, the girls came inside the bar, nudged the jeans maven and Camilo out of their way, and pulled up two chairs. One promptly began to run her fingers through my hair.

"Want braids like mine? Only five dollars—good price."

THROUGHOUT MY TRAVELS around the Bloc, I wrestled with the question of whether each nation's respective Revolution had been worth the Struggle. Was the end to imperial practices like female foot binding, the eradication of diseases like leprosy, and the building of schools and hospitals throughout the People's Republic of China worth the senseless deaths of so many millions to state-induced famines, political purges, and labor camps? Was the privilege of living in a major industrialized nation and world superpower worth the terror and oppression of the Soviet Union? If not, why the hell did so many Russians and Chinese reflect on their Revolutions with such nostalgia and continue to revere the men who led them? Were hundreds of millions of people living in total denial?

Cuba complicated matters even further. One set of statistics revealed that it was one of the wealthiest nations in Latin America prior to the Revolution and became one of the poorest afterward. That unknown thousands of Cubans had drowned in the sea while trying to escape on rafts constructed of tires and plywood. But other stats told how postrevolutionary Cuba became the first underdeveloped country in the world to totally wipe out hunger and malnutrition. How Fidel's public health care system was recommended as a "model for the world" by the World Health Organization in 1989 and how in literacy Cuba leads not only Latin America, but the United States as well.

But even if the Revolution had changed the average Cuban's life for the better, wasn't it time to move on?

One evening while Machi was conducting interviews, I decided to visit the Vedado district. Havana transportation offered public buses known as *guaguas* and state-run tourist taxis, but lacking the time to wait for the former (which can take hours) or the money for the latter, I opted for the third mode: the gypsy cab. As in Moscow, you need only stick your hand out in a Havana street before someone screeches to a halt and invites you aboard. This time, a vintage Plymouth Deluxe pulled over. As per Communist protocol, I hopped in the front seat next to the driver, who greeted me with a million-dollar smile wrapped around a half-smoked cigar. His graying hair was carefully combed; his dress shirt neatly pressed. He'd been listening to *Radio Liberación* but flicked it off so we could chat. I started by asking the age of his car.

"Nineteen forty-eight, same year as me!" He beamed. "Where are you from, *mi amor*?"

"I'm a Yankee."

"*¿¿Yanqui?!*" His eyes lit up with questions. "Cuba isn't like they say it is in America, is it?"

Before I wagered a reply, he answered himself. "Of course it isn't! Just look at our streets! See how tranquil they are?" he cried, then slapped the dashboard at each of his country's attributes. "No drugs. No weapons. All of our kids have shoes. No one is begging. No one is starving. Where else in the Caribbean can you find conditions like this? Where else in Latin America?"

In a way, he was right. At birth, Cubans could expect to live about seventy-five years—a rate on par with first world nations. All medical procedures, from eye examinations to brain surgery, were free of charge. Ration cards ensured that no one starved. Free education through the university level meant that everyone could read. Workers got paid vacations and received pensions when they retired. The government even picked up the tab for funeral expenses. For a taxi driver who spent his childhood under the social injustices of President Batista, these social services mattered most.

"I've got neighbors who moved to Miami, but I'll never leave. What for? I've got everything I need right here—my wife, my kids, my car, my job, my house. And when I retire, I'm going to be taken care of."

By this point, we reached my destination. I paid him a few dollars and bade him farewell. "You go back to America and tell everybody that Ricardo is doing fine over here," he said, then slapped his knee and belly laughed.

I would go on to see a few people begging on the streets of Havana during my stay. One was an elderly black woman standing in front of a store; the others were middle-aged and sitting on the stone steps of a church. All wore shoes (unlike the beggars I've encountered in Asia, the Middle East, and Latin America) and appeared to be healthy (unlike many street dwellers in the United States). I also saw a man with no legs pedal around in a hand-maneuvered bicycle, but while the disabled are generally a good barometer of how a society is faring, I couldn't help wondering if this particular man was a decoy of sorts (as he was circling around the heavily touristy Museo de la Revolución).

I did not, however, question Ricardo's sincerity or his claim to be perfectly happy living in Cuba.

On my way back to my casa a few hours later, I hailed a ride with Guillermo, a twenty-six-year-old computer programmer who supplemented his $9 monthly salary by freelancing his father's Oldsmobile 88. He wore blue jeans and a baseball cap; techno pulsed from his radio's speakers. After discovering I was a *yanqui*, he too asked what I thought of his country.

"*¡Me encanta!*" I gushed.

He grinned at my response, but when I added that I'd like to live in Havana someday, he stared at me as though I'd gone *loca*. "Why would you want to do that when you have everything in your country and we have nothing?" he asked incredulously.

In a way, he too was right. Cubans could not launch an opposition party to their government. Artists were sometimes persecuted. Dissidents were harassed, imprisoned, or shot. Their press was censored; their media monitored. Bureaucracy was omnipresent. They couldn't buy a house or car or travel overseas without official approval, which could take years. Moreover, they were broke. The average Cuban made between $8 and $12 a month, while a decent pair of shoes cost $35. For someone who spent his formative years in the Special Period, these oppressive restrictions mattered most.

"My mother, brother, and uncle are in America. I've been doing everything I can to join them, but your country won't let me. I've applied for a visa three times now, and every time they reject me. They think I'll try to immigrate." Guillermo reached into the glove compartment, pulled out a crumpled pack of cigarettes, and fired one up.

"Well, of course I'd try to immigrate. What Cuban wouldn't?" he muttered through the smoke.

28. REVOLUTIONARY REVERIES

**IF I'M TOLD 98 PERCENT OF THE PEOPLE NO
LONGER BELIEVE IN THE REVOLUTION, I'LL
CONTINUE TO FIGHT. IF I'M TOLD I'M THE ONLY
ONE WHO BELIEVES IN IT, I'LL CONTINUE.**
—*Fidel Alejandro Castro Ruz*

LIKE MANY CAMPUSES in Latin America, the University of Havana has a volatile past. Fidel carried a gun around when he studied law there in the 1940s, and that wasn't just an early warning sign of his strong arm to come. Antigovernment protests erupted on a regular basis back then. The university may have barred the police and military from patrolling its grounds, but politicians and mafiosi could wander around freely—and a few left a trail of blood as they did. The ashes of slain student leader Julio Antonio Mella (who founded the Cuban Communist Party) were stored in a monument at the foot of the university's entryway.

Machi and I visited during exam week, though, so most of the students were tucked away studying. We combed the campus for something redolent of its revolutionary past but found only commercial tributes to Che Guevara. (His rugged silhouette tattooed nearly every T-shirt, folder, key chain, and wallet in the store.) On our way out, we spotted three students relaxing beneath a shade tree, and one cheerfully waved us over. His name was Armando and he studied psychology; Netty and Gabriela were graduating that June in biology.

"What will you do with your degrees?" I asked.

"Whatever the government wants," replied Gabriela, an artsy girl in faded jeans and sandals. "Our education is free, but afterward we go to work for them for two years, wherever they need us. Then we can do what we want."

"What other obligations do you have to fulfill as students?"

"Whatever is needed," Armando said, his large brown eyes warm and friendly. "Last year, the elementary schools had a shortage of teachers and we got sent to help them. We also go to the countryside during summer break to help the farmers."

While I tried to picture how that mandate would go over at a frat house—"All right, boys, put down your beers and pick up your hoes!"—Machi slipped into journalist mode. "Do you like helping out?"

Surprised by her question, Armando paused before responding. "Well, our country is going through a very hard time right now, but it still pays for our books and our tuition and even gives us a small stipend when it can. So we think it is only fair that we help out, too, when we can."

Netty and Gabriela nodded in agreement. As in the old Soviet Union and People's Republic of China, Cuban youth were raised to be *estudiantes hoy, trabajadores mañana, soldados de la patria siempre*—students today, workers tomorrow, soldiers always.

Just then, Gabriela's boyfriend, Antonio, walked up with a fist full of tickets for a performance at the Gran Teatro de la Habana the following evening. Cuba heavily subsidized theater and other fine arts so that everyone could afford it, as the Soviet Union once did. "Who wants to go?"

We each took one and agreed to continue our conversation then.

BETWEEN MOSCOW, BEIJING, and New York City, I'd grown accustomed to watching hours-long theatrical performances and understanding hardly a thing. But sitting through an entire play of Spanish jokes I didn't get and stories that failed to move me was maddening. I tried to pin down individual words and decipher them, but they kept whizzing past my head the way those fly balls used to in Southside Little Miss Kickball (until my coach sent me farther back centerfield than any eight-year-old could kick).

Finally the curtain fell, and Machi and I wondered what to do. We wanted to spend time with the students, of course, but doing what and where? A *mojito* at a bar would likely cost more than they normally spent in two weeks, and we didn't want to insult Armando and Antonio by offering to pay (or worse, make them feel obligated to return the gesture). Fortunately, Armando had a better idea: How would we like to take a stroll along the Malecon?

Scores of young people had gathered there that night to catch up on gossip, pass around bottles of rum, and pair off and make out. As we wove through the crowds, Armando ticked off his favorite singers and songwriters to see if we had any in common. He was crushed that I hadn't heard of one. "But they're American!"

"Then how did *you* hear about them?"

"I downloaded them off Napster."

After a time, we came upon a row of ferries bobbing like apples in the ink-black sea. We lowered ourselves into one and tugged across the harbor to a suburb called Casablanca, where a gigantic statue of Jesus Christ crested a hill like the Second Coming. As we approached the stairwell at the hill's base, we heard a faint trace of salsa that rose as we ascended and crescendoed at the summit. Christ, it seemed, was having a fiesta: The entire hilltop pulsed with hundreds of locals slapping their pelvises in time to the beat.

Both Netty and Armando spoke English, so we sat together on the low stone wall overlooking Havana's sparsely lit skyline to talk. They had as many questions for me as I did them: Was it true there were homeless people in America, even in front of the White House? And crack sold in schoolyards, and students who shot other students, and tens of millions living without health care? Did the KKK still burn crosses in front of black people's homes and churches?

I answered them all, then tossed one back: "Is that all they teach you about my country?"

"We can tell by your cameras and clothes there are a few advantages to your system, too," Armando said, deadpan, before cracking a mischievous grin.

We laughed. "So what do you think about this tourist invasion?"

"It's good for our economy," Armando allowed, "but sometimes we don't like the way tourists treat us. They take pictures of us all the time, when we get on the buses, when we ride our bicycles, when we cross the street. Like we're animals. And then there are those old men who can't find any women to love them in their own country, so they come to ours and either take them away or use them for a night and leave them."

Armando was referring to *jineteras,* the invariably beautiful women who could be found in almost any bar, club, or restaurant snuggling up to bald-headed, beer-bellied tourists in hopes of trading their company for a drink, a meal, an evening at a disco, a night at a fancy hotel, or—for the lucky few—a ticket out of there. Such a scene could be found the world over, of course, but with a major difference. *Cubanas* weren't sold into sex slavery by their parents (as so often happened in Asia) or tricked into it with promises of lucrative jobs overseas (as in the former Soviet Union). Most entered the trade because they were sick and tired of sacrifice. Consequently, many were highly educated physicists, nurses, or librarians trying to give their families a better life. I have heard, however, that *jineteras* grow younger with each passing year, and it is not uncommon to see fourteen- and fifteen-year-olds selling themselves for T-shirts and lip gloss now.

Netty and Armando blamed these *jineteras* (and their hustling male counterparts, *jineteros*) for the "moral decay" of their society. This lament reminded me of Andrei's diatribes against the *Mafiya,* but when I said as much, they balked, insisting their nations could not be compared. (As with Beijingers, the Habaneros I met didn't seem terribly envious of their post-Soviet peers, despite their freedom to travel, vote, and publish. But while Liu and Yuer viewed Russia as "too dangerous," Armando and Netty declared it "no fun.")

"So what do you think about these Elián rallies?" I asked, switching topics.

They shook their heads in exasperation. "When the rallies first started, we took to the streets of our own free will. We wanted to participate. We *believed* in it. But it has gotten to be too much. Times are hard in Cuba and money is scarce, yet the government is putting so many resources into these rallies. Can you imagine—all these flags, T-shirts, and demonstrations, just for one child! It's crazy!" Armando said.

That seemed a natural transition to what I really wanted to know: "What do you think of the man behind them?"

"We really admire Fidel," Armando replied steadily. "Even Cubans who disagree with his politics admire him for his intelligence, his leadership, his charisma. He gave us our dignity."

"So what is going to happen when he . . . ?"

Netty's eyebrows lifted and collided. "We have no idea, absolutely no idea."

"Not only do we not know what will happen, we don't even know what we *want* to have happen," Armando added. "There are many aspects of our current system that we don't want to give up, but at the same time, things can't go on as they are. The problem is that we can't say we'd like to try a certain new system, because we don't really know any other. Take capitalism. What does that mean to us? In school, we learn it's a system based on the exploitation of men by men. The media tells us it's corruptive, bourgeois decadence. That's all we know—what we're taught."

"Do we live better than the Chinese?" Netty asked.

I had been contemplating the same since my arrival. Whose shoes would I rather fill: Liu's or Netty's, Yuer's or Armando's? "You guys definitely have more fun." I nodded at the dance party beneath the giant Jesus.

They smiled.

"But the Chinese eat better," I decided, weighing Beijing's sumptuous *xiao chi* stands against the forlorn ham sandwiches of Havana. "Their government cracks down harder on dissidents, but it's easier for people to leave the country. You have a more open society, but fewer opportunities. I guess it's a toss-up."

"Life is getting better now, but it is still very hard," Netty said. "I'll probably only make two hundred pesos [ten dollars] a month in my first job—and that is with a biology degree from our best university."

"We'll never be independent with those kinds of wages," Armando interjected. "We can't eat out, go out, move out. Gabriela and Antonio want to get married, but it will take years and years before they could even rent a room for themselves. I want to go to Paris, but how can I on so little money? I could work my whole life and never have enough for a plane ticket."

They weren't soliciting pity with these remarks, but it lodged in my throat regardless. Before I could utter some lame "that's too bad but others have it worse and someday things will get better" line, Armando popped off another question. "So why don't you speak Spanish if your mother is Mexican?"

It was the question I had been dreading that whole trip. I launched into the monologue I had perfected long ago, the one that deflected responsibility from me to the racial climate in which generations of my family had grown up. Armando and Netty nodded at the appropriate moments and made the corresponding murmurs of empathy. But when I finished, Netty clarified: "So you spent all those years learning Russian and Chinese, but not the language of your own family?"

It sounded pretty bad when put like that, didn't it? There wasn't much to say in my defense, though: I had made a conscious decision not to study Spanish because I couldn't fathom where it would get me besides my backyard. I was only beginning to understand that I should have gotten to know my own block before digging up someone else's.

"*Sí*, in Cuba, we have to fight harder for our dreams than you do in America," Armando allowed. "But in the end, the only thing that really matters is the knowledge you obtain of yourself and how you project this on your environment. The way you grew up negating your roots in order to be accepted by your society—that could never happen here. We all know we're Cuban."

I would think back on this comment many times after I left Armando's country, but at the time he said it, I could only nod and blink.

Just then, Gabriela walked over to announce it was 1:30 A.M. Both Armando and Antonio had hours-long bus waits and rides ahead of them, so we climbed down the hill toward the wharf. The return ferry was full of party revelers, the couples burrowing hungrily into each other for some last-minute loving while their friends drained the last of their rum. Back on the Havana side, we accompanied the students to a bus stop and hugged each of them good-bye. When I got to Armando, he sighed. "Sometimes I wish I grew up in the 1960s, in the beginning of the Revolution. Cubans were united back then. We had something to believe in. What a great time that would have been to be alive."

It was stunning to hear words I so often used come from the mouth of another—especially one who lived in a nation defined by Revolution. But here was someone else who wished he belonged to a time defined by activism rather than apathy, consciousness instead of consumerism. We both just wanted something to believe in.

29. THE CUBAN UNDERGROUND

BOUNCE TO THIS, SOCIALIST MOVEMENT
MY ENVIRONMENT MADE ME THE NIGGA I AM.
—*dead prez, "I'm a African"*

THE ONLY DOWNSIDE to staying with a host family is the not unfounded feeling you're imposing on their life. Machi and I always tried to get back at a decent hour, but after that night with the students, we didn't make it to Cecilia's doorstep till well past 2:00. Feeling extremely guilty, we rang the bell and braced ourselves for a bedraggled hostess rubbing her puffy eyes and pulling at her robe. But when the door flung open, Cecilia was clad in her usual spandexed glory, her eyes wide and lively. Every light was on in the house and we could hear the sound of music and laughter. Grabbing our hands, she led us through the foyer to the kitchen, where neighbors had gathered around the table. A light-skinned man with a handlebar mustache was strumming a flamenco guitar; a coffee-and-cream man was beating a conga. A black woman kept time by rapping a spoon against a half-drunk bottle of rum, while Gregorio—Cecilia's Creole husband—tilted his chair back and sang.

"*¡Baila! ¡Baila!*" they cried out to us. Dance! Dance!

That moment, perhaps more than any other, encapsulated

what I loved about Cuba: the spontaneity, the resourcefulness, the music, the laughter, and above all the camaraderie that seemed to transcend color lines. Having grown up in a nation where ethnicities were assigned to checkable boxes and people segregated themselves accordingly, Machi and I found this a hard concept to grasp. We once asked a cabdriver to pinpoint his identity—Spanish? Santero? Caribbean? white?—and he looked at us incredulously. *"Soy cubano, puro cubano,"* he claimed. I'm a Cuban, pure and simple.

And that's what the Revolution has tried hard to instill: the notion that national identity eclipses racial identity. It is an ambitious goal for a country bitterly divided by race for so many centuries. Like most nations, modern Cuba was built upon the backs of its people of color. Within decades of Columbus's landing, Spanish settlers had obliterated nearly the entire indigenous population through overwork, disease, and outright genocide. They looked first to Hispaniola (present-day Haiti and the Dominican Republic) for labor replacements in their prized sugarcane fields but then began importing tribespeople from Africa. The brawn of these men, women, and children turned Cuba into the sugar bowl of the world and the jewel of the Spanish Crown. The slave trade thrived for some 350 years, with at least 700,000 Africans sold into human bondage. (The United States, by comparison, imported approximately 427,000 slaves.)

Cuba's *grito de yara*—call to liberty—resounded in October 1868, when a fierce critic of Spain freed his slaves and then enrolled them in his army to fight against the *imperialistas*. Within a week, 1,500 other slave owners had followed suit, and war came quickly after. Fighting side by side, blacks and whites managed to abolish slavery and win their independence from Spain. But while Cuba never suffered the stringent segregation of the American South in the decades that followed, whites continued to hold undisputed power. Blacks and *mulatos* (a term commonly used in Cuba, without a negative connotation) were hired for only the most menial work and routinely refused entry to the best beaches, social clubs, theaters, restaurants, and schools. Even President Batista—a *mulato*—was shunned by the elite Havana Yacht Club. Upon his arrival one legendary evening, the white patrons turned off the lights to show their disapproval.

When Fidel seized power in 1959, he won immediate favor from blacks by opening all of the beaches and granting everyone equal access to health care and education. Black Cubans have since made strides in politics, sports, music, cinema, and dance that were unthinkable prior to the Revolution. To this day, poor and rural blacks constitute one of Fidel's most loyal bases, despite the fact that they occupy the bottom rung of Cuba's socioeconomic hierarchy and have failed to establish much of a political presence. Blacks have also suffered most in the Special Period, since fewer can rely on remittances from overseas families (as far more whites have gone into exile than blacks). Desperate for dollars, some have turned to hustling, crime, or prostitution to get by.

Ten days allowed for only the most topical of observations, and much of what we saw seemed contradictory. In some ways, Cuba did live up to its reputation as a nation of racial tolerance. I met African Americans who claimed they traveled there just to walk down streets where no one suddenly clutched their purse and switched to the other side. Some American blacks have even sought political asylum in Cuba, like activists Assata Shakur and Nehanda Abiodun. And what could be more rosy than stumbling home at 2:00 A.M. and finding a rainbow coalition dancing around your kitchen table?

But while restaurants and businesses had refreshing blends

of whites, blacks, and *mulatos* on staff, the former seemed to hold more positions of power than the latter two, particularly in the tourist industry. We also witnessed police stop far more blacks than whites on the street to conduct ID checks. And then there was that haunting wall-size painting in a Habana Vieja art gallery: *Difícil no es ser hombre, es ser negro*—It is difficult not to be a man [but] to be black.

WHEN MACHI TOLD me we'd be hanging with Pablo Herrera—Cuba's premier hip-hop producer—one evening, I pictured a Caribbean Puff Daddy in bright white sneakers and sunglasses with a model under each arm. We met him at a club that, from the moment we walked in, distanced itself from every other we'd seen. Gone were the tourists and their long-legged mistresses, the spit-polished bars with their bow-tied tenders. Jeans were worn baggy and low there, with baseball caps turned backward. Run-DMC's "King of Rock" was jamming on the sound system as we strode across the dance floor, and the mostly black and largely male clientele were rapping along: "To burn my kingdom, you must use fire / I won't stop rockin' till I retire."

Pablo was helping the DJ spin in back. A down-to-earth thirty-year-old in jeans and a T-shirt, he had produced most of Cuba's major rap acts (including the Orishas, before they defected to Paris) and became a cross-cultural music ambassador in the process. Over the course of the evening, he told us how rhymes and rhythm came to be the foremost means of self-expression for an entire generation of Cubans.

"This all started when somebody got hold of Sugar Hill Gang's 'Rapper's Delight' in the early eighties. We didn't connect with the lyrics so much as the beat, and our block parties filled the street," he said.

The music particularly took hold in Alamar, the suburb where the government built a colossal Soviet-style complex in the 1970s that now housed tens of thousands of the capital's poorest residents—most of whom were black. Teenagers constructed antennas on their balconies to beam in hip-hop from Miami and taught themselves how to break-dance while their homegrown *raperos* rhymed about their fine girlfriends. They also tried to imitate the latest in South Bronx fashion.

"People started walking around in hoodies and sweats in ninety-degree heat," Pablo said, laughing.

At first, the police deemed the music "capitalist" and "imperialist" and shut down neighborhood street parties. But hip-hop fast became such a world phenomenon, not even the state could suppress it—especially when groups like N.W.A and De La Soul politicized it in the late 1980s. Public Enemy's anthem lyrics " 'Cause I'm Black and I'm proud / I'm ready and hyped plus I'm amped" hit a raw nerve in the Cubans who'd been told race didn't matter for four decades. Once the government started barring its citizens from tourist resorts and beaches again, *raperos* began to incorporate social injustice into their own lyrics. This made police clamp down even harder—until Pablo started organizing meetings with government committees and persuading them that *el rap* was revolutionary, not reactionary. Young Cubans needed a voice in their society, he argued, and this music was the perfect medium. In the late 1990s, he helped secure an invitation for a New York–based alliance of grassroots organizations called the Black August Collective to visit Havana and promote hip-hop as a social movement. Soon after, Minister of Culture Abel Prieto declared that *el rap* was an "authentic expression of *cubanidad*" and promised *raperos* "the freedom to claim their power culturally." When the Cuban national baseball team blasted the group Doble Filo before their national championship game against the Baltimore Orioles instead of the usual salsa, the entire stadium rapped along—including, by many accounts, Fidel. The government also began to funnel money into the music.

Naturally, some restrictions came with state patronage. *Raperos* couldn't exactly shout "Down with socialism" into the mike—or anything else that might be construed as "counter-revolutionary." In fact, the more pro-Revolution a group, the better their chances of success. With lyrics like "I would give anything for my Cuba / I'm happy here," the wildly popular Anonimo Consejo had become a featured act of state-sponsored shows and toured with a state-run production company. But *raperos* could and did push the limits on other taboo topics like *jineteros*, racism, and police harassment. They also promoted black empowerment. In another song, Anonimo Consejo sang: "There's a fortune under your dark skin / The power is yours."

All in all, it was a story made for radio. Machi hit up Pablo for contacts and conducted some interviews. A few days later, we randomly met two of the rappers/producers—whom I'll call Yosvany and Dagoberto—on the street. Though they were missing the gold chains and Timberlands, they had other markings of their trade. Dagoberto wore a black beret and overcoat and walked with a carved wooden cane; Yosvany wore blue mirrored sunglasses and black cowboy boots. We invited them to lunch at Los Amigos, an especially good *paladar* in Vedado. (As in other family-owned and -operated restaurants, you dined right in Los Amigos' living room, surrounded by photographs of the people serving you, and walked through someone's bedroom to get to the bathroom.) Machi ordered us a *criollo* meal of fried chicken, plantains, french-fried potatoes, black beans, white rice, and a round of Cristal beer, and we asked about their music.

Being a *rapero* in the birthplace of rumba wasn't easy. Hip-hop was the art of production, but no one there had the equipment with which to produce. Even CDs were scarce in Cuba, so many *raperos* had to record their tracks on cassettes or DAT instead. Yosvany and Dagoberto had been waiting five years to cut an album but still hadn't rounded up the necessary equipment.

"Our album will come out someday," Yosvany said, cautiously optimistic.

"What do you rap about?"

"We rap about what we see; we rap about what we do," Dagoberto summed up. "We rap about the difference between good and bad."

"And what would that be?"

"The bad would be things like street crime, *jineteros*, violence, police harassment, racism. And the good would be the Revolution," he said.

The ironies were striking. Yosvany and Dagoberto obviously admired their brothers up north. But while Ice-T was telling his fans to "Fuck tha police," they were telling theirs to support the System. Their nemesis was capitalism and consumerism—what a good deal of American hip-hop had become. When I pointed this out, Dagoberto replied: "Yes, Cuban rap is very positive. We try to work within the System and push it to be its best."

"You could say that our music is the sound track of the new Revolution . . . just like rap is the voice of the new generation," Yosvany said. "This is also the only music movement in Cuba today that reaffirms what it means to be black."

"So hip-hop is mainly for blacks?"

Dagoberto shook his head. "No Cuban is one hundred per-cent black or one hundred percent Spanish. We are a fusion of each of these cultures, and over the years, this fusion has formed its own culture."

"We also share a revolutionary culture," Yosvany added.

"How about that Revolution?" Machi asked.

Dagoberto paused to collect his thoughts. "If you ask a Cuban that, their knee-jerk reaction is to complain about the bureaucracy, the lack of efficiency, the shortage of goods. But if you sit down and really talk with them, you'll find that deep down, they still believe the Revolution is the best thing for Cuba."

"Why?"

"Because it's ours. Our heroes are Cuban, our leaders are Cuban, our people are Cuban. Our ideology is formed by Martí, not Marx," Yosvany explained.

As the martyred revolutionary leader of Cuba's fight for in-dependence from Spain, José Martí was indeed the nation's most beloved figure—the one man whose bust could be found upon the mantels of Communists and exiles alike. The most frequent complaint we heard about Fidel was that he should have followed Martí's ideological path more than "that German philosopher's."

Having scheduled a session at Pablo's that afternoon, Yos-vany and Dagoberto needed to leave soon after our meal. As Machi finished her interview with Yosvany, Dagoberto took me aside and lowered his voice. "Getting back to your question about the Revolution, I can tell you one thing: Every Cuban left on this island *wants* to believe in the Revolution. Badly."

30. BACK IN THE U.S. OF A.

NO HAY MAL QUE DURA CIEN AÑOS
NI UN CUERPO QUE LO RESISTE.

THERE IS NO EVIL THAT LASTS A HUNDRED
YEARS, NOR A BODY THAT CAN RESIST IT.
—*Cuban proverb*

THE UNITED STATES has prohibited its citizens from trading with Cuba since Eisenhower, but it forced that law upon the rest of the world in 1996 with the Helms-Burton Act (which, among other things, allows Americans to sue foreign companies that conduct business in Cuba). Some say Clinton passed the law as a concession to the Miami exiles who helped him win reelection; others say it was because Cuban jet fighters had recently shot down two "Brothers to the Rescue" planes searching for refugees in the Straits of Florida. Still others swear that Fidel somehow masterminded the entire thing himself, as it united more Cubans against the United States than anything he'd dreamed up in years.

Whatever the case, the law has disastrously impacted the Cuban people—particularly in terms of health care. There is such a dearth of medicines and supplies in Cuba, some doctors must resort to acupuncture for anesthesia and sew wounds with hemp. The embargo also deprives American farmers of an estimated $1.24 billion annually and infuriates the governments of practically every other nation on the globe. But because it benefits a few Miami hard-liners, a handful of Washington bigwigs, a couple of corporations (namely Bacardi rum), and possibly Fidel—Helms-Burton seems here to stay.

This unconscionable policy is the reason Machi and I initially pretended that we were Canadians. It is also why, before leaving Texas, we stocked up on supplies we thought hospitals and schools might need. They sat at the bottom of our backpacks until our final morning in Havana, when we ventured out to distribute them. Our first stop was the Prado, the tree-lined boulevard leading up to the Capitolio. With its galleried walkways and vaulted ceilings, this was Havana's most prestigious address in the late 1700s. But when the Mafia bought it out in the twentieth century, the highborn moved out and the harlots checked in, transforming the strip into a red-light district of live sex shows and glitzy casinos. Soon after the Revolution, however, Fidel sent the call girls to training camp, replaced the blackjack tables with bookshelves, and turned the bordellos into classrooms, renaming the Prado "El Paseo de Martí." Machi and I ambled down its crumbling walkway and selected an old schoolhouse at random. As we pushed through its towering double doors, a middle-aged man in a neatly pressed guayabera, or traditional dress shirt, appeared.

"We brought gifts," we announced.

He pointed to a classroom with a wave and a smile. We peeked through its doorway. Inside were forty students working quietly around rectangular tables, each one wearing maroon shorts, a white blouse, and a blue neckerchief signifying their membership in the Union de Pioneros José Martí, or

Communist Youth League. They appeared to be in the third grade. Their spacious room was lined with bookshelves, a world map, and a poster of thumbnail sketches of select Sierra Maestra rebels. Above the blackboard hung a black-and-white framed photograph of Che Guevara smoking a cigar. (The pledge *Seremos como el Che*—We will be like Che—is recited by schoolchildren every morning.) Their teacher looked on from a three-legged stool, her own leg wrapped in an enormous white cast unraveling at the seams. Noticing us in the doorway, she beckoned us in, as if travelers often appeared there, wringing their hands uncertainly. The students watched, wide-eyed and excited, as we walked to the front of the room and piled stickers, notebooks, pens, and pencils onto a table. Then I looked at Machi and she looked at me. What now?

When I packed these supplies in Corpus, I rehearsed a little speech in my head—something along the lines of "Americans are your friends. We did not kidnap your classmate Elián. We hope he can return home to Cuba as soon as possible." But after ten days in Havana, I was starting to think my country really *had* kidnapped the little boy.

"We brought gifts," Machi finally said.

We passed out the supplies. The students sang out their appreciation. And then we left. No one asked who we were or where we came from, and we didn't tell them.

From there, we hailed a Rambler to the nearest children's hospital. I thought we'd be turned away for certain when I saw the little old lady sitting authoritatively behind the large empty desk, but when we asked if we could visit the patients, she chirped: *"Sí, cómo no?"* and waved us in.

We walked down a hallway and knocked upon a door marked PHYSICAL THERAPY. A curly-haired woman in a white lab coat welcomed us into a dimly lit room painted green. A boy with thick black curls smiled at us from a surgical table as a therapist massaged his spindly legs. A shriveled balloon dangled from one of the metal bedposts.

"We brought gifts," we said as we emptied our backpacks of cough syrup, aspirin, bandages, and rubbing alcohol. When I pulled out some bars of Ivory soap, the therapist gasped.

"*Mil gracias,*" she breathed. "We need soap so badly around here."

By the time we left the hospital, we had only an hour to spare. After my conversation with Netty and Armando, I had refrained from taking street photos but found myself wanting to capture the rich imagery around me. Momentarily stifling my nagging conscience, I pulled out my camera and started snapping pictures. Of a seventy-year-old man in a beret blowing smoke rings. Of three women sitting on the curb of a pharmacy. Of a college student strumming a guitar. I was freeze-framing a vintage Chevy Deluxe when Machi grabbed my shoulder and pointed out the good-looking guy in blue mirrored sunglasses walking toward us. It was Yosvany, *el rapero*. He kissed us hello and announced that he and Dagoberto had decided they liked us. "We're always getting burned by foreign journalists who come to Cuba, spend a few days interviewing us, and go off and write about how we are the counterrevolution. It's like they didn't hear a word we said. Don't they realize we have to live with what they write?"

There were a number of ways to take a comment like that. My Chinese colleagues might have said the editors of the newspapers in question thought their journalists had been "brainwashed" by Cuba's Communist regime and so tweaked their copy accordingly. My Russian friends might have called the hip-hop artists the "brainwashed" ones. But I tried to take it at face value (as an offhanded compliment) and clasped his hands with both of my own in thanks.

Our time rapidly diminishing, we said a last good-bye to Yosvany and then hurried into the street to flag down a car. Just as a Plymouth pulled over, a manly pair of hands suddenly wrapped themselves around my waist. It was Harold, the rumba king, in a collarless linen suit with seven strands of yellow and black beads clasped around his neck. (He'd left in a huff that night at La Loipa, offended when I started dancing with some guy with dreads.)

"*Llamame,*" he breathed into my ear. Call me.

"I'm leaving for Mexico in twenty-five minutes!"

"Stay."

A mental image of an extended life in Havana quickly formed. Of getting a job at *Granma* and supplementing my wages selling faux cigars to tourists. Of finding that jeans maven and trading my khakis and denim for her Lycra and spandex. Of finally learning to roll my *r*'s and speak in a tense other than present.

"*Te montas o no?*" the driver suddenly shouted, yanking me out of my fantasy.

"*Sí, sí,*" I assured him, then turned around to kiss Harold good-bye before climbing into the Plymouth. With that, Machi and I zoomed out of Vedado toward Centro Habana, marveling at the odds of running into two of our favorite Habaneros again, in a city of 2.2 million people. Back at our *casa*, we scrambled into our room to grab our things, kissed Cecilia and Rosaldo good-bye, then roared back down the Malecon one last time, past the lip-locked lovers and the strolling families, the *jineteros* on the prowl and their unsuspecting prey, past the schoolkids heading home for lunch and the fishermen waiting patiently for theirs.

Back at José Martí International, I plunked down my passport for the control officer and declared my love for his country. He grinned. *"Entonces, necesitas volver muy pronto,"* he said as he returned it, unstamped. Then you must hurry back very soon.

And then he buzzed me back through the little white doors.

FORTY-EIGHT HOURS LATER, our bus rolled up to the American border. Dirty and hungry, Machi and I staggered into the morning sunlight, grabbed our backpacks from beneath the bus, and shuffled into a line that consisted entirely of Mexican nationals in conservative skirts and trousers. Two female agents—a robust African American and a mousy-haired gringa—nabbed us the instant we stepped across the building's threshold.

"IDs?" one asked.

We handed them our driver's licenses.

"Where you coming from?"

"Mexico City," Machi said. That was actually true—our plane did land there from Havana.

"How long were you there?"

"A little over two weeks," I said.

"Okay. You come with me," she said to Machi, "and you go with her." She pointed me to the gringa.

My heart thumping, I followed the agent to the other side of the room. When she asked what I'd bought, I pulled out the knickknacks I'd purchased primarily for their garish HECHO EN MEXICO—MADE IN MEXICO—stickers.

"Anything else?"

I licked my lips contemplatively as I thought of the Commie paraphernalia stuffed inside my second bag. "Not really."

"Let's have a look." She patted a table.

Starting with my day pack, the agent pulled out my jar of

peanut butter, opened it, and sniffed. "So what did you do in Mexico City?"

"Ummmm . . . mmmm . . . museums! The Frida Kahlo Museum, the Anthropology Museum, the Trotsky—I mean, the Teotihuacán ruins. . . ."

"Did you go anywhere besides Mexico City?"

"Cuernavaca! Have you been? It's great! I've got my bus tickets right here." I patted the money belt tucked inside my jeans.

Her eyes narrowed in on the bulge around my belly. "Let's see 'em."

As I fumbled with its clasp, I remembered what else was stored in there: my Mexican tourist visa. I had tossed out all hard evidence of my trip to Cuba—airline tickets, receipts—except that one, and it stated clearly that I'd been in Mexico only a couple of days, not a couple of weeks. *Dios mio,* what had I done? My hands trembling, I removed the belt, unzipped its pouch, and pulled out its contents. There was the visa, tucked behind my passport. *HailMaryFullofGracetheLordIswithThee.* As the agent reached out to take it—*BlessedArtThouAmongWomen*— the other agent suddenly called her name from across the room. Reflex mandated that she turn her head, and I slipped the card beneath my poncho when she did. "Here you go."

She looked back at me, accepted the bundle of papers, and signaled me to open the second pack. Dread churning in my stomach, I undid the combination lock and pulled back the flap. She shoved aside my Guatemalan skirt and there they were: Cuban cassettes. Cuban CDs. Havana maps and guidebooks. Postcards of Che, Fidel, and Camilo Cienfuegos romping through the Sierras. A rumpled Cuban flag. She opened my journal and paused to read what I had scribbled in block letters on the first page: "CUBA OR BUST!"

For an unbearably long moment, she scrutinized the souvenirs as if choosing the most condemning one—the one that would send me to the slammer for good. Then she reached for the plastic bag of carrot and celery sticks I'd prepared that morning in Mexico City.

"You can put your things together," she said, then walked off with my papers and my lunch.

Machi and I stared at each other from opposite sides of the room as our agents huddled together, comparing our documents. Then they called us over to explain the discrepancy. Why did Machi's passport have a reentry stamp from two days ago while mine did not? In fact, it was because I had given the Mexican customs officials my driver's license and birth certificate in lieu of a passport on our return from Cuba so it wouldn't be branded with a reentry stamp. Having forgotten her birth certificate in Texas, however, Machi had to hand over her passport, which revealed she'd gone to a third country during our trip.

"Did you two always stick together?" the black agent—who clearly took no shit—demanded.

"Yes," I said as confidently as possible.

"Then why is her passport stamped and yours is not?"

"I don't know," I said, trying not to blink.

She looked at Machi, then at me. Hard. *Ay, Dios mio,* we are sooooo busted. . . .

"And where are your Mexican tourist visas?"

Fingering mine in my pocket, I lied: "They took them in Reynosa."

"Okay, ladies," she said briskly, rubbing her hands together.

Okay, ladies, what? 'Fess up? Call your lawyers? Into the slammer you go?

"Have a good trip back."

Careful not to look at each other, Machi and I gave thanks and bowed out of the building. Half a block down, a bus began to pull away from the curb. We raced toward it, our Che Guevara coins jingling in our pockets. As I reached the bus door, I turned triumphantly toward Machi. We clasped our hands together in a fast high five. Then we clambered aboard the bus and headed home to South Texas.

THE BLOC IS a hell of a teacher.

True, she has built within me a foundation that allows me to stroll the world's passageways with confidence. She has taught me the difference between being alone and being lonely and made me ever selective of my company. In fact, the Bloc has turned me into such a self-sustained, self-contained unit, I'm expecting to self-pollinate any day now.

But she has also shown me that I'm really not the militant-vegetarian-Chicana-feminist I prided myself on being at age twenty-one. My vegetarian loyalties drowned in a bowl of yak penis soup. I compromised my feminism by putting up with men who did me wrong. My inability to converse fluently with *cubanos*—and, more important, *mexicanos*—proved I still have some work to do before I can rightfully claim the Chicana label.

I'm still struggling with many of the Bloc's lessons, like the one first presented by Vova and Karina back in Moscow. Having realized the devastating ways state propaganda had clouded their nation's concept of reality for so many decades, they challenged me to do the same, about my own. I've been working on that lately and have found some disconcerting similarities between our respective ideological frameworks. The Soviets revered mass murderers; we honor presidents who kept slaves, sent indigenous people on death marches, and waged brutal wars on developing nations. China's news gets filtered through the state, ours through mega–media conglomerates. Cuba may not hold democratic elections, but can we really claim to after our disastrous 2000 presidential election? And what about our USA Patriot Act, or our clampdown on immigrants from Muslim nations, or our stifling of civil liberties, or George W. Bush's warning to the world: "You're either with us or against us"?

Rather than point out the holes in others' truths, we should be investigating the ones in our own.

The Bloc has also taught me a thing or two about activism. A year after my return from Beijing, tens of thousands of environmentalists, union organizers, and activists poured into the streets of Seattle to protest the World Trade Organization. I watched them on TV in amazement: Had the political activity I so eagerly sought overseas taken root in my backyard? Two weeks after September 11, 2001, I joined the movement at a peace rally in Tucson, Arizona, where I—ironically enough—got called a "fucking Commie" by a man in a truck for holding a peace sign. A month later, I moved to Park Slope, Brooklyn, where war resisters held rallies outside the subway station every Thursday. And once Washington began to beat the war drum against Iraq, dissenters united in protest worldwide. On February 15, 2003, up to ten million citizens from seventy-five countries took to the streets for peace, my friends and I among them.

But while it has been thrilling to witness and participate in this mass movement, I have realized that demonstrations are not—as I once thought—romantic acts of passion. It takes a pretty dire situation to rile millions of everyday citizens out of bed to march in the cold. Rather than lament the fact that my student body was so apathetic in the early 1990s, I should have been grateful that we didn't have quite so many heinous reasons to demonstrate. By early 2000, it was painfully apparent that the Red Scare that had terrorized our nation for half a century had been replaced by the Green Scare of Islam.

It devastates me that we have seemingly learned so little from the mistakes of our past. Will my niece and nephew someday fear a menacing green blob gobbling up Asia, Africa, and the Middle East on their own maps? How many people must die senselessly before our world leaders realize the insanity of branding entire populations "evil"?

Finally, the Bloc taught me the momentousness of culture. That's ironic, considering how fervently Stalin and Mao—and, to a far lesser extent, Fidel—tried to vanquish centuries of religion, tradition, and ritual by forcing their people to conform to socialist culture. Yet hundreds of thousands of citizens around the Bloc repeatedly defied these rulings, like the nonethnic Russians who risked the Gulag to distribute underground *samizdat* printed in their native language during the Soviet regime or the Uighurs and Tibetans who prostrated before their gods in their officially atheist "autonomous provinces." Meanwhile, those of us who haven't needed to fight for our culture have often deserted it. In some ways, capitalism has done an even better job of dissolving cultures than communism. My travels in the Bloc forced me to question why. How did I lose such a fundamental part of who I am? And why have I never invested time or energy recovering it?

This may be the lasting impact of my four-year journey: realizing the need to turn inward. I may have lived my high school nightmare—spending my twenty-fifth year home in

Corpus Christi—but it was there that I finally realized that of all the things I did to be "more Chicana" in college, I'd failed at the most important: learning Spanish. My time back in Mexico and South Texas showed me that a knowledge of Spanish would gain me a greater intimacy with my people, my family, and of myself.

And now, I *want* to speak the tongue of my ancestors—not just to make idle conversation, but to tell my *tías* a funny story, to soothe a frightened child, to philosophize, to sing, to pray. I want my grandchildren to be transfixed by my fingertips, singed and callused from heating up tortillas. I want to be able to call myself a Chicana in any crowd—and believe it.

So I basically traveled tens of thousands of miles to appreciate what had been in my block all along. But it probably would not have seemed this rich if I hadn't taken the long road.

IT WAS MUCH EASIER TO WIN
THE REVOLUTIONARY WAR THAN
IT IS TO RUN THE REVOLUTION NOW
THAT WE ARE IN CHARGE.

—*Fidel Alejandro Castro Ruz, 1959*

NOTES

SECTION ONE ★ MOSCOW

2. WHEN WE WERE KINGS

13 **When Sting sang, "What might save us"** Sting, "Russians," *The Dream of the Blue Turtles*, A&M Records, 1985.

14 **The King Ranch was "discovered"** Mona D. Sizer, *The King Ranch Story: Truth and Myth* (Plano, Tex.: Republic of Texas Press, 1999).

23 **At that time, the government owed** Jennifer Gould, *Vodka, Tears, and Lenin's Angel* (New York: St. Martin's Press, 1997).

23 **According to Alla Bodiereva** Stephanie Griest, "First Vote on a President Since Soviet Collapse in 1991," *Seattle Post Intelligencer*, June 11, 1996, A1.

24 **Russian schools were no longer** Taylor E. Dark, "No Illusions: Russia's Student Generation," *National Interest* (spring 1996).

25 **In Former Times (that is, while the Soviet Union was still intact)** Jim Riordan, "The Komsomol," in Jim Riordan, ed., *Soviet Youth Culture* (Bloomington and Indianapolis: Indiana University Press, 1989).

4. THE ABANDONED

42 **According to a 1998 Human Rights Watch report** Kathleen Hunt, "Abandoned to the State: Cruelty and Neglect in Russian Orphanages"

(New York: Human Rights Watch, December 1998), available at www.hrw.org/hrw/reports98/russia2/Russ98d.htm

45 **Soviet propaganda long ago instilled**   Hunt, "Abandoned to the State."

5. BOUNTIFUL BALAKHNA

52 **She wanted to relocate to the capital**   David Filipov, "In Moscow, They're Aliens in Their Own Nation," *The Boston Globe*, October 26, 1997, A2.

55 **But how can you blame**   Isabel Fonseca, *Bury Me Standing: The Gypsies and Their Journey* (New York: Knopf, 1995).

62 **By July 1996, some**   Michael Wines, "Scores Die as Bombs Ravage Chechen Capital," *The New York Times*, October 22, 1999, A3.

65 **I was under the impression**   Katherine Verdery, *The Political Lives of Dead Bodies* (New York: Columbia University Press, 2000).

66 **Gorky probably enjoyed his stay**   Gennady Gorelik, "Andrei Sakharov: Soviet Physics, Nuclear Weapons, and Human Rights" (College Park, Md.: American Institute of Physics, 1998), available at www.aip.org/history/sakharov.

6. THE VODKA CHRONICLES

74 **The average Russian (man, woman, or child)**   Geoff Winestock, "Russia's Vodka Politics," *Journal of Commerce*, April 2, 1996, 6A.

74 **Dr. Alexander Nemtsov**   Victoria Clark, "Killer Vodka Runs Riot in Russia," *The Observer*, November 26, 1995, 26.

7. FROM *DEVUSHKA* TO *ZHENSHINA*: FROM GIRL TO WOMAN

86 **Journalist and author**   Francine du Plessix Gray, *Soviet Women: Walking the Tightrope* (New York: Anchor Books, 1990).

86 **In 1996, Russia boasted**   Alessandra Stanley, "New Face of Russian Capitalism," *The New York Times*, August 14, 1996, D3.

89 **She became one of Russia's**   Lori Cidylo, "Russia Discovers the Rape Victim," *Financial Times*, August 13, 1994.

89 **After sharing some grisly statistics**   Eileen O'Connor, "Domestic

Abuse: Russia's Tragic, Hidden Secret" (*CNN World News*, March 7, 1997), available at www2.cnn.com/WORLD/9703/07/russia.domestic/index.html

90 **On the order of Ivan the Terrible** Gray, *Soviet Women.*

90 **Then came the Bolsheviks** Wendy Goldman, *Women, the State and Revolution: Soviet Family Policy and Social Life, 1917–1936* (Cambridge: Cambridge University Press, 1993).

91 **When the socialized kitchens** Goldman, *Women, the State and Revolution.*

91 **The collapse of the Soviet Union in 1991** Vanora Bennett, "Violence Against Women in Russia Grows Worse," *Los Angeles Times,* December 6, 1997.

91 **Russian women also have to contend with** Naomi Neft and Ann Levine, *Where Women Stand: An International Report on the Status of Women in 140 Countries* (New York: Random House, 1997).

91 **Some employers stipulate quite openly** Bennett, "Violence Against Women in Russia Grows Worse."

91 **. . . others ask female applicants to send in photos** Gould, *Vodka, Tears, and Lenin's Angel.*

92 **Yet not a single sexual harassment case** Bennett, "Violence Against Women in Russia Grows Worse."

96 **According to folklore, *banya*** Genevra Gerhart, *The Russian's World: Life and Language* (Fort Worth, Tex.: Harcourt Brace, 1995).

8. *NASTAYASHII RUSSKII MUZHIK:* A REAL RUSSIAN MAN

100 **Leo Tolstoy once defined him** Forward to N. Orlov's 1909 book, *Russkie Muʒhiki* (St. Petersburg, Russia: T-vo R. Golike and A. Vilborg), available at www.russianart.dk/EarlierExhibitions.

103 **Its graphite moderator burst** Jessica Matthews, "The Chernobyl Curse," *The Washington Post,* April 23, 1996, A17.

109 **In 1994, a Moscow *propiska* cost** David Hoffman, "Moscow Remains a Perk for Permit Holders," *The Washington Post,* January 20, 1997, A19.

109 **Without one, Kari couldn't** Clara Germani, "Russia, Home to Legal Nonentities," *Baltimore Sun,* May 19, 1997, 2A.

9. THE WILD EAST

115 **Russian *Mafiozi* were generally classified** Andrian Kreye, "RA-BORKA! The Emergence of the Moscow Mafia in the Mid 90s," available at http://users.rcn.com/akreye/Moscow.html. English translation of an excerpt from Kreye's book *Berichte aus der Kampf-zone* (*Dispatches from the Combat Zone*) (Munich: Droemer Knaur, 2002).

116 **By the mid-1990s, the underworld** Jack Kelley, "Mafia Has Death Grip on Russia," *USA Today*, November 4, 1996, 4A.

116 **By 1996, there were nearly eight thousand** David Remnick, *Resurrection: The Struggle for a New Russia* (New York: Vintage, 1998).

116 **Unlike Kirill, the bulk of contract assassins** Kelley, "Mafia Has Death Grip on Russia."

116 **and Russia's murder rate was roughly double** Remnick, *Resurrection*.

119 **Journalist and author David Remnick** David Remnick, *Lenin's Tomb: The Last Days of the Soviet Empire* (New York: Vintage, 1994).

123 **But over the years, it evolved** Doug Steele, "The End of an Era: The Hungry Duck," available at www.hungryduck.com/exile.htm.

124 **The Hungry Duck was finally shut down in 1999** John Helmer, "Dying Swan Kills Hungry Duck," *Moscow Tribune*, March 26, 1999.

10. FREE LOVE, RUBLE BEER

132 **It was the Bolsheviks who introduced "free love"** James Riordan, "Introduction," in Igor Kon and James Riordan, eds., *Sex and Russian Society* (Bloomington: Indiana University Press, 1993).

132 **Feminist Alexandra Kollontai** Goldman, *Women, the State and Revolution*.

132 **A few years later, Stalin halted** Lynne Attwood, "Sex and the Cinema," in Kon and Riordan, eds., *Sex and Russian Society*.

133 **Brothels, massage parlors, porn flicks** Riordan, "Introduction," in Kon and Riordan, eds., *Sex and Russian Society*.

133 **It has been widely rumored that** Carrie McVicker, "Russia's Prostitution Trade," *TED Case Studies: An Online Journal* 8, no. 1 (January 1988), available at www.american.edu/projects/mandala/TED/RUSSSEX.HTM.

134 **When the Soviet Union dissolved**   John Daniszewski, "Russian Coalition Fights Sex Slavery," *Los Angeles Times*, May 17, 2001, A3.

134 **Lured into cartels with promises**   McVicker, "Russia's Prostitution Trade."

134 **The Soviet Health Ministry never**   Riordan, "Introduction," in Kon and Riordan, eds., *Sex and Russian Society*.

134 **Women who took the pill**   Larissa Reminnick, "Patterns of Birth Control," in Kon and Riordan, eds., *Sex and Russian Society*.

135 **The Bolsheviks were a progressive bunch**   Goldman, *Women, the State and Revolution*.

135 **Some reports claim the average**   Reminnick, "Patterns of Birth Control," in Kon and Riordan, eds., *Sex and Russian Society*.

135 **. . . others show the rate between seven**   Lee Hocksteader, "Anti-Abortion Activists Backed by America's Church Drive in Russia," *The Washington Post*, May 19, 1994.

135 **In 1920, the average woman gave birth**   David Adamson and Julie DaVanzo, "Russia's Demographic Crisis: How Real Is It?" RAND Issue Paper (Santa Monica: Center for Russian and Eurasian Studies, July 1997), available at www.rand.org/publications/IP/IP162

136 **Homosexuality was actually fairly accepted**   Igor Kon, "Sexual Minorities," in Kon and Riordan, eds., *Sex and Russian Society*.

136 **Homosexuality was finally decriminalized**   James Meek, "Out of the Gulag but Still Outcast," *The Guardian*, June 24, 1995, 16.

11. DEMOCRACY 101

142 **Vladimir Ilyich Ulyanov Lenin had one dying wish**   Bill Wallace, "Can Russia Bury Its Past?" *The Scotsman*, June 5, 1999.

143 **As Felix Dzerzhinsky, founder of the KGB, put it**   Ilya Zbarsky, *Lenin's Embalmers* (London: Harvill Press, 1997).

143 **Reds across the world met similar fates**   Andrey Yarushin, Olga Kostromina, Lyudmila Yermakova, and Inna Zhukova, "Russia Marks Lenin's Death Anniversary with Mixed Feelings," Itar-Tass News Agency, January 21, 1999.
   Christopher Thomas, "Sun and a Faulty Fridge Bedevil Hero's Tomb," *The Times* (London), October 30, 1985.

143 **Whenever the controversy started brewing** Verdery, *The Political Lives of Dead Bodies.*

145 **As the story goes, a Party Congress** Ibid.

146 **The Politburo promptly banished** Zbarsky, *Lenin's Embalmers.*

146 **Lenin utilized famine as a political weapon** David Remnick, "Vladimir Ilyich Lenin," *Time,* April 13, 1998.

146 **Then he was succeeded by a man** Remnick, *Resurrection.*
Information and statistics on the 1996 Russian presidential election (pp. 147–58) came from David Remnick, "The Black Box," *The New Yorker,* March 27, 2000, and Remnick, *Resurrection.*

153 *Eto est' nash poslednij* Lyrics to "The Internationale" available at www.geocities.com/yrraph/int_russian.htm.

12. *MOSKVA CLYEZI NE VERIT:* MOSCOW DOESN'T BELIEVE IN TEARS

162 **A crew of 2,500 had been** Gould, *Vodka, Tears, and Lenin's Angel.*

162 **Indeed, I would later learn** Ibid.

SECTION TWO ★ BEIJING

13. THE CULINARY REVOLUTION

176 **In addition to creative misspellings** Shai Oster, "Foreign Brains in Beijing," *The Wall Street Journal Interactive Edition,* March 17, 2000.

15. UNHEARD OF: INSIDE A CHINESE NEWSROOM

193 **The results were often catastrophic** Harrison Salisbury, *The New Emperors: China in the Era of Mao and Deng* (New York: Avon Books, 1993).

194 **Headlines claimed that wheat fields were so thick** Jianying Zha, *China Pop* (New York: New Press, 1995).

194 *People's Daily* **replaced classroom textbooks** Jung Chang, *Wild Swans* (New York: Anchor Books/Doubleday, 1992).

197 **He read aloud the first few lines** Bruce Springsteen, "I'm on Fire," *Born in the U.S.A.*, Columbia, 1984.

198 **Even its name—*aizibing*** Orville Schell, *Mandate of Heaven: A New Generation of Entrepreneurs, Dissidents, Bohemians, and Technocrats Lays Claim to China's Future* (New York: Simon & Schuster, 1994).

198 **But the virus soon exploded** Elisabeth Rosenthal, "AIDS Scourge in Rural China Leaves Villages of Orphans," *The New York Times*, August 25, 2002, A1.

200 **"The 15th National Congress of the Communist Party"** Xu Dashan, "Meeting to Lead Nation into the 21st Century," *China Daily*, September 12, 1997, A1.

202 **In *China Pop*, Jianying Zha quotes** Jianying, *China Pop.*

208 **His inaccuracies were so absurd** "Death by Default: A Policy of Fatal Neglect in China's State Orphanages" (New York: Human Rights Watch, January 1996), available from www.hrw.org/summaries/s.china961.html#shanghai.

16. *LAOWAI:* THE FOREIGNER

212 **When the army finally drove out** "The Roots of Racism Rubbed Raw," *U.S. News & World Report*, January 9, 1989, 10.

212 **In 1839, a Chinese commissioner** Michael Cooper, "New Mission for Lin Ze Xu, Hero of Old," *The New York Times*, June 2, 1996.

17. CLOSE ENCOUNTERS WITH EMBALMED COMMUNIST NO. 2

226 **The tradition started out of genuine reverence** Schell, *Mandate of Heaven.*

227 **One *China Daily* centerfold** Lu Shaohe, "Couple Sculpts Mao for Love," *China Daily*, December 5, 1997, A10.

227 **After his death in 1976** Schell, *Mandate of Heaven.*

228 **Like Lenin, Mao never asked** Lincoln Kaye, "Leaders Under Glass," *World Press Review*, December 1994, 30.

229 **The leader who organized one hundred thousand men** Jeremy Atiyah, David Leffman, and Simon Lewis, *China: The Rough Guide* (London: Penguin, 1997).

18. THE JUNE 4 REBELLION/INCIDENT/MASSACRE

233 **Yet after the April 15, 1989** Salisbury, *The New Emperors.*

233 **The Western press summarized** Linda Jakobson, "Lies in Ink, Truth in Blood: The Role and Impact of the Chinese Media During the Beijing Spring of '89" (Discussion Paper D-6, the Joan Shorenstein Center on the Press, Politics and Public Policy, John F. Kennedy School of Government, Harvard University, August 1990), available at www.ksg.harvard.edu/presspol/publications/papers.htm.

234 **The students won support** Schell, *Mandate of Heaven.*

234 **Even pickpockets announced publicly** Liu Binyan, *Tell the World: What Happened in China and Why* (New York: Pantheon Books, 1989).

234 **"We, the children, are ready to use our lives"** Ian Buruma, *Bad Elements: Chinese Rebels from Los Angeles to Beijing* (New York: Random House, 2001).

234 **The young protesters made far sexier** Jan Wong, *Red China Blues* (New York: Anchor Books/Doubleday, 1997).

235 **The top student leaders became** Jakobson, "Lies in Ink, Truth in Blood."

235 **Between the failed Sino-Soviet Summit** Wong, *Red China Blues.*

236 **Incredibly, few troops** Salisbury, *The New Emperors.*

236 **The Chinese Red Cross released figures of 2,600 casualties** Jakobson, "Lies in Ink, Truth in Blood."

236 **The New York Times put the death toll at 400 to 800** Nicholas Kristof and Sheryl WuDunn, *China Wakes* (New York: Vintage, 1995).

236 **The Chinese government said** Editorial Board of the Truth about the Beijing Turmoil, "The Truth About the Beijing Turmoil" (Beijing: Beijing Publishing House, 1990).

236 **It is doubtful the real number will** Schell, *Mandate of Heaven.*

236 **In the months that followed, as many as forty thousand Chinese** Buruma, *Bad Elements.*

239 **On May 4, some two hundred journalists** Jakobson, "Lies in Ink, Truth in Blood."

239 **"We tell lies. Don't believe us."** Salisbury, *The New Emperors.*

239 **Less than a week later** Liu, *Tell the World.*

240 **According to Jasper Becker's The Chinese** Jasper Becker, *The Chinese* (New York: Free Press, 2000).

242 **Never in its history** Buruma, *Bad Elements.*

243 **Several foreign journalists witnessed**   Schell, *Mandate of Heaven*.

243 **According to the Party**   Liu, *Tell the World*.

244 **Computer "hacktivists" have programmed**   Schell, *Mandate of Heaven*.

19. UIGHUR DREAMS

246 **During the Long March**   Becker, *The Chinese*.

246 **By 1997, the Uighurs had dropped**   "People's Republic of China: Gross Violations of Human Rights in the Xinjiang Uighur Autonomous Region" (London: Amnesty International, April 1, 1999), available at web.amnesty.org/library/index/engASA170181999.

246 **Government troops grazed down scores**   Todd Crowell, "Days of Rage in Xinjiang; A Mosque Scuffle Flares into Ethnic Violence," *Asiaweek*, February 28, 1997.

246 **According to Amnesty International**   "People's Republic of China: Gross Violations of Human Rights in the Xinjiang Uighur Autonomous Region."

247 **Xinjiang is in such a geographically strategic position**   Lena Sun, "Ancient Silk Road Oasis Restive; Amid Crackdown, Anti-Chinese Sentiment in Xinjiang Grows," *The Washington Post*, September 25, 1990.

252 **This is said to be the oldest dance form**   Stephanie Elizondo Griest, "Proof Man's Belly Has a Higher Purpose Than Beer," *The New York Times*, July 13, 1997.

21. TABOO TO WHO?

264 **One of literature's most debaucherous books**   Salisbury, *The New Emperors*.

264 **Soon after taking power, Mao**   Jianying, *China Pop*.

264 **Yet he was as big a hypocrite**   Salisbury, *The New Emperors*.

264 **. . . so he could penetrate them**   Buruma, *Bad Elements*.

264 **But while he encouraged his countrymen**   Kristof and WuDunn, *China Wakes*.

264 **The Masses weren't supposed to enjoy**   Jianying, *China Pop*.

264 **Under Deng Xiaoping's "Campaign Against Spiritual Pollution"**   Ma Jian, *Red Dust: A Path Through China* (New York: Pantheon, 2001).

265 **The porn trade emerged in the mid-1980s** Jianying, *China Pop*.

265 **Concubine villages have also made** Becker, *The Chinese*.

271 **"You can get yourself cleaned"** Village People, "YMCA," *We Want You: The Very Best of Village People*, EDEL, 1998.

272 **For two centuries at the height of the Han dynasty** Bret Hinsch, *Passions of the Cut Sleeve: The Male Homosexual Tradition in China* (Berkeley: University of California Press, 1990).

273 **Gay culture noticeably reemerged when lesbians** Lisa Rofel, "Qualities of Desire: Imaging Gay Identities in China," *QLQ: Journal of Lesbian and Gay Studies* 5, no. 4 (1999).

274 **Even gay activists contend** Rofel, "Qualities of Desire."

23. SUNSET OVER CHINA

293 **Tens of thousands of practitioners would be arrested** Danny Schechter, *Falun Gong's Challenge to China* (New York: Akashic Books, 2000).

298 **Classical texts describe this** Schell, *Mandate of Heaven*.

SECTION THREE ⁎ HAVANA

24. *LA EXTRANJERA*

305 **Under the Trading with the Enemy Act** Christopher P. Baker, *Cuba Handbook* (Chico, Calif.: Moon Travel Handbooks, 1997).

25. WAITING FOR FIDEL

312 ***"No hay que llorar / No hay que llorar"*** Celia Cruz, "La Vida Es un Carnaval," *Mi Vida Es Cantar*, RMM Records, 1998.

316 **According to author Jon Lee Anderson** Jon Lee Anderson, "The Old Man and the Boy," *The New Yorker*, February 21–28, 2000.

316 **That might sound paranoid** Ann Louise Bardach, *Cuba Confidential: Love and Vengeance in Miami and Havana* (New York: Random House, 2002).

316 **When his yacht *Granma* crash-landed off the southeastern shores** Jon Lee Anderson, *Che Guevara: A Revolutionary Life* (New York: Grove Press, 1997).

317 **He even issued one hundred thousand college students** Tzvi Medin, *Cuba: Shaping of Revolutionary Consciousness* (Boulder, Colo.: Lynne Rienner, 1990).

318 **He legalized the U.S. dollars (USD)** Anderson, "The Old Man and the Boy."

318 **Finally, he opened the doors to tourism** Andrew Phillips, "Preparing for the Pope," *Maclean's*, January 19, 1998.

318 **According to *Granma*, 1.8 million tourists responded** "The Year 2000 Put Tourism to the Test" (Havana: Digital *Granma Internacional*, March 22, 2001), available at www.granma.cu/ingles/marzo3/12turism-i .html

26. THE RUMBA QUEEN

324 **Santeria originated with the advent** Harry G. Lefever, "When the Saints Go Riding In: Santeria in Cuba and the United States," *Journal for the Scientific Study of Religion*, September 1996.

324 **They quickly noticed important similarities** John W. Kennedy, "Santeria Holds Cuba in Thrall," *Christianity Today*, January 12, 1998.

324 **But while he canceled Christmas** Lefever, "When the Saints Go Riding In."

324 **My favorites: As a child** Georgie Anne Geyer, *Guerrilla Prince: The Untold Story of Fidel Castro* (Boston: Little, Brown & Company, 1991).

324 **...as a revolutionary, he was blessed by a *babalao*** Anderson, "The Old Man and the Boy."

328 **This was classic Cuban rumba** Jon Pareles, "Rumba, the Heartbeat of Cuban Music," *The New York Times*, June 11, 2000.

27. AN AFTERNOON AT EL CASTILLO DE FARNES

334 **This was especially tragic considering that the Cuban Revolution** C. Peter Ripley, *Conversations with Cuba* (Athens: University of Georgia Press, 1999).

335   **But other stats told how postrevolutionary Cuba**   "Summary Report of American Association of World Health on Impact of U.S. Embargo on Health of Cuban People" (San Francisco: Global Exchange, 2003), available at www.globalexchange.org/campaigns/cuba/foodAndMeds/healthImpact.html.

335   **and how in literacy Cuba leads**   Bardach, *Cuba Confidential*.

28.   REVOLUTIONARY REVERIES

339   **Fidel carried a gun around**   Geyer, *Guerrilla Prince*.

339   **The university may have barred**   Baker, *Cuba Handbook*.

343   ***Cubanas* weren't sold into sex slavery**   Lynn Darling, "Havana at Midnight," *Esquire*, May 1995.

29.   THE CUBAN UNDERGROUND

347   **Bounce to this, socialist movement**   dead prez, "I'm a African," *Let's Get Free*, Relativity, 2000.

348   **Within decades of Columbus's landing**   Lefever, "When the Saints Go Riding In."

348   **Cuba's *grito de yara*—call to liberty**   Hugh Thomas, *Cuba, or the Pursuit of Freedom* (New York: Da Capo Press, 1998).

350   **"To burn my kingdom, you must use fire"**   Run-DMC, "King of Rock," *King of Rock*, Profile Records, 1985.

351   **The music particularly took hold in Alamar**   Danny Hoch, "Not Only Built 4 Cuban Bronx," *The Village Voice*, September 29–October 5, 1999.

351   **" 'Cause I'm Black and I'm proud"**   Public Enemy, "Fight the Power," *Fear of a Black Planet*, Def Jam, 1990.

351   **Soon after, Minister of Culture Abel Prieto**   Annelise Wunderlich, "Cuban Hip-Hop, Underground Revolution" (University of California at Berkeley, Graduate School of Journalism, 2001), available at journalism.berkeley.edu/projects/cubans2001/story-hiphop_printable.html.

352   **... and promised *raperos* "the freedom"**   Brett Sokol, "Rap Takes Root Where Free Expression Is Risky," *Miami New Times*, September 3, 2000.

352   *Raperos* **couldn't exactly shout "Down with socialism"**   Wunderlich, "Cuban Hip-Hop, Underground Revolution."

30. BACK IN THE U.S. OF A.

355   **The United States has prohibited its citizens**   Bardach, *Cuba Confidential*.

355   **... some doctors must resort to acupuncture**   Tim Golden, "Health Care in Cuba," in Irving Louis Horowitz and Jaime Suchlicki, eds., *Cuban Communism* (New Brunswick, N.J.: Transaction Publishers, 1998).

356   **The embargo also deprives**   Bardach, *Cuba Confidential*.

356   **With its galleried walkways and vaulted ceilings**   Baker, *Cuba Handbook*.

357   **The pledge** *Seremos como el Che*   Anderson, *Che Guevara*.

ACKNOWLEDGMENTS

THEY SAY NO ONE under fifty should write a memoir. Having just done so, I'd like to concur. That I am still standing is a testament to the incredible support of the following friends, mentors, colleagues, and family.

Without David Barboza, this book simply would not be. He convinced me I was capable of writing it and then counseled/advised/cheered me the whole way through. Michael Robertson was the dinner partner/party starter who kept my sanity intact. Rachel Day Star served as the book's midwife during its first trimester; Priya Naman—future M.D.—monitored my breathing in the last; and Stephanie Emory and Ann "Ni hao Kitty" Rogers nurtured my prose and my spirits throughout. No matter how rough the road, Daphne Sorensen and Tyra Robertson could always make me laugh; I would have been lost and lonely without them. My Odyssey family—Nick Tilsen, Neda Farzan, Jennifer Peskin, Irene Lin, Stephen Danner, Becky Kroll, and our *jefe máximo*, Jeff Golden—and my Luce family—including Lareina Yee, Jacinda Mawson, Lisa Bosler, Nicole Fraser, and Harley Feldbaum—were infinite sources of strength. Fellow writers Amy Schapiro, Jake Dyer, and Jeffrey Hogrefe sent muses and comfort my way. Other beautiful people include Sonya Tsuchigane, Paulette Beard, Daniel Doremus, Shea Daugherty, Joy Carver, Melissa Moloney, Michelle Trautwein, Paul Stekler, Milena Worsham-Roshen, Irene Carranza, Melissa Mann, Svetlana Mintcheva, Aliana Apodaca, Karen Hsu, Kavitha Rao, Patricia Rojas, Maria Sacchetti, Viktoriya Drukker, Sherry Shokouhi, and Cheryl Holz. These friends formed my backbone during this process, and I thank them immensely.

At the University of Texas at Austin's College of Communication, Charles Whitney, Darrell Rocha, Rosental Calmon Alves, Gigi Durham, and Bob Mann taught me the tenets of journalism, wrote countless letters to get me where I needed to go, and became lifelong mentors and friends. Elena Lifschitz and Tom Garza in the Slavic Department prepared me linguistically (and otherwise) for Moscow.

I am most grateful to the Henry Luce Foundation for the extraordinary opportunity to spend ten months in Asia with such fantastic people. Thanks also to the Asia Foundation and the Ford Foundation, which secured my work placement and made my stay so enjoyable. *Feichang ganxie* to *China Daily* for allowing me into their newsroom.

This book was conceived in the High Times Cafe (RIP) in Austin, Texas, written in the Lotus Cup and Café Calypso in Corpus Christi, Texas, and revised at Ozzie's on Seventh Avenue in Brooklyn, New York. Many thanks to the sympathetic staff who allowed me to sit for so many (thousands of) hours on single mugs of tea. Heartfelt thanks also goes to the Ragdale Foundation, in whose dreamy cloister I completed this manuscript.

Tom Miller, Bill Broyles, Esmeralda Santiago, and Michele Serros provided invaluable counsel and amazing support throughout the writing and selling of this book. The wise suggestions of Robert Smith, Monica Gomez, and Irene Lin improved each draft dramatically. Anna Kushner, Karina Alexanyan, and Sarah Johansson Locke graciously shared their knowledge, and Megan Rehn, her access to a coveted database. Huge thanks to the *jefes* who kept a roof over my head: Michael Holmes at the Associated Press, Marjorie Heins at the Free Expression Policy Project, and Joan Bertin at the National Coalition Against Censorship. *Muchas gracias* to Dolores Prida at *Latina* magazine and *Traveler's Tales* for giving my work an outlet.

Literary angels transformed my stories into the book you are now holding. Sarah Jane Freymann was the agent/fairy godmother/friend whose faith in this project brought it to fruition. My eternal devotion also goes to the staff of Villard, especially Katie Zug for acquiring and beautifully editing the manuscript and Robin Rolewicz for insightful comments and for guiding it through production with such enthusiasm and expertise.

Now for those who motivated me to pick up a pen in the first place. My touchstone in Moscow was Elena Shishkina, whose family welcomed me as their own. Ines Brand's gifts of empathy and compassion remain my constant inspiration. *Spacibo bolshoi* to Irina Vovrik for her *druzhba* and to *babushki* everywhere for their resilience. Words defy my love and gratitude to "Liu" and "Yuer" for sharing their lives with me. *Xie xie* to my tutor Mei, dear friend Jufang, and *China Daily* colleagues. My man in Havana will forever be "Armando"—*muchísimas gracias por tu confianza y amistad*. Kandy Kelly, "Ming," and "Machi" were the greatest travel companions one could ask for—thanks for the tasty memories.

I wrote this book in memory of my cousin Nicole Elizondo, my friends Jason Wisniewski and Virginia Dominy, and my grandma Madge Griest. Rest in peace.

Finally—*mi familia*. I derive great pride from *mis tías y tíos* and *primas y primos* down in South Texas, my Griest clan up in Kansas, and Barbara, Alex, Jordan, and Analina. And now for my parents. Dad brought me Subway sandwiches for lunch and cooked me dinner every day for a solid year; Mom patiently read and edited nine versions of the book proposal, four complete drafts of the manuscript, and was my on-call, 24/7 therapist. They gave me confidence to explore this world, support to write about it, and a home to always return to. I dedicate this book to the two of them, with all of my love.

INDEX

ABOUT THE AUTHOR

STEPHANIE ELIZONDO GRIEST has written for
The New York Times, *The Washington Post*, the
Associated Press, *Latina*, and *Travelers' Tales*.
As a national correspondent for The Odyssey, an
educational website for kids, she once drove forty-
five thousand miles across America, documenting its
history. She now runs an anticensorship activist
organization called the Youth Free Expression
Network out of New York City. Visit her website
at www.aroundthebloc.com.